THE DISCOURSE OF SLAVERY

Aphra Behn to Toni Morrison

Edited by Carl Plasa and Betty J. Ring

London and New York

First published 1994
by Routledge
11 New Fetter Lane, London EC4P 4EE

Simultaneously published in the USA and Canada
by Routledge
29 West 35th Street, New York, NY 10001

Typeset in Bembo by
Ponting–Green Publishing Services,
Chesham, Buckinghamshire
Printed in Great Britain by
T.J. Press (Padstow) Ltd, Padstow, Cornwall

British Library Cataloguing in Publication Data
A catalogue record for this book is available from
the British Library

Library of Congress Cataloging in Publication Data
The Discourse of Slavery: Aphra Behn to Toni Morrison/
edited by Carl Plasa and Betty J. Ring;
foreword by Isobel Armstrong
Includes bibliographical references and index.
1. English literature–History and criticism.
2. American literature–History and criticism.
3. Slavery and slaves in literature.
I. Plasa, Carl   II. Ring, Betty J. (Betty Joan)
PR408.S57D57   1994
820.9'355–dc20   93–27522

ISBN 0–415–08151–3   0–415–08152–1 (pbk)

CONTENTS

NOTES ON CONTRIBUTORS

Isobel Armstrong is Professor of English at Birkbeck College, University of London. She is author of numerous articles and books on Romantic and Victorian literature and critical theory. Her most recent publication is *Victorian Poetry: Poetry, Poetics and Politics*.

Anne Fogarty is a Lecturer in the Department of English, University College Dublin. She has published articles on Renaissance literature and Irish women's writing. She is presently working on a study of sixteenth- and seventeenth-century colonial writing in Ireland, entitled *Colonial Plots*.

Jon Hauss is an Assistant Professor of English at Rhode Island College. He has published on *Benito Cereno* and is currently preparing a book-length manuscript entitled *Masquerades in Black: Narratives of Slavery in Ante-bellum America*.

April Lidinsky is a graduate student and instructor in the Department of English at Rutgers University. She is currently writing a dissertation examining working-class women's self-representations in nineteenth-century Britain and the United States.

Jane Moore is a lecturer in the Centre for Critical and Cultural Theory, University of Wales College of Cardiff. She is co-editor of *The Feminist Reader: Essays in Gender and the Politics of Literary Criticism* and has published articles on Mary Wollstonecraft and on critical theory. Her current projects include a book on theory in fiction and a study of Mary Wollstonecraft.

Carl Plasa is a lecturer in the School of English, University of Wales College of Cardiff. He has published articles on Keats, Tennyson, T. S. Eliot and Jean Rhys. He is currently working on a study of inscriptions of colonialism in Austen, Charlotte Brontë and Rhys.

Betty J. Ring is a graduate student in the Department of English at Birkbeck College, University of London. She is currently completing a doctoral thesis on post-war consciousness in the work of William Golding.

David Lawrence Rogers is an Associate Lecturer at Kingston University. He has published on *The Unvanquished* and is currently writing a book on form and gender in Faulkner's novels.

Elizabeth Jean Sabiston is an Associate Professor of English at York University, Toronto. She is author of *The Prison of Womanhood: Four Provincial Heroines in Nineteenth-Century Fiction* as well as articles on Henry James, Sherwood Anderson, William Faulkner and Philip Roth. At present she is working on a book-length manuscript entitled *"Letters to the World": Six Women Novelists*.

Steven Vine is a lecturer in the Department of English at the University College of Swansea. He is author of *Blake's Poetry: Spectral Visions* and articles on Coleridge and Mary Shelley. He is currently writing on Emily Brontë.

ACKNOWLEDGEMENTS

The editors would like to thank the following for their advice, support and assistance: Annie and Michael Lowry, Mary (for hermeneutic illumination of passages from the Bible), Sue and Linda and R. Claire Hall. Special thanks are due to Elizabeth Jean Sabiston for her patient involvement in the project from its earliest stages and April Lidinsky, whose resourcefulness helped mitigate occasional moments of transatlantic panic.

Additional thanks are due to the Trustees of the British Museum for permission to reproduce plate 2 of William Blake's *Visions of the Daughters of Albion*. The two Blake designs are reproduced from Robert N. Essick, *William Blake's Commercial Book Illustrations: A Catalogue and Study of the Plates Engraved by Blake after Designs by Other Artists*, Oxford, Clarendon Press, 1991, by permission of Oxford University Press: figs. 167 and 170. The permission of Alfred A. Knopf, Inc., to quote from Toni Morrison's *Beloved* is also gratefully acknowledged.

FOREWORD

Isobel Armstrong

Virginia Woolf's *To the Lighthouse* (1927) records an instant of disquiet, when Mr Ramsay thinks of the social inferiority of the liftman who both literally and metaphorically facilitates his ability to move upward. He recalls, in a quickly repressed moment of guilty recognition, that the achievements of ancient civilizations were dependent upon slavery. The irony of this reflection is redoubled because slavery was actually historically much nearer to Mr Ramsay – and much more uncomfortably at issue – than were the tyrannies of the ancient past. It had existed in the nineteenth century barely a generation before him. Its ideological and economic repercussions, just before the First World War when the novel opens, were with him still.

This book of essays recognizes that the effects of slavery continue to assert themselves in the 1990s. The discourses on slavery, both in attack and in defence, are a matter of living debate as well as the object of historical analysis. The book's contributors are aware that the accounts of race and nation that were implicated in the institution of slavery have not disappeared in a grand narrative which charts emancipation. On the contrary, the metaphors and categories intrinsic to the post-enlightenment imagination, and which shaped the slavery debate, are present in our own thought.

Through particular instances of the discourse of slavery from Aphra Behn to Toni Morrison, the chapters demonstrate the complexities of the questions which that discourse raises, not the least of these being the problematics of thinking and imagining the unspeakable nature of slavery for those who have not been slaves as well as for those who have. Anne Fogarty and Carl Plasa, for example, warn against conflating different forms of oppression – whether of gender or class – with the condition of slavery. Jane Moore argues that the universalizing concept of rights actually functions as a form of exclusion from definitions of the fully human because it abstracts and transcendentalizes. For these critics the careful work of historical investigation and deconstruction is prerequisite to comprehending the ideological complexities and anguish of slavery. The insistent dialectic theorized by Hegel, but which has remained an untheorized part of European and American consciousness for so long, *can* give way to other models. Such new models are explored, in different contexts, by Steven Vine's discussion of Blake and April Lidinsky's reading of Morrison.

A major concern of the book is to understand the power-structures that permitted slavery. Only through this understanding is it possible to conceive of different political structures and paradigms of relationship which dissolve the master–slave pattern. *The Discourse of Slavery: Aphra Behn to Toni Morrison* is a timely book, as the consequences of colonial and imperial oppression continue to be felt today throughout the world.

INTRODUCTION

Carl Plasa and Betty J. Ring

The essays in this collection address the problematic of slavery within the literary, cultural and political discourses of Britain and America from the late seventeenth century to the present. The breadth of historical period they cover is complemented by the variety of the texts they examine – fiction, poetry, political philosophy and the slave-narrative, among others. Contributors also deploy a range of frequently overlapping critical insights – those primarily of poststructuralism, black criticism and feminism. Such diversity of generic focus and critical approach is offset, however, by the essays' implication in a shared concern with and analysis of forms of *difference* (especially racial and sexual) as they operate in and across a number of historically specific contexts.

The collection is further integrated by two assumptions. First, the essays recognize the historically and culturally specific nature of their *own* contexts in the 1990s. They are grounded accordingly in the claim that reading is always – to whatever degree – a political act and means of intervention, both determined by and consequential for the moment in which it is performed. As such, the book is part of a wider cultural critique, a particularly striking recent expression of which is to be seen in the controversy arising from the "celebration" of the quincentenary of Columbus's "discovery" of the Americas.

The second assumption, related to the first, is that history is never a thing of the past. Forms of historical reflection play a crucial role in any attempt to counteract oppression in the present: a culture that seeks to evade the more violent aspects of its own history will only perpetuate them. The institutions of British and American slavery were formally eradicated by means of legislation carried out during the course of the nineteenth century: the slave-trade was outlawed by both Britain and America in 1807, full emancipation of slaves eventually brought about in British colonies between 1834 and 1838 and slavery in the United States finally abolished by the Emancipation Proclamation in 1863 and the Thirteenth Amendment in 1865. The dates in the calendar of "liberation" are well known. Yet as April Lidinsky puts it in her reading of Toni Morrison's *Beloved* (1987), we can never "neatly sunder past from present." Ideologies of racial difference continue to be produced and enacted in the 1990s – not only in Britain and America but throughout the world. The histories of such ideologies need constantly to be examined, as a means of developing an understanding of the ways in which differences are constructed in contemporary societies: one of the most brutal, systematic and far-reaching of those histories is slavery.

Much of the current debate about slavery takes place in America and through American publications. This situation is itself the result of a widespread and ongoing interest in African-American studies occurring within institutions of Higher education in the United States and is outlined, for example, by Henry Louis Gates, Jr. in his introductory article to the January 1990 issue of *PMLA*. In this light the book can be seen not only to offer a contribution to those debates already firmly under way in America but to supplement and broaden the terms of current critical discussion within the context of literary and cultural studies in Britain. The need for this broadening derives from the fact that in Britain the subject of racial oppression has been examined primarily in relation to colonialism, postcolonialism and imperialism but much less fully with regard to the problematic of slavery.

One of the effects of the outburst of critical theory beginning in the 1970s is registered, in the 1990s, as an unsettling of the boundaries between disciplines within the Humanities – shifts and changes encouraged by some, resisted by others. What might once have been safely designated as "literary studies" is now a cultural practice marked by an expansion and redefinition of critical possibilities. This has opened up what might be said in the course of reading a text, how one might say it and the kinds of text to which critics might legitimately turn their attention, along with the question of the positions from which they speak. For many, such changes in the discursive horizon have resulted in precisely the kind of *politicization* of the reading of texts of which this volume is an example. Situated amid these intellectual and institutional shifts, the collection thus addresses a wide constituency of readers concerned with questions of power, language and the politics of difference.

Focusing on British and American contexts, the book also emphasizes the interplay and dialogue between them. In this respect it represents a significant departure from previous collections which deal with slavery and black oppression in literature and culture. These have tended principally to confine themselves to either the one context or the other, as is, for example, the case with David Dabydeen's *The Black Presence in English Literature* (1985), Moira Ferguson's *Subject to Others: British Women Writers and Colonial Slavery, 1670–1834* (1992) or Deborah E. McDowell and Arnold Rampersad's *Slavery and the Literary Imagination* (1989). Without wishing to deny the importance of the cultural specificity on which such works are based, *The Discourse of Slavery: Aphra Behn to Toni Morrison* deliberately counterpoints both contexts in acknowledgement of the sense in which British and American slavery are economically, historically, politically and culturally interlinked. This aspect of the book is in turn underlined by the ordering of the essays: chapters 1 to 4 focus on writers within the British tradition (Aphra Behn, Mary Wollstonecraft, William Blake and Charlotte Brontë) while the last four chapters direct themselves toward African-American and American contexts, providing readings of Frederick Douglass, Harriet Jacobs, William Faulkner and Morrison. The two groups of essays are bridged by a chapter on Elizabeth Gaskell and Harriet Beecher Stowe whose intertextual method – like its placement – precisely emblematizes the connections between British and American slave-histories and their representation through cultural forms.

The book opens with a chapter by Anne Fogarty on Aphra Behn's *Oroonoko* (1688), commonly read as one of the earliest examples within English literature of an anti-slavery text. Beginning with an account of the "multifarious critical responses" to *Oroonoko* in the twentieth century, Fogarty argues that they are marked alike by a failure fully to recognize the "tensions and contradictions" of Behn's novella. These are made especially manifest, it is shown, in Behn's use of slavery as a medium for articulating other power-structures, relating, specifically, to female oppression and the struggle for political ascendancy in seventeenth-century England. In discussing slavery as metaphor, Fogarty's reading of Behn introduces one of the book's recurrent emphases, evident, to varying degrees, in a number of other chapters – Steven Vine's on Blake, Elizabeth Jean Sabiston's on Gaskell and Stowe, and, particularly, Carl Plasa's on Brontë.

Slavery is predicated upon a denial of particular rights to the human subject including, indeed, the right to humanity and rights have been a central element in traditions of enlightenment and revolutionary thought from the eighteenth century onward. Yet as Jane Moore's chapter on Mary Wollstonecraft illustrates, the principle of rights – reliant as it is upon a transcendental notion of "truth" – is not unproblematic either in theory or practice, particularly from deconstructionist and feminist perspectives. Discussing Wollstonecraft's *A Vindication of the Rights of Men* (1790) and *Vindication of the Rights of Woman* (1792), while also examining a range of contemporary feminist arguments, Moore suggests that the discourse of rights has the potential to "enslave" as much as liberate the subject.

For Steven Vine, the radical potential of Blake's work is not defined by an unambiguous dialectic of freedom and oppression but located elsewhere – in the contradictory and ironic energies of Blakean language. This assumption forms the basis for Vine's analysis of the representation of enslavement, sexuality and enlightenment in *Visions of the Daughters of Albion* (1793). In reading this text Vine relates it to Wollstonecraft's *Vindication of the Rights of Woman*: *contra* Wollstonecraft, Blake figures the female body not simply as "enslaving" but as a site of political conflict and hence emancipatory potential. Vine also examines the relations between Blake's text and J.G. Stedman's *Narrative, of a Five Years' expedition, against the Revolted Negroes of Surinam* (1796) for which Blake provided several engravings during the period in which *Visions* was produced. Both the poem that refigures him and the engravings are shown to expose Stedman's collusive and duplicitous relation to colonialism, just as *Visions* itself illuminates the contradictions inherent to the ideology of enlightenment.

Carl Plasa's chapter on *Jane Eyre* (1847) develops recent rereadings of Brontë's novel which recover precisely those questions of race and colonial slavery that are marginalized by the text itself as by Anglo-American feminist critics. The chapter focuses upon the language – specifically the metaphorics – of mastery and enslavement within the text and seeks to illustrate the politically double-sided nature of its operations. On the one hand, the language of slavery systematically constructs and empowers the narrative. The fictional self is thus apparently able to understand its own identity, just as Brontë herself secures a means of elaborating a critique of class- and gender-relations within early-nineteenth-century England. However, the very power that the figurative structures accord to heroine and authoress alike is also one they re-appropriate, taking it back across the gap between enslavement-as-metaphor and the literal experience of colonial oppression obliquely inscribed at the novel's margins in the shape of British exploitation of African and Creole slaves in the West Indies. Yet, even as it co-opts the slave-trope to its own ends, *Jane Eyre* simultaneously comments upon and disputes the legitimacy of its rhetorical procedures, offering a complex gloss on the political problems they entail.

British and American contexts are explicitly brought together in Elizabeth Jean Sabiston's intertextual analysis of the relation between the work of Gaskell and that of Stowe. Sabiston's reading of *Mary Barton* (1848) in conjunction with *Uncle Tom's Cabin* (1852) demonstrates the way in which the interplay between oppression through class (in Gaskell) and through slavery and race (in Stowe) extends its effects beyond the realm of the figurative and allows itself to be read in terms of a certain parallelism of plot between the two texts. The reworking of *Mary Barton* in and by *Uncle Tom's Cabin* is thus one of the sources through which Stowe's anti-slavery novel might be said to be enabled. Yet, on the other hand, the parallel between class- and racial oppression – writ large in a parallelism of plot – reveals the degree to which the radical potential of Stowe's work is simultaneously compromised by the text in which it is asserted.

For Betty J. Ring, *Narrative of the Life of Frederick Douglass, an American Slave* (1845) elaborates a complex response to the material conditions of enslavement in antebellum America. While considering the "representative" or "exemplary" status of both Douglass and his texts, Ring combines close analysis of

Douglass's writings with an emphasis on the historical, political and cultural – particularly religious – contexts in which slave- and ex-slave narratives are produced. This involves exploring the strategies of textual appropriation of religious discourses that Douglass enlists in order to negate the power of those discourses themselves to appropriate the freedom of blacks and to legitimate and maintain oppression. For Douglass, as Ring shows, birth into language by means of the deployment of an alternative hermeneutics is integral to the possibility of freedom – the self's bodily and intellectual crossing from slavery to emancipation and history achieved through nothing less audacious than an appropriation of the Word itself.

As outlined in a chapter by Jon Hauss, the importance of Jacobs's *Incidents in the Life of a Slave Girl* (1861) lies in its foregrounding of the gaps and disjunctions between different social experiences within antebellum America, elements elided – he argues – in Stowe and Douglass. It is these differences – the effects of slavery and patriarchy – that Linda Brent, Jacobs's pseudonymous narrator, seeks to negotiate through strategies of storytelling. These strategies, whose cultural specificity Hauss demonstrates and emphasizes, are designed to facilitate networks of "transsocial understanding," particularly with re-gard to the sexual violence and coercion of slave-masters. For Brent the difficult possibility of others' understanding of slavery creates the potential for resistance and a "passage" to freedom. Such a "passage" is doubly textual: *Incidents* not only drama-tizes the attempts of slave-women to fashion structures of alliance but in so doing offers a model for its relations to a white Northern readership.

Despite his close identification with the American South, Faulkner represents the material conditions of slavery only rarely. Nevertheless, in the texts examined by David Lawrence Rogers (from *Soldiers' Pay*, 1926, to *Go Down, Moses*, 1942) it is shown to be a pervasive concern, legible through processes comparable to the "literariness" and "Signifyin(g)" outlined as a feature of African-American writing by Henry Louis Gates, Jr., in *The Signifying Monkey* (1988). Faulkner's fiction stages a revisionary deconstruction of slavery's "idealist" discourses and the fixed hierarchical divisions of race and gender that char-acterize them. The sites of this procedure are the interrelated figures of the mulatto and epicene, increasingly promoted and affirmed throughout the Faulknerian *œuvre*. However, in a brief coda, Rogers suggests that Faulkner's public stance in the 1950s toward questions of race ultimately compromises the radical potential embodied in his fiction.

April Lidinsky concludes the book with her chapter on *Beloved*. Relating Michel Foucault's notion of the "fictioning" or "imaginative reproduction" of history to the work of "re-memory," Lidinsky shows how *Beloved* challenges those proprietary models of body and identity that at once underpin slavery and are underpinned by it. This challenge is nowhere greater than in the visionary spirituality of Baby Suggs, whose Call in the Clearing to "Love" constitutes both a re-imagining of the self and its communal relations and a way of effecting a movement toward collective political action. While Baby's liberative energies draw upon nineteenth-century Holiness currents of the Methodist and African Methodist Episcopal Churches, they are shown to resonate strongly with postmodern theories of the construction of subjectivity in and through discourse. The corollary to the kind of "re-invention" of traditional models of self propounded by *Beloved* is a re-invention of the possibilities for political action and life alike.

1

LOOKS THAT KILL
Violence and representation in Aphra Behn's *Oroonoko*

Anne Fogarty

Aphra Behn's novella with its violent account of the execution of an African slave who was once a king was published – significantly – in 1688, the year that saw the bloodless deposition of King James II in England.[1] The social unrest that led to the dismemberment of the slave-king in Behn's fiction is matched by a similar discord in late-seventeenth-century England that issued in the ousting of the final Stuart king from his throne. Reality and fiction seem to mimic each other yet, as this chapter will show, the symmetries that *Oroonoko* suggests are ultimately spurious ones. In this reading of the intricacies of *Oroonoko*, I shall argue that Behn utilizes the ambiguity and eccentric vision of the woman writer in order to indicate that a confluence of perspectives between the black slave Oroonoko and his sympathetic white female friend is an impossibility. The partisan and divisive nature of political and ethnic identity, as of sexual desire, ultimately prevents the harmonious and non-exploitative co-existence of different races. This reading of *Oroonoko* consequently runs counter to many recent interpretations that celebrate it as an unproblematic and pioneering document in the history of anti-slavery literature. In particular, it contests the finding frequently proposed as a key to Behn's liberalism – namely the belief that slavery functions in *Oroonoko* as a means of tracing a parallelism between the subjugation of other races and the oppression of women. This view holds that Behn's narrator identifies with the fate of a black slave because she sees his powerlessness as homologous with her own.

Such a reading of *Oroonoko* ignores patent tensions and

contradictions in the text: Behn's novella is built around a series of disjunctions and displacements as well as a set of identifications. The narrator is torn between her fascination with other cultures and an unremitting ethnocentrism. In addition, she is divided between her admiration for the central male protagonist and a regard for female virtue and courage as represented by Imoinda. Such, moreover, is the ambivalence and complexity of Behn's political allegory that all the central figures in her drama of colonial unrest may be seen in diametrically opposed ways. Oroonoko, the oxymoron embedded in the subtitle reminds us, is a "Royal Slave"; he is simultaneously at the bottom of the social scale and at its pinnacle. Conforming to two shifting and conflicting registers of meaning, Oroonoko is both a renegade and a falsely deposed sovereign. Paradoxically, he acts as an allegory both of royal power and of social anarchy. Similarly, Imoinda, Oroonoko's wife, plays a double part in Behn's multi-layered allegory. She is at once an image of female oppression and a sign of otherness, simultaneously representing – like Oroonoko himself – moral order and savagery. While she has a civilizing effect on the world around her, she is also the cause of a family feud in Coramantien and the instigator of the slave-revolt in Surinam.

In analysing the pivotal function of these contradictions in Behn's text, I shall make the case that *Oroonoko* is ultimately fractured by the twofold political causes that Behn espouses. Her lifelong support of royalism is at odds with her passionate defence of the rights of women. The conflicting allegories and shifting viewpoints of her novella and its repeated questioning of the boundaries between reality and fiction map out the dissonances and discontinuities in Behn's attempt to write an account of history from the perspective of those who remain outside it. The permanent dilemma for the author is that she discovers not only that there is a lack of congruence between the needs and desires of women and slaves as marginalized subjects in the colonial world of Surinam, but that these two groups are also often dismayingly at odds. Far from making common cause, women and slaves seem forced into positions of conflict.

The reception of *Oroonoko* has been a peculiarly troubled one. Indeed, the heated debate that this text generated through-out the twentieth century has until recently ignored Behn's representations of ethnic otherness and concentrated instead on questioning the authenticity of the female author. Tellingly, the issue of gender was allowed to displace that of race in analyses of the text. The problem of misrecognition which is such a prominent theme of Behn's novella (whereby the viewpoint of one particular social group occludes that of another) seems to be amply illustrated by the critical misreadings that the text has spawned. By tracing the interpretative battles which *Oroonoko* has instigated, I want both to give an account of the multifarious critical responses to this work and to pinpoint their elisions and shortcomings. However, in the crosscomparison of the many analyses of Behn's narrative, the objective is not to formulate a reading that will act as a corrective to previous interpretations; rather, I shall suggest that this tale of romance and injustice brings its audience face to face with the problem of representativity. *Oroonoko* is predicated on a crisis in authority. Those interpretations that attempt to stabilize the text by defining it as the mouthpiece of one particular ideology – be it colonialism, royalism, or some embryonic version of feminism or abolitionism – cancel out the hesitancies and contradictions that are integral to its workings.

In her dedicatory epistle and introduction to the tale itself, Behn is insistent that the story she is about to relate is not a fictive invention but rather a truthful and accurate reconstruction of historical events. Those aspects of the narrative that strike us as "new and strange" are a measure not of the writer's fertile imagination but of the distance that separates us from the exotic world she is depicting.[2] In this manner, Behn attempts to defuse the otherness of *Oroonoko* by insisting on its factuality. The most vociferous of Behn's detractors refuse, however, to recognize the subtlety of her framing devices which have the function of protecting both author and text. Instead, they query the authenticity of her descriptions and sometimes even go so far as to call her very existence into question.[3] Ernest Bernbaum discovers many inconsistencies in Behn's biography which he feels prove that she never visited Surinam at all. In addition, he accuses her of plagiarism and comes to the damning conclusion that in writing *Oroonoko* she "deliberately and circumstantially lied."[4] For him the likelihood that Behn used George Warren's *Impartial Description of Surinam* (1667) as a source for many of her vivid renderings of Surinam entirely invalidates her work. His debunking of the novella bears out Behn's own fears that a text written by a woman and centring on the plight of a slave will never be given credence by the world. The circularity of his reasoning is further indicative of the plight of the female writer. Bernbaum dismisses *Oroonoko* because it does not correspond with his version of Behn's biography. By questioning the facts of her existence he simultaneously casts doubt on the facts of the story she produced. Both her life and her work are shown to be equally fictive and hence equally dubious. His reading is, effectively, a double erasure: by denying that Behn could have had experience of other cultures, he not only discredits her but also obscures the colonial history that she commemorates.

Bernbaum's ill-founded and cantankerous attack on *Oroonoko* has long been refuted. In particular, Behn's biographers have succeeded in dispelling many of the doubts about the nature and the extent of her travels.[5] It has now been established that, no matter how clouded the evidence, she did indeed spend a short period in Surinam and that moreover her portrayal of this country and of Oroonoko's African homeland is precise and informed rather than fanciful.[6] Other critics, including most prominently B.G. MacCarthy, demonstrate that Bernbaum's concept of realism is so narrowly defined that he inevitably fails to appreciate the complexity of Behn's mode of romantic verisimilitude.[7] However, all the many attempts to rehabilitate this text still insist, problematically, on invoking criteria of truth and accuracy as a means of legitimating Behn's work. Where once her biography and her gender were utilized as weapons to invalidate her writing, it now frequently appears to be the case that her life-story and perspective as a woman are the very things that act as a warranty for the history she records. Critics rising to Behn's defence set out to prove either the realism of her writing or the purity and coherence of her vision.

Early feminist accounts of her work have been especially guilty of such simplifications. Behn is championed, for example, by both Virginia Woolf and Vita Sackville-West as the first professional woman writer. For them, Behn's texts have an automatic resonance because they represent for the first time in English literature a female perspective on the world. Woolf famously declared that "all women together ought to let flowers fall upon the tomb of Aphra Behn," while Sackville-West pronounced with equal insouciance that Behn's having written at all is "much more important than the quality of what she

4

wrote."[8] Much later appraisals of Behn continue to echo this euphoric celebration of her work as establishing a representative female voice in English literature. Dale Spender awards her a prominent ranking in her list of the forgotten mothers of the English novel. Behn's writing deserves special praise because it measures men by women's standards.[9] Spender assumes that the particular merit of these standards lies in their seemingly pre-given moral superiority, finding in Behn not just a singularly female point of view but an ability to sympathize with the political oppression of others. In Spender's reading of *Oroonoko*, therefore, the expansiveness and openness of the woman writer explain Behn's exaltation of the black hero. For all his flaws and contradictions, not least among these being the fact that he too trades in slaves, Oroonoko is shown to possess a nobility lacking in his white counterparts. Elaine Campbell makes a similar case in defence of *Oroonoko*. For her the vigour and breadth of Behn's imagination is of a piece with her ability to empathize with the problems of people outside her own culture. Behn's work, she declares, is fuelled by a "transcendental quality of compassion."[10]

More recent readings of Behn have attempted to question the all-too-ready assumption that speaking as a marginalized white woman is equivalent to or compatible with speaking for a black African slave. Vron Ware points out, for instance, that an anti-slavery politics should not be equated with a challenging of ideologies of racial domination.[11] Laura Brown and Moira Ferguson are more far-reaching still in their contestations of the view that Behn's assertion of women's right to write and express themselves freely naturally feeds into a desire for the emancipation of slaves. For Brown, the very instability of the narrator in *Oroonoko* ensures that she act as a vehicle for colonial ideology. Notwithstanding her sympathetic insights into the life both of African slaves and of Surinamese Indians, the narrator nevertheless cements the exploitative connections between the colonizing English and native cultures by acting as a mediator between them.[12] Moreover, Brown feels that Behn celebrates her hero more on the grounds of his royal status than on those of his enslavement. Oroonoko is a tragic figure because he is a dispossessed king – not because he is a man denied his freedom. Ferguson, in a similarly trenchant revisionist reading of *Oroonoko*, contends that Behn sets out to attack not the institution of slavery but the inequities and inefficiencies in the running of the colony of Surinam.[13] While she notes the many equivocations in the text, she is nevertheless of the opinion that to see it as an argument in favour of the abolition of slavery is a misreading. Heidi Hutner similarly redresses the anachronistic accounts of Behn's liberal politics that have influenced interpretations of *Oroonoko* until recently.[14] She maintains that Behn indicts not slavery as the source of human oppression but the violence and savagery of colonial expansionism.

From being a paradigmatic text in the history of women's literature and politics and a representative early female voice in the battle against social oppression, *Oroonoko* has become symptomatic of the blind spots and omissions in feminism itself. It is now, it transpires, a prescient narrative because it mirrors the failure of western feminism adequately to address the problem of racism and to recognize the way in which white women themselves play the role of oppressor with regard especially to their black counterparts.[15] Indeed, Ros Ballaster points out, in her persuasive analysis of the politics underlying feminist interpretations of *Oroonoko*, that, perhaps in keeping with Behn's own disengagement with this figure, critics have tended to disregard the role of the black female slave in the text.[16] It is Imoinda and not Oroonoko who acts finally as a figure of alterity in Behn's story of slave-rebellion. Where Oroonoko is Europeanized and depicted as alluring and eloquent, she remains alien, remote and largely silent. Doubly oppressed, Imoinda is an emblem of both sexual and racial otherness. Her physical presence, at once commemorated and yet held at a distance by the narrator, is symbolic of the material existence of the "other woman" who, as Gayatri Spivak argues, western feminism is so much at pains to disavow.[17]

The original feminist reception of *Oroonoko* is now surprisingly reversed. Where once this text was emblematic of the optimism and utopianism of feminist politics, it currently is seen by many critics as a register of the shortcomings and mistaken goals of the fight for women's liberation. Uncomfortably, too, the rereading of the historical contexts of Behn's writing and the concomitant insistence on the political embeddedness of her work seem to indicate that the woman writer is more entrenched in the ideologies of her day than are even her male contemporaries.[18] Her marginalization appears to restrict her vision rather than to allow her a more unblinkered view of the world. The myth of Behn the revolutionary champion of women and slaves has now been scotched by the sobering discovery of her royalist sympathies and seemingly ineradicable racist attitudes. Indeed, it appears to be the case that studies of Behn have come full circle. The earlier sexist denunciations of her deficiencies as a woman writer have now given way to feminist pronouncements on the limitations of *Oroonoko* as a narrative purportedly written in defence of an African slave. The one-time complaint that Behn's writing is false and inauthentic has been replaced by the finding that it is biased and contradictory.

This re-adjusted account of Behn's text runs the risk, I would suggest, of furthering an overly narrow view of her novella and its import. By simply swapping Behn the feminist for Behn the racist we fail to do justice to the complexity of her work. Moreover, in accepting historicist readings of her text that see it as irrevocably rooted in the political beliefs of her day, we fall into the trap of assuming that ideologies are monolithic and pre-empt all critique. In the interpretation of *Oroonoko* that occupies the latter half of this chapter, I want to analyse the tensions and anxieties around which it is built. Moreover, I shall argue that the excessive violence that forces itself upon our attention at the end of the text in the two scenes describing the punishment and killing of Oroonoko is an indication of those racial and sexual conflicts that the writer cannot succeed in resolving. It will be demonstrated that Behn's narrative centres on the problems of authority and representativity.[19] Her text is woven around the rival voices of the woman writer and the slave-king. The story of a dispossessed African king sanctions her presumption in daring to write in the first place. Also, in telling us about the fate of Oroonoko she is afforded the opportunity of depicting her own life, albeit indirectly and allusively. The need to relate the story of the wronged king cancels the impropriety involved in assuming a command of language as a woman. However, at the same time Behn is aware of the danger of her position. In the most frequently cited passage in the text she points to the incongruity of her celebration of Oroonoko:

> I ought to tell you, that the Christians never buy any slaves but they give 'em some name of their own, their native ones being likely very barbarous, and hard to pronounce;

so that Mr. Trefry gave Oroonoko that of Caesar; which name will live in that country as long as that (scarce more) glorious one of the great Roman: for 'tis most evident he wanted no part of the personal courage of that Caesar, and acted things as memorable, had they been done in some part of the world replenished with people and historians that might have given him his due. But his misfortune was, to fall in an obscure world, that afforded only a female pen to celebrate his fame.

(63–4)

The chronicle of the life of Oroonoko is an equivocal one. Aiming to be a story of heroism, it turns into a register of loss. Oroonoko, the narrator indicates, is demeaned by the fact that his biographer is female. The oddity of her perspective as a woman means that she is incapable of relating the epic tale of courageous exploit required by her central subject as a fitting tribute. However, at the same time, the narrator suggests it is not just incapacity that prevents the woman writer from producing a record consonant with the male view of history as a chain of heroic deeds. Instead, the account of Oroonoko is one of power-conflicts between men and women and slaves and slave-owners. The heroicizing testimonial to Oroonoko that the putative male historian might have produced would have glossed over and suppressed such conflicts. By contrast, the decentred vision of a woman facilitates the narration of a double story. In her version, Oroonoko has both his native African name and his European title. Unlike the male pen, the female does not deny otherness or shirk the reality of the racial, sexual and colonial conflicts which link the English community with that of the black slave. Yet Behn does not suggest that a feminization of history allows us a more balanced and inclusive account of events. Indeed, the problem for the narrator is that by assuming the role of historian she must also admit to her collusion with male coercive force. The text does violence to Oroonoko because it obliterates rather than celebrates him, making the narrator also part of the process whereby the African prince is transformed into the mutilated body of a European slave. Moreover, in presuming to write at all it seems as if the female pen produces rather than questions the horror of this atrocity. Her very powerlessness makes her personal responsibility for his death all the more shocking. The averted gaze of the narrator who is absent, she informs us, from the scene of Oroonoko's execution, nevertheless partakes in this spectacle of violence.

Julia Kristeva has made the point that the presence of the foreigner in our society turns the pronoun "we" into an impossibility.[20] *Oroonoko*, I would argue, registers this dilemma. The narrator is torn between giving an account in the first-person singular of her experiences abroad – thus emphasizing the private intensity of her connection with Oroonoko – and producing a narrative in the first-person plural that stresses membership of the community of white female colonists in Surinam. On the one hand, her relationship with Oroonoko is personal and sympathetic, while on the other her admiring but distancing view of him is part of the collective response of a colonizing society to those it views as foreign. The initial passages of the story map out a conflict between a use of "I" and "we" in describing the fate and personality of the hero. The narrator depicts herself as having an independent point of view: "I was my self an eye-witness to a great part of what you will find here set down." Yet she also indicates that such freedom of vision is compromised and mediated by the English view of racial others. She confides to us that "we who were perfectly charm'd with the character of this great man, were curious to gather every circumstance of his life" (27). Where her statement made in first-person singular suggests a positive interaction with her African friend, the declaration made in first-person plural reminds us of her complicity with the violently dismembering vision which turns the ethnic other into a curiosity and a dreadful spectacle.

Oroonoko may indeed be interpreted as the tragic story of the "looking relations" that structure the interaction between different cultures.[21] Initially, Behn tries to construct a picture of the mutual and noncompeting gazes that symbolize the harmonious co-existence of the various communities living in Surinam and inhabiting the imaginative space of the narrative. In describing the customs of the Surinamese Indians and the life led by Oroonoko prior to his enslavement, Behn fleetingly manages to envisage societies where looking has nothing to do with violence and domination. In addition, by presenting us with positive accounts of these other ways of seeing, she attempts to dissociate herself from the destructive and appropriative gaze that the colonizer brings to bear on other societies.[22] She describes the natural innocence of South American Indians who live in a blameless sphere of purity, where nakedness is not a reminder of dangerous desires:

> And though they are all thus naked, if one lives for ever among 'em, there is not to be seen an undecent action, or glance: and being continually us'd to see one another so unadorn'd, so like our first parents before the fall, it seems as if they had no wishes, there being nothing to heighten curiosity; but all you can see, you see at once, and every moment see.
>
> (29)

In the prelapsarian world of this native culture there is no place for the commandeering "curiosity" that is a feature of English ways of looking. Moreover, in a comic reversal of positions, it is the English traveller who is turned into a sight when the narrator and her friends undertake a trip to visit the local tribes. She describes the consternation that the Indians feel when they first catch sight of the English and the disproportionate exuberance of their attire:

> They had no sooner spy'd us, but they set up a loud cry, that frighted us at first; we thought it had been for those that should kill us, but it seems it was of wonder and amazement. They were all naked; and we were dress'd, so as is most commode for the hot countries, very glittering and rich; so that we appear'd extremely fine: my own hair was cut short, and I had a taffety cap with black feathers on my head; my brother was in a stuff-suit, with silver loops and buttons, and abundance of green ribbon. This was all infinitely surprizing to them.
>
> (78)

Here, it is the colonizers and not the natives who are qualified by their visibility and difference.

In her description of the amorous relationship between Imoinda and Oroonoko in Africa, Behn similarly imagines ways of looking that are the result of the desire for mutuality rather then domination. The exchange of gazes, "the parley of the eyes" (45) between these two lovers, is symbolic of the powerful attraction they feel for one another and the ease with which they can circumvent the obstacles that separate them. Above all, the ideal harmony of the love between Imoinda and Oroonoko is located beyond the divisive sphere of language. Their looks of love constitute an alternative mode of expression which heals all divisions:

> But as soon as the King was busy'd in looking on some fine thing of Imoinda's making, she had time to tell the Prince, with her angry, but love-darting eyes, that she resented his coldness, and bemoan'd her own miserable captivity. Nor were his eyes silent, but answer'd hers again, as much as eyes cou'd do, instructed by the most tender and most passionate heart that ever lov'd: and they spoke so well, and so effectually, as Imoinda no longer doubted but she was the only delight and darling of that soul she found pleading in 'em its right of love, which none was more willing to resign than she.
>
> (41–2)

The narrator tries to recreate this affirmative mode of seeing in her admiring descriptions of Oroonoko. She depicts him as someone visually familiar and attractive yet also strange and exotic. She both acknowledges his cultural difference and attempts to reduce his otherness. Although she Europeanizes his appearance, at the same time she insists that his colour cannot be ignored:

> His nose was rising and Roman, instead of African and flat. His mouth the finest shaped that could be seen; far from those great turn'd lips, which are so natural to the rest of the Negroes. The whole proportion and air of his face was so nobly and exactly form'd, that bating his colour, there could be nothing in nature more beautiful, agreeable and handsome.
>
> (33)

However, the gaze of "surprize and wonder" (32) which the narrator centres on Oroonoko throughout the text can never escape the social differences and power-structures that contour their relationship. Her admiration for him, lingering on his physical beauty as it does, sexualizes and commodifies him. Despite the insistence that she is a nonpartisan observer, the narrator nevertheless uses the fetishizing language of the colonizer in order to control Oroonoko. Similarly, she Europeanizes him not so much to indicate a shared sphere of interests as to cancel and deny ethnic difference. Oroonoko acts as a surface onto which the narrator projects her own political and religious convictions. She tells us that he laments "the deplorable death of our great monarch" (33) and also that her conversations with him are motivated in part by a desire to convert him.

Paradoxically, however, the more she endeavours to erase Oroonoko's difference, the more prominent it becomes. It is not just his colour that refuses to disappear but also his sexuality and masculinity. The narrator's attempt to domesticate her hero underlines his otherness. The power that she wields over him is a phantom one. Oroonoko may call her "great mistress" but in the end is divided from her because of his ethnic otherness and gender difference. Indeed, while the narrator's insistence on the sexuality and physicality of Oroonoko is certainly a means by which she asserts the racial superiority of the white woman over the black native, it simultaneously functions as an index of her own lack of presence and power.[23] His visibility and threatening potency underscore her powerlessness and vulnerability. Momentarily, she co-opts Oroonoko to an ideal female domain of shared feeling and mutual concern. She declares that he "liked the company of us women much above the men" (69). Yet when Oroonoko rebels and delivers his speech exhorting his fellow slaves to revolt it is precisely the feminized sphere to which he is consigned that he cites as the ultimate sign of his social degradation: thus, he upbraids the other slaves by pointing out that they "are bought and sold like apes or monkeys, to be the sport of women, fools and cowards" (83).

At the end of the story, even the ideal love between Imoinda and Oroonoko becomes symbolic of the inequity of the power-relations between men and women. In order to protect her from possible assault, Oroonoko kills Imoinda in advance of leading an attack on his white enemies. His sexual ownership of her justifies the sacrificial mutilation of her body:

> the lovely, young and ador'd victim lays her self down before the sacrificer; while he, with a hand resolved, and a heart-breaking within, gave the fatal stroke, first cutting her throat, and then severing her yet smiling face from that delicate body, pregnant as it was with the fruits of tenderest love.

(94)

Oroonoko is physically transformed by this ritual killing. The narrator views him not from the intimate perspective of friendship but through the horrified eyes of her community:

> We ran all to see him; and, if before we thought him so beautiful a sight, he was now so alter'd, that his face was like a death's-head black'd over, nothing but teeth and eye-holes.
>
> (97)

It is significant that Oroonoko in the closing moments of the narrative is no longer seen as desirable. Instead, he has become an image of abjection and horror. His body is now a sign not of exotic otherness but of savagery. Far from finding him alluring the narrator informs us that she is repelled by his "earthy smell." Yet her attempt to dissociate herself from him only links them all the more. Oroonoko's debilitated condition is mirrored by her own melancholic illness. In addition, her decision to leave the place for some time seems to provoke the final attack on Oroonoko by Banister, "a wild Irish man" (98). The "frightful spectacles" of Oroonoko's execution dominate the ending of the text:

> He had learn'd to take tobacco; and when he was assur'd he should die, he desir'd they would give him a pipe in his mouth, ready lighted; which they did: and the executioner came, and first cut off his members, and threw them into the fire; after that, with an ill-favour'd knife, they cut off his ears and his nose, and burn'd them; he still smoked on, as if nothing had touch'd him; then they hack'd off one of his arms, and still he bore up, and held his pipe; but at the cutting off the other arm, his head sunk, and his pipe dropt and he gave up the ghost, without a groan, or a reproach. My mother and sister were by him all the while, but not suffer'd to save him.
>
> (98–9)

The grotesque and harrowing account of the pipe-smoking Oroonoko being slowly hacked to death acts as a final and lasting reminder of the gulf separating white women and slaves in a colonial society. The bizarre comfort that he draws from tobacco becomes a mocking commentary on the nature of colonial trade. The sadistic excess involved in the slaughtering

13

of Oroonoko and his apparent imperviousness to physical pain once again emphasize his ethnic otherness and archetypally masculine courage. Disturbingly, too, the narrator's mother and sister seem by their very inactivity to collude in this savage killing. Oroonoko's dismemberment appears in part to be a retribution for his role as the object of female desire and fear throughout the text.

Indeed, the ambivalence of Behn's parting description of Oroonoko suggests that the white colonial woman and the black male slave are trapped in an unavoidable pattern of reversal and betrayal. In asserting his masculinity and dis-affection with the English colonial regime Oroonoko breaks the bonds of sympathy that linked him with the narrator, thus assuring his downfall. Likewise, the narrator's collapse into female melancholia and sudden expression of fear of the alien world in which she is living render her complicit with the inhuman massacre of the black slave once held to be her friend. The things that link these figures are one and the same with those that pit them against each other. In particular, the experi-ence of slavery both unites and divides the central personae. As a consequence, the final sentence of *Oroonoko* is circular and inconclusive:

> Thus died this great man, worthy of a better fate, and a more sublime wit than mine to write his praise: yet, I hope, the reputation of my pen is considerable enough to make his glorious name to survive to all ages, with that of the brave, the beautiful, and the constant Imoinda.
>
> (99)

The text ends with an acknowledgement of the separate and disparate nature of its chief protagonists, the narrator, Oroon-oko and Imoinda, and with a recognition that because of the different political positions of these individuals the tale that we have read has fallen short of its purpose. Behn succeeds neither in attacking slavery nor in proving that marginalized groups such as women and slaves have a shared experience of the world. The figure of the heroic black slave cannot act as a unifying metaphor for the specific injustices done to kings, women, oppressed ethnic groups and colonized peoples. Fit-tingly, *Oroonoko* concludes with a desire to circle back on itself and make good its omissions and inconsistencies. Finally and helplessly it gestures at the stories which it can never relate and the list of political causes – those of dispossessed kings, aspiring women writers and black women among them – it can never hope fully to interweave. It seems appropriate that the final name in this catalogue of disparate and incommensurate personae should be that of the black woman slave, Imoinda. Her name remains as a final, lingering reminder of the guilty complicities and contradictions in Behn's attempt to celebrate those forgotten by history. By using the figure of the black slave as a metaphor for the oppression of white political leaders and white women she has been guilty of a double erasure. Imoinda represents the point at which Behn's conflicting beliefs in the rights of colonizing sovereigns and of marginalized women are called most fully into question.

NOTES

1 For an account of the revolution of 1688 see J.R. Jones, *Country and Court: England 1658–1714*, London, Edward Arnold, 1978, 234–55.
2 A. Behn, *Oroonoko and Other Stories*, ed. M. Duffy, London, Methuen, 1986, 25, 27 (cited hereafter by page number only in parenthesis).
3 A. Goreau provides an account of the many disputes about the details of Behn's life, also noting the attempts made by Behn's "de-biographers" to discredit her. See *Reconstructing Aphra: A Social Biography of Aphra Behn*, Oxford, Oxford University Press, 1980.
4 E. Bernbaum, "Mrs. Behn's Biography a Fiction," *PMLA* 28 (1913) 432–53. The phrase occurs on 434.
5 See M. Duffy, *The Passionate Shepherdess: Aphra Behn 1640–89*, London, Jonathan Cape, 1977, and Goreau, *Reconstructing Aphra*.
6 For evidence of Behn's accuracy in her account of both West African and South American culture see E. Campbell, "Aphra Behn's Surinam Interlude," *Kunapipi* 7: 2–3 (1985) 25–35, B. Dhuicq, "Further Evidence on Aphra Behn's Stay in Surinam," *Notes and Queries* 224 (1979) 524–6, H.G. Platt, Jr., "Astrea and Celadon: An Untouched Portrait of Aphra Behn," *PMLA* 49 (1934) 544–59, J.A. Ramsaran, "*Oroonoko*: A Study of the Factual Elements," *NQ* 205 (1960) 142–5, K.M. Rogers, "Fact and Fiction in Aphra Behn's *Oroonoko*," *Studies in the Novel* 20 (Spring 1988) 1–15, and W. Sypher, "A Note on the Realism of Mrs. Behn's *Oroonoko*," *Modern Language Quarterly* 3 (1942) 401–5.
7 B.G. MacCarthy, *Women Writers: Their Contribution to the English Novel, 1621–1744*, Cork, Cork University Press, 1944, 148–88.

8 V. Woolf, *A Room of One's Own* and *Three Guineas*, ed. Morag Shiach, Oxford and New York, Oxford University Press, 1992, 85, and V. Sackville-West, *Aphra Behn: The Incomparable Astrea*, London, Gerald Howe, 1927, 12.

9 D. Spender, *Mothers of the Novel: 100 Good Women Writers before Jane Austen*, London, Pandora Press, 1986, 47–66.

10 See Campbell, "Aphra Behn's Surinam Interlude," 33.

11 V. Ware, *Beyond the Pale: White Women, Racism and History*, London, Verso, 1992, 50–3.

12 L. Brown, "The Romance of Empire: *Oroonoko* and the Trade in Slaves," in F. Nussbaum and L. Brown, eds, *The New Eighteenth Century: Theory, Politics, English Literature*, New York and London, Methuen, 1987, 41–61.

13 M. Ferguson, "*Oroonoko*: Birth of a Paradigm," *New Literary History* 23 (1992) 339–59.

14 H. Hutner, "Aphra Behn's *Oroonoko*: The Politics of Gender, Race, and Class," in D. Spender, ed., *Living by the Pen: Early British Women Writers*, New York, Teachers College Press, 1992, 39–51.

15 The failure of feminism to reflect upon its unspoken acceptance of white privilege has become a vital area of debate in recent political writing. See especially b. hooks, *Ain't I a Woman? Black Women and Feminism*, London, Pluto Press, 1982, and E.V. Spelman, *Inessential Woman: Problems of Exclusion in Feminist Thought*, Boston, Beacon Press, 1988.

16 R. Ballaster, "New Hystericism: Aphra Behn's *Oroonoko*: The Body, the Text and the Feminist Critic," in I. Armstrong, ed., *New Feminist Discourses: Critical Essays on Theories and Texts*, London, Routledge, 1992, 283–95.

17 G.C. Spivak, "French Feminism in an International Frame," in *In Other Worlds: Essays in Cultural Politics*, New York, Methuen, 1987, 134–53.

18 For discussion of the royalist politics of many seventeenth-century women writers see C. Gallagher, "Embracing the Absolute: The Politics of the Female Subject in Seventeenth-Century England," *Genders* 1 (March 1988) 24–9.

19 For an analysis of the problem of representativity and the difficulty involved in the assumption that a woman writer can speak on behalf of everyone who is marginalized and oppressed see N.K. Miller, *Getting Personal: Feminist Occasions and Other Autobiographical Acts*, London, Routledge, 1991, 72–100.

20 J. Kristeva, *Strangers to Ourselves*, trans. L.S. Roudiez, Hemel Hempstead, Harvester, 1991.

21 As J. Gaines points out, the insistence on normative white ways of looking is a typical feature of racial discrimination. See "White Privilege and Looking Relations: Race and Gender in Feminist Film Theory," *Cultural Critique* 4 (Fall 1986) 59–79.

22 H.K. Bhabha analyses the way in which colonial regimes use a fetishizing gaze in order to insist on the inferiority of other races

and cultures and justify the domination of them. See "The Other Question: Difference, Discrimination and the Discourse of Colonialism," in F. Barker, P. Hulme, M. Iversen and D. Loxley, eds, *Literature, Politics and Theory: Papers from the Essex Conference 1976–84*, London and New York, Methuen, 1986, 148–72.

23 F. Fanon shows that white culture links blackness with sexual excess, corporeality and hypervisibility. See *Black Skin, White Masks*, trans. C. Lam Markmann, London, Pluto Press, 1986.

2

SEX, SLAVERY AND RIGHTS IN MARY WOLLSTONECRAFT'S *VINDICATIONS*

Jane Moore

Mary Wollstonecraft's *A Vindication of the Rights of Men* (1790) and *A Vindication of the Rights of Woman* (1792)[1] both begin with the premise that the inalienable right to liberty is a necessary condition for the creation of a society based on principles of justice and reason. The recognition that in the eighteenth century the right to liberty was operative for only some men – the propertied classes – and hardly any women does not, for Wollstonecraft, invalidate the *principle* of universal rights. The "truth" of rights is not at issue in these texts: the category of the universal is not called into question because rights have been exclusively applied. Thus when *Vindication of the Rights of Woman* takes account of the specificity of women's individual and civil rights it does so with the aim of refining and adding to the category of the universal, not repudiating it.

In the two hundred years since Wollstonecraft's intervention in the debate on women's rights, western liberal feminism has retained a conviction as to the political utility of rights. Nevertheless, the relationship between feminism and rights from the eighteenth century to the present has been a troubled one. Feminists have continually found that universal rights do not embrace women's specific needs. Yet while they have expressed dissatisfaction with the exclusionary practices of existing rights, this has rarely led to a fundamental questioning of the *principle* of rights itself. When feminists in the 1890s called for the rights of married women over their own person they were extending rather than rejecting the existent legal ideology and its discourse of rights. A century later, when feminists campaigned for a woman's right to choose to be pregnant, or not, they were amplifying the earlier demand. The aim was to expand, not problematize, the *principle* of rights, though, of course, the two projects overlap.

Insofar as a distinction can be made between the *principle* and the *content* of rights, this chapter's emphasis falls upon the former. The concern is not to debate the truth of individual rights but to analyse the way that truth is conceptually inscribed within the language of rights, examine its function and question its effects. Focusing on Wollstonecraft's writing, but also taking account of subsequent feminist work on rights, the chapter raises as a problem the possibility that one of the effects of the authenticating function of truth in rights discourse is to *enslave* – as to well as liberate – the subject.

To emphasize the enslaving effect of rights over their liberative function polemically reverses John Locke's theory that rights entail duties and require submission to the law in order to preserve rather than to destroy individual freedoms. The *"end of Law,"* Locke insists, "is not to abolish or restrain, but *to preserve and enlarge Freedom."*[2] Wollstonecraft's writing, in common with other enlightenment declarations, yokes rights to duties. The texts take as their premise the idea that in order to acquire rights, duties must be performed. Those people who do not "willingly resign the privileges of rank and sex" to take on civic duties, writes Wollstonecraft, "have no claim" to "the privileges of humanity," to human rights (*VRW* 220). The imbrication of rights and duties (circumscribed by the concept of citizenship) can also be seen in late-twentieth-century texts – for example, the British government's declaration of national rights, *The Citizen's Charter*. This document states that "citizenship is about our responsibilities . . . as well as our entitlements."[3] However, one of the problems with the duality of rights and duties is that rights easily slide into duties, the latter sometimes taking precedence. In practice, as the contemporary French feminist Luce Irigaray has observed, it often happens that "rights . . . become mainly duties, especially for women: the duty to have children, sexual duties."[4]

The implication of Irigaray's argument is that for women, at least, the duties that accompany rights can be a form of sexual servitude, if not enslavement. Nevertheless, Irigaray also argues that the causal link between rights and duties is a historical, theoretical and political necessity. She proposes that the absence of "civil rights and duties adapted to today's civil persons" is responsible for our consumer-culture, where

> Man is not concerned with improving the quality of man. "No time . . .", "Nostalgia . . .", "Oh, how archaic . . ." "All that's out of date", etc. All these unthinking reactions passively expressed by irresponsible citizens seem to me to be the result of a lack of rights and duties.[5]

It could be argued, on the other hand, that Irigaray's desire for an ethics of rights (and duties) does not solve the dilemma that rights have been superseded, in historical practice, by duties. As later suggested in connection with *Vindication of the Rights of Woman*, the rights/duties pairing remains highly contentious for the *practice* of rights, especially for women. What needs to be underlined, for the moment, is that what makes the enunciation of the problem of rights and duties possible – fixing the "truth" of their relationship – is the metaphysical language within which a western discourse of rights and reason is inscribed. In what follows I propose that "truth" is at the core of the problem of rights, because the power of truth is, ultimately, the power to enslave.

Jacques Derrida's notion of logocentrism is pertinent here. Logocentrism attributes to the word a prior concept (logos) located beyond the order of language and culture, a signified which holds the signifier in place.[6] This order is in turn made secure by a single transcendent Truth, the transcendental signified (Logos), God, or his surrogates, reason and nature. In common with American and French eighteenth-century declarations of rights, Wollstonecraft's *faith* in man's immutable right to liberty is indissociable from and dependent upon acceptance of God – the "transcendental, divine guarantee of the principle of humanity."[7] God, the creator of all life, signifies the idea of absolute goodness and omnipotence. He is the supreme authority. According to Christian myth, God exists above and beyond those orders of language and culture that he created. This has two disturbing consequences. The first is that his divine will, outside history, beyond language and therefore immune to the play of the signifier, is inscrutable and inaccessible. Since God's intention is inaccessible it is also incontrovertible. This produces the second consequence of enslaving humanity to a "truth" that is eternally fixed and therefore, ultimately, dictatorial. Authorized by God, rights are similarly legitimated by a single, unquestionable truth. The incontestable nature of this truth is the point where I begin this analysis of the relationship between enslavement and rights in Wollstonecraft's writing.

"THE RIGHTS OF MEN"

The concept of rights in *A Vindication of the Rights of Men* is "strictly linked to the destiny of the *universal*."[8] From its beginning Wollstonecraft's text confirms and conforms to an enlightenment faith in the *principle* of an abstract human nature, undifferentiated by national, religious or sexual identities. Despite the gendered noun "men," the text is addressed to the whole of humanity, aiming to establish the existence of a universal self.

The text's opening paragraph immediately draws attention to the universality of its declaration of human rights: "I war not with an individual," states Wollstonecraft, "when I contend for the *rights of men* and the liberty of reason" (*VRM* 7). This emphasis on the universal is what defines the difference between Wollstonecraft's view of liberty and Burke's. For Burke, who deplored the abstract rights of the French Revolution and contrasted them with "the rights of an Englishman," liberty was essentially a national and political concept.[9] His *Letter to the Citizens of Bristol* (1774–5) proposes that "A right is merely an abstract metaphysical conception which can never be imposed on society without disaster."[10] In contrast, for Wollstonecraft, the meaning of liberty transcends national or political differences and exceeds the concerns of any historical moment. Arguing that it is exactly the abstraction of the rights of man from the political that ensures and safeguards the principle of social justice for all, she declares, in the spirit of enlightenment humanism, that the meaning of liberty is the "birthright of man" (*VRM* 9). The "truth" of this birthright is guaranteed by the transcendental signified – God.

THE TRANSCENDENTAL SIGNIFIED

"Man" is the destination of rights in Wollstonecraft's text; yet he is not the transcendental signified. It is God, not man, who is enlisted as the origin and guarantor of rights. The text states adamantly that God gave men reason, thus authorizing their rights:

> It is necessary emphatically to repeat, that there are rights which men inherit at their birth, as rational creatures, who were raised above the brute creation by their improvable faculties; and that, in receiving these, not from their forefathers but, from God, prescription can never undermine natural rights.
>
> (VRM 14)

For Derrida the transcendental signified denotes an original meaning that exceeds and governs all other meanings. In the sense that the transcendental signified is a term borrowed from linguistics it is not strictly commensurate with a theological discourse. Even so, I have retained it, rather than the (Althusserian) Subject, or the (Lacanian) Other, to designate the *function* of God in Wollstonecraft's text, because it seems that at the level of meaning, of language, *A Vindication of the Rights of Men* inscribes God precisely as meaning, as *the* meaning which holds all other meanings in place and fixes the *truth* of rights.

Absolute and complete, the transcendental signified does not depend on any other signifier for its meaning. Thus it *appears* to be independent of language, a concept "which in and of itself, in its essence, would refer to no signifier, would exceed the chain of signs, and would no longer itself function as a signifier."[11] It is important to note, however, that, for Derrida, the linguistic autonomy of a transcendental signified is illusory: this is because there is no meaning outside language and "every signified [in language] is also in the position of a signifier."[12] According to Derrida, language is a structure of signifiers, with the result that meaning is endlessly deferred. It is therefore incapable of producing a single, self-identical meaning; any search for an absolute meaning, a signified that would transcend the plurality of meanings denoted by the ceaseless interplay of signifiers, is metaphysical.

Wollstonecraft's text is imbued with a metaphysical essentialism. The argument it makes for the existence of "natural" rights depends on invoking God as their transcendental signified. This is because without God in place as the divine Logos, rights become arbitrary and differentiated. By locating the truth of rights outside language, in God, the text strives to make truth independent of the arbitrariness of meanings produced in language. Rights that result from the "everlasting foundation" of God's "immutable truth" (*VRM* 9) possess a sacred inviolability: "neither open enmity nor hollow homage destroys the intrinsic value of those principles which rest on an eternal foundation, and revert for a standard to the immutable attributes of God" (*VRM* 60).

In contrast, Wollstonecraft identifies laws that result from political and, by derivation, individual interests through their difference from natural/divine rights. The "truth" of inheritance laws and property rights, for example, is not transcendental, but culturally specific and circumscribed by particular rather than universal interests. Individual interests – whether these are economic, parental, religious or national – are consistently figured in terms of slavery and oppression. References are made to parents who treat their children like slaves, to the "iron hand of property" and to the tyranny that characterizes the clergy's management of inferiors (*VRM* 22, 24, 39).

The following passage, attacking Burke's belief that the American Revolution should be understood as the assertion of traditional English liberties, uses the historical example of slavery as a means of critiquing his privileging of national rights to the exclusion of the universal rights of mankind:

> But on what principle Mr Burke could defend American independence, I cannot conceive; for the whole tenor of his plausible arguments settles slavery on an everlasting foundation. Allowing his *servile* reverence for *antiquity*, and prudent attention to *self-interest*, to have the force which he insists on, the slave trade ought never to be abolished; and, because our *ignorant* forefathers, not understanding the *native dignity of man*, sanctioned a traffic that outrages every suggestion of reason and religion, we are to submit to the inhuman custom, and term an atrocious insult to humanity the love of our country, and a proper submission to the laws by which our property is secured. – Security of property! Behold, in a few words, the definition of English liberty. And to this *selfish* principle every nobler one is sacrificed. – The *Briton* takes place of the *man*, and the *image of God* is lost in the *citizen*!
>
> (*VRM* 14–15, emphasis added)

What is objected to here, above all, is the substitution of the "being of the *national citizen*" for that of the "*universal and natural man.*"[13] The effect of putting national interests before universal rights is to create a conflict between the two. English property laws, based on antiquity, not reason, come into conflict with the universal right to liberty, "self-interest" compromising the humanity of reason and religion. For Wollstonecraft, universal rights embrace national interests, whereas the laws peculiar to specific nations are not always commensurate with the dignity of universal "man."

The resistance to privileging individual or national laws above universal or natural rights is crucial to Wollstonecraft's belief that liberty can be secured for all only by maintaining the principle of a universal human dignity, which reflects God's image, and is authorized in his name. Yet does the principle of an eternal, universal truth, sanctioned by God, guarantee rights for all humanity? Moreover, is it possible to have a notion of universal rights without invoking simultaneously the different and often conflicting interests of nation, class, sex and commerce?

One of the consequences of fixing the truth of rights on the inalienable ground of the transcendental signified is the elision of such questions. The trouble with the transcendental signified is that, located outside language, it is also outside meaning. There is no meaning beyond language and meaning in language depends on difference. If the transcendental signified is undifferentiated fullness, it follows that it is also without meaning, or at least one that is knowable. Consequently, the idea of God, of the transcendental signified, resides at the level of the *imaginary*. To this extent, its existence is illusory and the meaning, the truth that it fixes, is destabilized simply because it is, ultimately, unknowable.

Alternatively, if the transcendental signified is returned to language, as when it is inscribed in the notion of universal rights, then it becomes automatically subject to the play of the signifier, the differences that structure the signifying chain. This is so because rights involve interests and meanings and differences. The universal is not an empty category – its principle cannot be separated from its content. Not so much a void as an umbrella under which individual differences shelter, the universal is comprised of entities and groups, which are the site of struggle over the meaning, over the truth of rights.

24

Language is where the battle over meaning is conducted. At the beginning of *A Vindication of the Rights of Men*, Wollstonecraft announces to Burke that she "glow[s] with indignation" in the attempt "to unravel [his] slavish paradoxes, in which [she] can find no fixed first principle to refute" (*VRM* 10). Wollstonecraft's polemic is designed to discredit Burke, but translated into the broader terms of a suspicion of rhetoric and metaphor, her frustration with Burke's linguistic twists and turns indicates a recognition of language's dangerous capacity for deferring, or as Wollstonecraft would have it, distorting, meaning. Misunderstanding is linked to slavery – to Burke's "slavish paradoxes." Is it language that is culpable, or Burke? There is no obvious answer, but Wollstonecraft's rejection of Burke's argument on the grounds of his (mis)use of language provides, at the very least, a context for her desire to locate truth outside the order of language.

However, at the moment that the transcendental signified is posited as an extralinguistic guarantee of the truth of rights, Wollstonecraft's text confronts, but cannot concede, the limits of its own metaphysical essentialism. One of these limits is that the idea of God, the notion of full meaning, cannot be made present in language. God is an absent presence in *A Vindication of the Rights of Men*. So too by extension are the rights that originate with him. This has the consequence of making the discourse of rights teleological. "Liberty," for example, is reported to be

> a fair idea that has never *yet* received a form in the various governments that have been established on our beauteous globe . . . . But that it results from the eternal foundation of right – from immutable truth – who will presume to deny, that pretends to rationality – if reason has led them to build their morality and religion on an everlasting foundation – the attributes of God?
>
> (*VRM* 9, emphasis added)

The conditional word "yet" immediately betrays the argument as teleological and gives to Wollstonecraft's doctrine of rights a utopian quality, which simultaneously introduces an aspect of faith into the argument. In the above citation, faith and truth are related concepts: the assertion that liberty results from the "eternal foundation of right – from immutable truth" would appear to depend on "reason," but reason itself is strictly linked to "the attributes of God." Furthermore, since these are beyond the full comprehension of his subjects, reason and, by extension, truth, belong to the order of faith.

FAITH

Jacques Lacan has observed that one of the constraints of reason, law or rights is that outside an acceptance in principle of an agreed faith, or rule, these concepts have no fixed meaning, no essential truth:

> What is called logic or law is never more than a body of rules that were laboriously drawn up at a moment of history duly certificated as to time and place, by agora or forum, church, even party. I shall expect nothing therefore of those rules except the good faith of the Other, and, as a last resort, will make use of them, if I think fit or if I am forced to, only to amuse bad faith.[14]

The problem with fixing truth in faith is that faith itself cannot be analysed or questioned, only re-iterated. Perhaps this explains why, in practice, rights are written to be read, in both senses of the word. Often, rights are spoken out loud, as when a person is "read" his or her legal rights. American school-children come to "know" the meaning of freedom and citizenship by reciting from the Constitution: "I pledge allegiance to the flag of the United States of America and to the Republic for which it stands, one nation indivisible under God, with Liberty and Justice for all." In America – as in Britain – a person learns rights, not through processes of analysis, but in the practice of reading and reciting.

Citation is also the means by which *A Vindication of the Rights of Men* communicates the idea of the transcendental signified that guarantees the truth or principle of rights. For example, the truth of Liberty, which rests, finally, with God, is something that cannot be determined by analysis of either the concept in itself or the transcendental signified that seeks to ground it.[15] Rather, the "truth" of God, and in consequence, rights, is inscribed in a series of repeated references which have the quality of a citation or catechism – "Liberty . . . results from the eternal foundation of right – from immutable truth"; "I reverence the rights of men. – Sacred rights!"; "What can make us reverence ourselves, but a reverence for that Being, of whom we are a faint image?" (*VRM* 9, 34, 39).

These examples illustrate the closed nature of citational knowledge. Citation is an indirect knowledge, "composed of reported statements that are incorporated into the metanarrative of a subject that guarantees their legitimacy."[16] To repeat the point made earlier, outside an acceptance in principle of an agreed faith, or rule, the discourses of reason, law or rights, have no fixed meaning, no essential truth. Yet a truth that is affirmed by faith is beyond redress. There thus arises the possibility that a discourse of rights legitimated by faith is part of the logic, not of liberty, as *A Vindication of the Rights of Men* proposes, but of enslavement – to a truth that is ultimately unknowable, and all the more desirable for being so. What could be a more seductive and effective mode of control than a truth that is tangible enough to be acknowledged yet mysterious to the point where full comprehension is withheld?

AUTHORITY

The treatment of God's authority in *A Vindication of the Rights of Men* is ambiguous. On the one hand it is asserted beyond question that God is the "Supreme Being," the first and final authority; the text insists on this point. Yet it also stresses that God is not a despot. On the contrary, he is absolute goodness, reason, truth. Thus when Wollstonecraft announces "I *FEAR* God!" she makes the important qualification that the source of her humility is not God's power but rather his reason: "It is not his power that I fear – it is not to an arbitrary will, but to unerring *reason* I submit" (*VRM* 34). In giving men and women rational faculties, God also gave them freedom to choose. Reason is coterminous with freedom of choice, and there is a difference, the text asserts, between chosen submission to God's law based on rational understanding, and blind obedience, which is the result of slavish or habitual devotion. The Creator of all human life is the essence of pure reason. Consequently, "the more man discovers of the nature of his mind and body, the more clearly he is convinced, that to act according to the dictates of reason is to conform to the law of God" (*VRM* 51). The argument produces a perfect syllogism: God is the eternal foundation of reason and truth; rights result from reason; therefore rights are true. In this fashion, the subject is simultaneously an active thinking being and *one subjected* to a truth that transcends worldly interrogation. There is certainly an ambiguity here regarding the omnipotence of God and the power of the subject to resist his truth. Yet there is also closure, because God's truth is finally inviolable and ultimately inaccessible, with the result that it is able to operate as a mode of control, regulating what subjects can legitimately say and do.

EXCLUSION

I wish in what follows to take the American Declaration of Independence (1776) as an example of how the metaphysical essentialism of truth produces in practice forms of enslavement and exclusion. My aim is not, however, to cite the Declaration as an instance of the "abuse" of universal rights. Rather, at this juncture, I wish to raise the possibility that exclusion is a *theoretical necessity* of the argument from national rights. Here is the opening paragraph of the Declaration:

> When in the course of the human events, it becomes necessary for one people to dissolve the political bands which have connected them with another, and to assume among the powers of the earth the separate and equal station to which the laws of nature and of nature's God entitle them, a decent respect to the opinions of mankind requires that they should declare the causes which impel them to the separation.[17]

The constitutional and political purpose of the text is to transfer power from England to the American states. However, the language mystifies this constitutional purpose as a general principle – that of the nation – the "one people." The notion of a "people" or "nation" assumed in the Declaration is seen as natural, given, universal and, though paradoxically, above politics. In this respect, it can be said that here "'natural' man is immediately *political*, hence *national*."[18] This slippage from "natural" to "national," from "man," to "citizen," is striking in its difference from Wollstonecraft's much more "abstract" definition of liberty in *A Vindication of the Rights of Men*, where the interests of "national" man, Burke's "Briton," are potentially in conflict with those of "natural" universal man. Both texts, though, appeal to God as the transcendental signified of rights. Ultimately, it is in God's name that the Declaration asserts its truth.

This is particularly apparent in the second, more famous paragraph of the American Declaration, which raises politics, under the common principle of nationhood, to the level of metaphysics:

> We hold these truths to be self-evident: that all men are created equal, that they are endowed by their Creator with certain unalienable rights, that among these are life, liberty, and the pursuit of happiness.[19]

The emphasis here falls on both universal dignity, "all men are created equal," and the transparency of this statement: "We hold these truths to be self-eviden." The transparency of truth is an effect of the transcendental signified, God. Before God, all men are equal: the triumph of the transcendental signified is to make truth the same for everyone, and to erase, in the abstract at least, the inequalities that fragment humanity.

Or perhaps this is not the case, at least in historical practice. History has demonstrated that the American Declaration is a divisive document. Ironically, the Declaration's most renowned words, cited above, were addressed to a society that countenanced slavery. Moreover, a considerable number of those who signed the Declaration were themselves slave-holders, Jefferson included. Slavery was not finally made illegal in the United States until Lincoln's Emancipation Proclamation (1863) and the Thirteenth Amendment (1865), and even then extensive controversy raged over the proclamation's constitutionality and legal effect. No complete agreement was reached.

The Declaration also shows how the discourse of nationhood that it employs ties the acquisition of "natural" rights to the concept of citizenship, with the result that the exclusion of non-citizens – foreigners and slaves – is a theoretical inevitability of the argument from national to universal rights. In this text, an eighteenth-century *faith* in the universal self and its accompanying ideology of universal rights thus reveals its blindnesses when confronted with slavery and national interests.

Can this example lead us to deduce anything about the status of the enlightenment universals themselves (Humanity, Liberty,

Truth) with regard to the issue of exclusion? Is exclusion a theoretical inevitability of these universals in themselves? Or can rights simply be equally extended to everyone and everything? To address these questions, it is necessary to make a distinction between universals and truth, which raises in turn the issue of whether it is possible to retain a version or ethics of universal rights that does not, ultimately, rely on the metaphysical essentialism of an underlying truth rooted in the transcendental signified.

To take the question of exclusion first, Patricia Williams, a contemporary US legal theorist, and herself the descendant of a slave, argues in *The Alchemy of Race and Rights* that exclusion from universal rights is an empirical and historical contingency, not a theoretical necessity. While recognizing that documents such as the American Declaration did indeed exclude black people from its universal embrace, she suggests that the symbolic meanings responsible for this exclusion also provide the material for a different outcome. Under the significant heading of "Excluding Voices," she writes:

> If one looks at documents like the Declaration of Independence and the Constitution, one can see how they marry aspects of consent and aspects of symbology – for example, concepts like the notion of freedom. On the one hand there is the letter of the law exalted in these documents, which describes a specific range of rights and precepts. On the other hand there is the spirit of the law, the symbology of freedom, which is in some ways utterly meaningless or empty – although at the same time the very emptiness provides a vessel to be filled with possibility, with a plurality of autonomous yearnings.[20]

Williams's analysis of the Declaration and the Constitution problematizes the symbolic aspect of rights and refuses to take on trust the truth of the transcendental signified. Although God is absent from her text, the transcendental signified is not. It is there in "the spirit of the law, the symbology of freedom," and, as Williams shows, is an empty signifier, "in some ways utterly meaningless." As a consequence, Williams implies that the effect of the transcendental signified is imaginary, not securing but destabilizing the truth. Abstract to the point of meaninglessness, it can signify at all only in context, in "the letter of the law."

Precisely because the transcendental signified lacks a positive meaning, Williams suggests, it "provides a vessel to be filled with possibility . . . a plurality of autonomous yearnings." She thus celebrates the transcendental signified as a site where meaning is multiple and changing, not single and fixed. On this ground she is able to envisage a new and plural concept of universal rights. What is at issue in rights, Williams argues, is not the universal category, which is capable of embracing a range of meanings, but the category of truth. Her point is that "truth" needs to be unmasked, and since this cannot be done without destroying the balance of things – the existing universals – the possibility arises of constructing a universal that would respect the differences dividing nations and subjects, rather than uniting them in a single reified truth.[21]

In sum, what Williams proposes is a theory of rights that could tolerate the strains of division and difference in language and would not fix meaning in a single truth. Yet does Williams's notion of universal rights solve the problem of exclusion? She concludes her discussion by arguing that rights should be extended to everyone alike:

> society must *give* them away. Unlock them from reification
> by giving them to slaves. Give them to trees. Give them to
> cows. Give them to history. Give them to rivers and rocks.
> Give to all of society's objects and untouchables the rights
> of privacy, integrity, and self-assertion; give them distance
> and respect.[22]

At this point Williams's argument becomes problematic since it is unclear exactly who could authorize the distribution of rights in a way that would avoid their "abuse" by specific political and national parties. Williams resolves this dilemma through recourse to "society." In practice, however, government authorizes the giving of rights in society, and because governments are national bodies, the possible exclusion of universal humanity from the rights given to national citizens returns as a problem. It thus seems that within the framework of democratic government, at least, exclusion is a practical and theoretical inevitability of the argument from rights.

The problem of exclusion in rights discourse is further addressed in Julia Kristeva's *Strangers to Ourselves*. Discussing enlightenment universals Kristeva argues that one can be aware

31

of their limitations and exclusions – the French Revolution "triggered the demand for the national rights of peoples, not the universality of mankind" – without calling the principle into question.[23] That an "*inalienable horizon,* irreducible to that of national political conscience and its jurisdiction"[24] was beyond the reach of many citizens, let alone foreigners who were, *de facto,* not citizens, does not in itself, Kristeva argues, invalidate the principle of universal human dignity. "Abstraction" for her is not the problem:

> The Nazis did not lose their humanity because of the "abstraction" that may have existed in the notion of "man" ("the abstract nakedness of being nothing but human"). On the contrary – it is because they had lost the lofty, abstract, fully symbolic notion of humanity and replaced it with a local, national, or ideological membership, that savageness materialized in them and could be practiced against those who did not share such membership.[25]

If abstraction is not the problem, what is? Kristeva's reply is twofold. It is the notion of national interests on the one hand, which entails the concept of citizenship, and the concept of truth on the other. In an attempt to address this issue, by opening it up for debate, rather than providing the illusory comfort of a single answer, Kristeva makes the case for a modification of enlightenment universals that involves replacing the transcendental signified with an ethics of difference and otherness which would provide the basis for a non-totalizing principle of universal human dignity.[26] "Such a modification," she writes, "is not within the competence of the courts of law alone: it implies not only *rights* but *desires* and *symbolic values.* It falls within the province of ethics and psychoanalysis."[27] What is required is the shift at every level of meaning – discursive, psychic, personal and political – from unity to difference, essence to position. In addition, if we are to prevent the collapse of difference into sameness then there is a need for a continual awareness of what Kristeva calls "that infernal dynamics of estrangement at the core of each entity, individual, or group."[28]

Perhaps it is not coincidental that it should be two women, both of whom speak from cultural margins – Williams because she is black, Kristeva because of the status of psychoanalytic discourse in political thought – who neither fully believe in rights, nor want to discard them. Instead, they share the project of revising rights so that we can live with them, at least in the spirit if not the letter of the law. Perhaps, however, it is the case that we never had problems with the spirit of the law and its abstract universality; maybe the problem has resided more at the level of the letter and its logocentrism and with the belief that behind the word lies a mysterious and transcendent truth of being. It seems to me that what Williams and Kristeva are urging us to resist is exactly the fixing of a single truth. What they are encouraging us to notice is that it is the struggle for meanings in relation to liberty, truth, man, woman, citizen, rather than the fixing of those meanings in formalized declarations of rights, that releases the plurality of signification and mobilizes change in consequence.

"THE RIGHTS OF WOMAN"

A Vindication of the Rights of Woman implicitly recognizes in its title that one effect of fixing truth in the category of the universal is the exclusion of others and their different interests. In this respect, the text goes some way towards acknowledging that plurality of meaning repressed in *A Vindication of the Rights of Men*. The reason for this, I suggest, is the difference made by the emphasis on sex. Starting from the premise that culture treats women "as a kind of subordinate beings, and not as a part of the human species" capable of reason (*VRW* 73), the text shifts rights discourse from the fully symbolic, sexless notion of humanity inscribed in *A Vindication of the Rights of Men* and replaces it with a concept of "citizenship" that foregrounds sexual difference. A key consequence of the transition from "man" to "woman" is a refinement of the category of universal rights.

This is not to imply, however, that the text abandons either the universal or the notion of a general humanity in its argument for female rights. Far from it. The emphasis falls on the damaging consequences of women's exclusion from universal rights and the project of the text is to affirm women's place in general humanity and thus restore to them their rights. Only after considering "women in the grand light of human creatures, who, in common with men, are placed on this earth to unfold their faculties," is the text prepared to particularize the sexual difference of those faculties, "to point out their peculiar designation" (*VRW* 74). Sexual difference is in this way presented as supplementary to the first category of general humanity. Thus, when the text takes account of sexual distinctions it does so with the aim of expanding the category of the universal.

SEXUAL SERVITUDE

A Vindication of the Rights of Woman resolutely rejects the dominant view held by Jean-Jacques Rousseau and his male contemporaries that women think and feel differently from men. According to Rousseau, women are less capable of rational thought than men and more inclined to be swayed by feelings, particularly sexual. Not only does this difference make women the social and intellectual inferiors of men, it also debars them from taking part in public life. Denied access to the worlds of politics, employment and education, woman is also deprived of agency, self-propriety and citizenship. In this context, Wollstonecraft rails against the sexual passion she sees as the chief cause of women's subordination, inscribing it in a series of slave-metaphors: a woman's body is the "gilt cage," the "prison" of her mind (*VRW* 113). With no "duty to fulfil, more noble than to adorn their persons," women become "the slaves of casual lust . . . standing dishes to which every glutton may have access" (*VRW* 208).

Sexual passion is dangerous, not so much in itself as in its consequences. Of these, the most important is that, treated largely as sexual, feeling creatures, women are seen as unfitted for public life and hence denied the duties of citizenship that would permit them to claim the rights accompanying those duties. However, given their principal role as sexual slaves, Wollstonecraft is unable to envisage a situation where women can contract into the rights and duties of citizenship. The text's solution to this problem is to urge women to reject the sexual advances of male gluttons, together with their own sexual appetites, and apply themselves instead to fulfilling the rational duties of motherhood. By prescribing a system of domestic duties peculiar to women, Wollstonecraft demands that women's distinctive qualities and tasks should become part of citizenship – and that women should be citizens in their own right.[29] It is proposed that:

The being who discharges the duties of its station is independent; and, speaking of women at large, their first duty is to themselves as rational creatures, and the next, in point of importance, as citizens, is that, which includes so many, of a mother.

(VRW 216)

Meanwhile, the woman who lavishes attention either on herself or on her husband, at the expense of maternal duties, "scarcely deserves the name of a wife, and has no right to that of a citizen" (VRW 217).

The interdependence of duties and rights is emphasized throughout *A Vindication of the Rights of Woman*. Yet, as the above citations illustrate, duties appear to take precedence over rights. Moreover, a notion of nature lies behind them. The duties of motherhood are fundamentally sexed, thus raising the question of whether it is possible for women to be citizens, and therefore possess rights, without enacting maternal duties which, for the twentieth- and perhaps also eighteenth-century woman, come dangerously close to a new form of enslavement.

The text is ambivalent about motherhood. At the same time as denouncing women who do not fulfil their maternal duties, it raises the problematic question of how "exceptional" (educated) women who reject motherhood can gain the right to be called citizens. "I cannot help lamenting," writes Wollstonecraft, that

> though I consider that women in the common walks of life are called to fulfil the duties of wives and mothers, by religion and reason . . . women of a superiour cast have not a road open by which they can pursue more extensive plans of usefulness and independence.

(VRW 217)

There is a tension here between what reason and religion sanctify and what women desire. The relationship becomes still further strained later in the argument as Wollstonecraft looks forward to a time when women will have female parliamentary "representatives, instead of being arbitrarily governed" by men (VRW 217); when they might "be physicians as well as nurses," "study politics" or pursue business of various kinds (VRW 218).

These are moments of great optimism in the text, arising in part from the instability surrounding the truth of the meaning of woman. In the scenes projected there is no transcendental signified – no truth – to hold the meaning of sexual identity in place. In the absence of a metaphysical essence – nature – the text moves beyond the notion of woman as a fixed psychic, sexual or social being. The future Wollstonecraft envisions is arguably the present of our own society, where women are also, but not *only*, mothers. What, then, is the relation of contemporary feminist theory to law, rights, duties and what is *their* relation to sexual difference?

"SEXUATE RIGHTS"

There is, of course, no short answer to the question. Nor is it possible here to give a representative account of feminist work in this area. Irigaray has consistently addressed the issue of law and rights from the perspective of sexual difference. Certainly her views, though not typical, are extraordinarily influential, *Je, Tu, Nous* (1990) taking as its project the definition of a code of "sexuate rights."

Insofar as Irigaray sets out to define rights and duties peculiar to women, her project seems remarkably similar to Wollstonecraft's. Yet while Wollstonecraft aims, ultimately, to include women in the category of universal rights, Irigaray seeks to establish a separate set of rights for them, thus preventing the erasure of sexual difference within a universal that has historically served the interests of men. In common with Kristeva and Williams, she does not, however, reject the principle of universal human dignity:

> The first universal to be established would be that of a legislation valid for both sexes as a basic element in human culture. That does not mean forced sexual choices. But we are living beings, which means sexuate beings, and our identity cannot be constructed without a vertical and horizontal horizon that respects that difference.[30]

Irigaray goes on to elaborate a theory of "sexuate rights" which would give women and girls a different "positive identity."[31] These rights centre on the assertion of a separate identity for women, which principally involves giving them full control over their virginity and status as potential mothers. At times, these proposals seem strikingly akin to Wollstonecraft's declaration of women's rights, particularly with respect to the key role played by maternal rights – and duties. Irigaray asserts, among other demands, "The right to *motherhood* as a component in female identity," arguing that "If the body is a legal issue, and it is, the female body must be identified in civil terms as virgin and potentially mother."[32]

It is no surprise that God – patriarch *par excellence* – is absent from Irigaray's declaration of women's rights. What is surprising – even shocking – from the perspective of post-structuralism, is the establishment of a new transcendental signified, the *sexed* body. Moreover, the female body is cast in the most stereotypical terms: as virgin and then, potentially, mother. The status of these female stereotypes in Irigaray's theory is problematic. On the one hand, it could be argued that she is re-appropriating these terms, turning them back upon the patriarchal culture that prescribed them. On the other hand, the body has had such a tenacious hold on notions of sexual identity that it seems dangerous to exalt it as the origin and truth of ourselves. Mysterious as the idea of God, with desires and drives never fully knowable, Irigaray's sexed body transcends history, culture, language. Yet, of course, the definition of sexual identity – the qualities attributed to men and women – takes place in culture. It is at the level of culture, of language, where meanings are produced and deferred, that change takes place. Rights become problematic, I wish to suggest, when meanings freeze into a truth that is presumed to be autonomous from the different social and political interests it is called on to guarantee.

The discourse of rights is integral to the meanings that circulate in culture. More than this, rights have played a central role in the history of emancipatory struggles from at least the eighteenth century to the present. However, it is the contest for meaning, together with the denaturalizing of accepted truths, that produces rights. This is where the potential for change is located. The enslavement to a metaphysics of truth hinders change, and rights have also been part of this tradition. The aim of this chapter has been to problematize the discourse of rights and question the assumption that rights, in principle and practice, can exist in a pure state, free from the ideological and divisive interests that structure their "truth." It is impossible, I suspect, to discard the relevance of rights in contemporary culture, but neither should we take their truth on trust. Rights are never simply *given*.

NOTES

1 For all references to and citations of these texts the edition used is *The Works of Mary Wollstonecraft*, ed. J. Todd and M. Butler, 7 vols, London, Pickering, 1989. Both texts appear in Volume V and are respectively cited hereafter as *VRM* and *VRW* with page number in parenthesis.

2 Cited in J.P. Reid, *The Concept of Liberty in the Age of the American Revolution*, Chicago and London, University of Chicago Press, 1988, 64.

3 J. Major, "Foreword" to *The Citizen's Charter*, London, HMSO, 1991, 2. The political left in Britain have received the Charter with scepticism and denounced it as phoney, a fake, a travesty, in fact, of the "rights of man." See, for example, *New Statesman and Society*, 31 July 1992, 5. Translated into the terms of postmodernist debate, the Charter's critics seem to be saying that it is a parody, or even a pastiche, of an enlightenment discourse of rights. It would be interesting to make this argument at length, not out of a neo-humanist nostalgia for the truth of human rights, but from a position that would theorize what the Charter's critics perceive to be its emptiness of meaning as symptomatic of the metaphysical assumptions that structure the western discourse of reason and rights.

4 L. Irigaray, "The Necessity for Sexuate Rights," *The Irigaray Reader*, ed. M. Whitford, Oxford, Blackwell, 1991, 198–203, at 201.

5 Irigaray, "How to Define Sexuate Rights?" ibid., 204–12, at 206.

6 For an accessible account of the concept of logocentrism and the metaphysics of presence see J. Derrida, "Semiology and Grammatology: Interview with Julia Kristeva," in *Positions*, trans. A. Bass, London, The Athlone Press, 1981, 17–36.

7 J. Kristeva, *Strangers to Ourselves*, trans. L.S. Roudiez, Hemel Hempstead, Harvester, 1991, 152.

8 E. Laclau, "Beyond Emancipation," paper delivered at the Cardiff Critical Theory Seminar, Cardiff, March 1992, 12, (emphasis added). From the perspective of a postmodern pluralism, Laclau's paper questions the teleology of enlightenment thought, which seeks to fix a single and final truth, such as emancipation.

9 Kristeva, *Strangers*, 152.

10 Cited in the "Introduction" to E. Burke, *Reflections on the French Revolution and Other Essays*, ed. A.J. Grieve, London and Toronto, Dent, 1929, ix.

11 Derrida, "Semiology," 19–20.

12 ibid., 20.

13 Kristeva, *Strangers*, 150.

SEX, SLAVERY AND RIGHTS

14 J. Lacan, *Ecrits: A Selection*, trans. A. Sheridan, London, Tavistock, 1977, 140.
15 On the difficulty of analysing the truth of universal, symbolic concepts see Laclau, "Beyond Emancipation," 14.
16 J.-F. Lyotard, *The Postmodern Condition: A Report on Knowledge*, trans. G. Bennington and B. Massumi, Manchester, Manchester University Press, 1984, 35.
17 P.M. Angle, ed., *By These Words: Great Documents of American Liberty*, New York, Rand McNally and Co., 1954, 93.
18 Kristeva, *Strangers*, 150.
19 Angle, *By These Words*, 93.
20 P. Williams, *The Alchemy of Race and Rights*, Cambridge, Mass., Harvard University Press, 1991, 16.
21 ibid., 163–5.
22 ibid., 165.
23 Kristeva, *Strangers*, 151.
24 ibid., 150.
25 ibid., 153.
26 ibid., 152–4.
27 ibid., 153.
28 ibid.
29 On the problems posed by the concept of citizenship for feminist political theorists from Wollstonecraft onwards see C. Pateman, *The Disorder of Women: Democracy, Feminism and Political Theory*, Cambridge, Polity Press, 1989, 14.
30 Irigaray, "How to Define Sexuate Rights?," 205.
31 ibid., 208.
32 ibid.

39

3

"THAT MILD BEAM"

Enlightenment and enslavement in William Blake's *Visions of the Daughters of Albion*

Steven Vine

"Enslav'd, the Daughters of Albion weep":[1] Blake's *Visions of the Daughters of Albion* (1793) begins with the sighs of Albion's enslaved Daughters toward America, and ends with the complaint of the female "soft soul of America" (1.3), Oothoon, whose lament is in turn echoed by her British sisters (8.13). However, despite these songs of shared female enslavement, Oothoon's fate in the poem – together with that of the Daughters – is to be a "solitary shadow wailing on the margin of nonentity" (7.15), severed from collective utterance and political possibility. In fact, Oothoon-as-America is confident only that her cries are heard by her patriarchal and colonial oppressor, Bromion, an ideological amalgam of British imperialism and masculinist aggression: "And none but Bromion can hear my lamentations" (3.1), she says.

Even though she speaks some of the most powerful emancipatory lines in English poetry, Oothoon's words remain a lament, a faint cry delivered on the margins of history. It seems that neither Oothoon nor the Daughters of Albion, in fact, reap much benefit from the revolutionary fires of Orc which consume British colonialism in Blake's *America* (1793) and European monarchy in *Europe* (1794), for both Oothoon and the Daughters lack a political constituency that can voice their demands. Moreover, the very utopian energy of Oothoon's protestations becomes the measure of her historical marginality, for she struggles in vain to find a place from which to

40

speak within the violent hierarchies that constrain her. Politically, like the Daughters of Albion (who, as the opening lines of the poem hint, *are* a "trembling lamentation" 1.1), Oothoon is condemned to vocal insubstantiality. In a bitter irony, she shifts between ringing declaration and silence, unheard.

Throughout Blake's *Visions*, Oothoon figures both repression and revolutionary possibility. She acts out an ideological ambivalence in her own person, for she opines in the divided voice of both revolutionary enlightenment and historical enslavement; her speeches veer disconcertingly between subjection and fierce autonomy, and she seems unable to find a position from which to speak that is free from contradiction. Oothoon's language, as we will see, explodes under the pressure of the contradictions that inhabit it. However, her capture in contradiction is far from a simple enslavement, for *Visions* strives to discover political possibility *within* contradiction. Indeed, "vision" in the poem *is* the discourse of contradiction. Thus the poem's subtitle, "The Eye sees more than the Heart knows," suggests that the "more" broached by vision goes beyond the ideological certainties of the "Heart": the heart's knowledge is submitted to an otherness (or, in Oothoon's idiom, a "difference") that exposes what the heart represses. "Vision" opens up contradiction within the known and the familiar, invoking marginalized possibilities in opposition to dominant ideologies. Indeed, the "more" belonging to vision in the poem is a mode of incertitude rather than knowledge; the visions of the Daughters (and of Oothoon in particular) look beyond the patriarchal system that enslaves them, but equally the poem's visions *of* the Daughters scrutinize the contradictions that obscure their insights. At once seeing and seen, the Daughters – divided, like Oothoon, between patriarchy and prophecy – command visionary vistas, but are also shadowed by discursive and historical ironies which cloud the horizons of their utopia.

This chapter examines the critical energies in *Visions*' account of the body, sexuality and slavery, and maps the struggle of the poem to expose structures of sexual and colonial enslavement in the name of a visionary enlightenment. Yet it also shows how, while affirming its radical potential, Blake's language dramatizes the historical and ideological uncertainty of its own illuminations.

SLAVES TO THEIR SENSES[2]

Sighing toward America, Albion's Daughters watch Oothoon with a divided longing, caught between hope and fear. Wandering in woe "Along the vales of Leutha seeking flowers to comfort her" (1.4), Oothoon is an image of awakening and vulnerable desire; and the account of her aroused and violated sexuality given in *Visions* is both a feminist addendum to the narrative of political revolution charted in *America* and an acknowledgement that, like the Daughters of Albion, Oothoon is part of a continuing history of subjection. Oothoon and her sisters *remain* enslaved subjects – victims, as will be seen, of a vicious colonization of the body.

Oothoon's impetuous flight at the beginning of the poem to the object of her desire, Theotormon, is interrupted by her rape at Bromion's hands. Her violation is framed explicitly in the language of colonization and enslavement

> Bromion rent her with his thunders. on his stormy bed
> Lay the faint maid, and soon her woes appalld his
>   thunders hoarse
>
> Bromion spoke. behold this harlot here on Bromions bed,
> And let the jealous dolphins sport around the lovely
>   maid;
> Thy soft American plains are mine, and mine thy north
>   & south:
> Stampt with my signet are the swarthy children of the
>   sun:
> They are obedient, they resist not, they obey the
>   scourge:
> Their daughters worship terrors and obey the violent:
>   (1.16–23)

As a multiple oppressor, Bromion is both rapist, slave-agent[3] and executor of British colonial power: a rabid imperialist, he appropriates Oothoon's body, American territory and the flesh of the "black African"[4] in a riot of colonial and sexual enslavement. For David Erdman, indeed, Oothoon's violation invokes the rape of the "virgin slave" by the brutal slave-owner, performed so that her "pregnancy enhances her price."[5] This savage sexual colonization is prefaced in the poem by Oothoon's

42

tremulous approach to the life of the body, as she "pluck[s]" the flower of desire and places it between her breasts (1.11–12); but her desire is brutalized by Bromion's violence. In this light, the opening section of *Visions* moves from the body's expansion in the "swift delight" (1.14) of desire to its colonial and sexual enslavement. The body as a site of desire and possibility becomes, in a terrible inversion, the body as a site of domination and subjection. From the instant of Oothoon's rape onward, in fact, the significance of the body in *Visions* is profoundly divided: it is at once the abject site where patriarchal domination enforces itself most powerfully, and the place from which Oothoon declares her desire most fiercely. In her alternate songs of lament and liberty, Oothoon intones the meaning of the body as both enslavement and enlightenment. Her body is a prison enclosing a limitless mind ("they inclos'd my infinite brain into a narrow circle," 2.32) and a threshold through which her visions are opened:

> Oothoon is . . . a virgin fill'd with virgin fancies
> Open to joy and to delight where ever beauty appears
> If in the morning sun I find it: there my eyes are fix'd
>
> In happy copulation;
>
> (6.21–7.1)

Against the closure of the senses, Oothoon affirms the *plurality* of sense, bodily and intellectual, in a hymn to incommensurability:

> With what sense is it that the chicken shuns the
>   ravenous hawk?
> With what sense does the tame pigeon measure out the
>   expanse?
> With what sense does the bee form cells? have not the
>   mouse & frog
> Eyes and ears and sense of touch? yet are their
>   habitations.
> And their pursuits, as different as their forms and as
>   their joys;
>
> (3.2–6)

Here Oothoon's doxology to difference celebrates a multiplicity that cannot be reduced to the "one law" (4. 22) proclaimed by

Bromion. Her language transgresses the separation of bodily and intellectual "senses," and traverses the opposing realms aggressively colonized by the poem's male antagonists: Theotormon's piously spiritual "reign" (1.15) and Bromion's "stormy bed."

However, Oothoon's affirmative embrace of what *The Marriage of Heaven and Hell* (1790) calls "numerous senses" (11.5) conceals a political contradiction. For Oothoon's plight in *Visions* reveals the body as a site of ambiguity, and "sense" as a theatre of ideological conflict. As several critics have pointed out,[6] the language of *Visions* frequently echoes Mary Wollstonecraft's account of woman's enslavement to the body in *A Vindication of the Rights of Woman* (1792).[6] In *Visions* Oothoon is schooled by nameless patriarchal tutors in an ideology of the bodily senses, but this is a lesson whose implications she identifies and resists:

> They told me that I had five senses to inclose me up.
> And they inclos'd my infinite brain into a narrow circle.
> And sunk my heart into the Abyss, a red round globe hot
>   burning
> Till all from life I was obliterated and erased. (2.31–4)

The enclosure of Oothoon's "infinite brain" in the prison of the five senses is not so much a Platonic lament for the fall into bodiliness as a recognition of the *political* implications of the senses. Like Blake's poem, Wollstonecraft's *Vindication* reveals and critiques an ideology of "sense" that, against the emancipatory categories of reason and enlightenment that Wollstonecraft (if not Blake) espouses, insistently entrenches woman in the somatic. Time and again, Wollstonecraft asserts that late-eighteenth-century culture conspires to "enslave women by cramping their understandings and sharpening their senses."[7] She shows how, through an entire system of education, marital relations, political structure and sexual ideology, women are rendered "slaves to their bodies"[8] and their "senses" – excluded from the masculine community of enlightened citizenship and rational exchange to which they ought rightfully to belong. Denied the status even of "rational creatures"[9] – as in Rousseau's *Emile* (1762), Wollstonecraft's central counter-text throughout *Vindication*[10] – women are reduced to living in the gap or hiatus of masculine reason. Woman appears only in reason's absence:

Gentleness, docility, and a spaniel-like affection are . . .
consistently recommended as the cardinal virtues of the
sex . . . . She was created to be the toy of man, his rattle,
and it must jingle in his ears whenever, dismissing reason,
he chooses to be amused.[11]

Woman appears when reason is absent, and she is absent when
reason is at work. This violent dialectic prompts Wollstonecraft
to demand that women be incorporated in the community of
enlightenment from which they are excluded by the force of law,
social education and Rousseauist sexual ideology. In Wollstonecraft, women take up their place in the march of male enlightenment; they become part of a revolutionary historical narrative
whose logic is one of progressive improvement and emancipation under the aegis of reason. With an eye upon contemporary political transformations in France, Wollstonecraft's
text calls upon women to assume their role as rational subjects
in a newly enlightened social order. As Cora Kaplan puts it,
Wollstonecraft's text is dedicated to "the optimistic, speculative
construction of a virtuous citizen subject for a brave new
egalitarian world."[12]

However, both Kaplan and Mary Jacobus argue that there is
a renunciative logic implicit in *Vindication*'s espousal of the
discourse of "reason." Jacobus comments:

The Rights of Woman, in claiming sense for women rather
than sensibility, pays a price that is reflected in its own
prose. Putting herself outside the confines of a despised
femininity, aligning herself with "sense," Mary Wollstonecraft also eschews "pretty feminine phrases" as a male
conspiracy designed to soften female slavery. Linguistic
pleasure (literary language) is placed on the side of the
feminine, then banned, like female desire.[13]

For Jacobus, Wollstonecraft's enlightenment woman – as if to
compensate for Rousseau's representation of woman as a
monster of passion – repudiates desire, literariness and imagination as forces designed to underscore her capture in the prison of
"sensibility." As Kaplan writes, "feeling" in Wollstonecraft's
argument is

reactionary and regressive, almost counter-revolutionary.
Sexuality and pleasure are narcotic inducements to a life of

lubricious slavery. Reason is the only human attribute appropriate to the revolutionary character, and women are impeded by their early and corrupt initiation in the sensual, from using theirs.[14]

For the Wollstonecraft of *Vindication*, the woman writer who does not distinguish herself from indulgent fancies and the errors of sensibility fatally excludes herself from the enlightenment to which she should belong.

Jacobus argues that this renunciation of feeling in *Vindication* is woman's loss as much as her gain. It is not that woman sets *herself* outside the empire of reason, but rather that the language of reason works ideologically in patriarchal culture to exclude woman. In political and cultural terms, woman is caught between a language of reason which debars her and a language of sensibility which debases her; as Jacobus says, "if 'sense' excludes women, 'sensibility' confines them."[15] Far from being innocent, the language of eighteenth-century reason functions to subject woman to the body; woman is consigned, like Blake's Oothoon, to a realm of the "senses," to a colonized cultural space from which she is unable to intervene in the dominant order. Against Wollstonecraft's best hopes, enlightenment reason unreasonably subordinates woman to a patriarchal cultural law that, despite the egalitarian promises of rationality, forbids the access it seems to proffer. Indeed, Kaplan argues that the "categories of independent subjectivity" propounded by enlightenment discourses as the rational foundation of new revolutionary and republican freedoms were

> marked from the beginning by exclusions of gender, race and class. Jean-Jacques Rousseau, writing in the 1750s, specifically exempted women from his definition; Thomas Jefferson, some twenty years later, excluded blacks.[16]

In this sense, enlightenment reason has a sinister underside and reason's light casts ideological shadows. This might be called the inescapable political irony of *Vindication*: the text appeals for judgement to the court of reason, but it also shows how, in the politics of late-eighteenth-century culture, reason shuts out women from the emancipatory discourse of enlightenment which in another respect it guarantees. Ironically, reason dispossesses woman of the rights it should – by rights – give her.

Near the end of *Vindication*, Wollstonecraft figures reason's self-certainty as the violent subjection of woman. Woman is seen as a quiescent slave sweetening the rational life of a master who brutally extracts his pleasures from her. Wollstonecraft asks:

> Is sugar always to be produced by vital blood? Is one half of the human species, like the poor African slaves, to be subjected to prejudices that brutalize them, when principles would be a surer guard, only to sweeten the cup of man? Is not this indirectly to deny woman reason?[17]

Woman is a sugar which sweetens man's bitter cup. The rigours of masculine reason are made bearable by the other of man and reason: woman. Man's reason tempers, refreshes and sustains itself by means of woman. Outside reason, woman is a bodily balm which allows reason to depart from itself, forgetting itself in pleasure – but only to return the more vigorously to itself. Like the "poor African slaves" who, in a cruel irony, manufacture sugar yet suffer bitterly for it, woman's mind is enslaved in order that her body may yield sweetness. Her senses cloy while her sense is brutalized. Almost against itself, Wollstonecraft's metaphor shows how masculine reason – like masculine pleasure – is constituted as jealously conserved *power* rather than as general or rational enlightenment. Politically, then, the cachet of reason works to maintain the enslavement of women as much as, in Wollstonecraft's terms, it presages their emancipation and enlightenment. Wollstonecraft's twin theme of woman's enslavement to sense and exclusion from reason reveals, therefore, a politics of *reason* as much as a politics of the body.

Like *Vindication*, Blake's *Visions* anatomizes the enslavement of woman. Indeed, as if in homage to Wollstonecraft's critique, Blake's poem often echoes the metaphors of the earlier text. As Blake's Oothoon begins by wandering through "the vales of Leutha seeking flowers to comfort her," so Wollstonecraft's hapless virgin "wander[s] through flowery lawns" in a "dream of passion"; and as, after her rape, Oothoon becomes a "solitary shadow wailing on the margin of non-entity," Wollstonecraft's "creature of sensibility," similarly violated, finds herself on the margins of a "sneering, frowning world . . . alone in a waste."[18] Yet if Wollstonecraft locates woman's enslavement in the body, sensibility and desire, Blake's *Visions* seems to politicize desire in the opposite direction. Analysing the problem of "female

sensibility and sexuality" in *Vindication* and Blake's poem,
Nancy Moore Goslee remarks:

> Blake appears to correct Wollstonecraft, but not by agree-
> ing with Rousseau. Instead, he employs Wollstonecraft's
> deductive method of arguing from a premise about human
> nature: Oothoon's premise, however, is not universal
> reason but universal desire.[19]

As Goslee suggests, Blake's poem reverses Wollstonecraft's
premises: instead of desire acting as the agent of female
oppression, reason as such (in a dialectic which it fails to
recognize) contrives ideologically to subjugate and exclude
women. If Wollstonecraft's metaphors, as we saw, hint that the
category of reason contains a violence within itself, Blake's
poem works to make that violence explicit. Oothoon, for
example, exultantly affirms "The moment of desire!" (7.3), but
discovers to her cost that desire is legislated by Blake's baleful
demigod of the enlightenment, Urizen, whose name puns his
function as the patriarchal law of "reason." Oothoon complains
to Urizen:

> O Urizen! Creator of men! mistaken Demon of heaven:
> Thy joys are tears! thy labour vain, to form men to
>   thine image.
> How can one joy absorb another? are not different joys
> Holy, eternal, infinite! and each joy is a Love.
>
> (5.3–6)

As Goslee observes:

> If we read the word "men" . . . as universal, a substitute for
> "human," then the mistake of Urizen is to believe that these
> "men" can be formed to mirror and thus duplicate his
> demonic rational singleness. . . . If we read "men" as
> "males" . . . then Urizen becomes even more clearly a
> presiding demon of mistaken patriarchal social structures.[20]

Oothoon's critique of Urizen's patriarchal rational law exposes
his false dreams of subjecting multiplicity to uniformity, and
including difference under homogeneity; but, more than this, it
shows how Urizen's rational singleness is founded on a politics
of male narcissism in which the world becomes the passive
reflection of his tyrannous and totalizing self-image. As Oothoon

acknowledges earlier, the political consequence of this is that woman – including herself – is banished from man's imperious act of rational self-mirroring: woman is "obliterated and erased." In *Vindication*, Wollstonecraft calls for woman to be included under reason's law, but Blake's Oothoon argues that such a principle itself effaces woman. However, despite the fact that *Visions* politicizes and problematizes the role of "reason" in this way, the text declines to affirm the body unambiguously. Indeed, like *Vindication*, Blake's *Visions* demonstrates the way in which female subjection to the body functions as one of patriarchy's strongest ideological props. Like *Vindication*, *Visions* exposes the body's politics. For instance, even though Oothoon affirms the body as a mode of emancipation, her language also shows it to be the very image of oppression:

> I call with holy voice! kings of the sounding air,
> Rend away this defiled bosom that I may reflect.
> The image of Theotormon on my pure transparent
>   breast.
>
> The Eagles at her call descend & rend their bleeding
>   prey;
> Theotormon severely smiles. her soul reflects the smile;
> As the clear spring mudded with feet of beasts grows
>   pure & smiles.

$$(2.14–19)$$

In a violent tableau, Oothoon calls on Theotormon's "Eagles" to "rend" her defiled body away in order that she may the more completely mirror his piously narcissistic self-image. Submitting herself desperately to her lover's tormented theological law, she asks that her body be erased before his self-regarding spiritual gaze.[21] Her "bosom" effaced, her "soul" will then "reflect" his devout narcissism all the more capably, like the glassy surface of a clear spring. However, what *seems* to be an effacement of Oothoon's body turns out, in fact, to be the opposite: Oothoon's "bosom" is not purified but bloodied, not spiritualized but brutalized in a terribly material assault upon the flesh. In this light, Theotormon's gaze *subjects* Oothoon to the body rather than abstracting her from it. Moreover, Oothoon's speech and its bloody aftermath make explicit the violence that inhabits Theotormon's apparently disembodied spirituality: for his fearful "smile" is raised on the basis of a viciously enforced dualism – the body is bruised to pleasure soul, and Theotormon's spirituality smiles on Oothoon's battered flesh. Ironically, however, Theotormon's beloved self-image returns to him soiled with its own violence, for the "clear spring" in which he sees himself is indistinguishable from Oothoon's bloodied bosom.

Throughout *Visions*, the ideological significance of the body is split: the body is affirmed in opposition to Urizenic rationality, and yet it is shown to be helplessly complicit with the forces of subjection. However, if Urizen and Theotormon subjugate woman in order to shore up their absurd narcissisms, obliterating her in order to enthrone themselves, the critical energies of *Visions*, as we will see, demolish the specular narcissism that underpins such fantasies of domination.

SLAVERY AND SPECULARITY

Theotormon enslaves Oothoon to his spiritualized self-image, but the purity of his self-reflection is sullied by Oothoon's flesh. Yet, in addition to being a critique of sexual politics, Blake's *Visions* dramatizes – as Erdman has shown – the violent logic of the slave-trade. Indeed, in the illuminated version of the poem, immediately beneath Oothoon's words, "that I may reflect./The image of Theotormon on my pure transparent breast," Blake depicts a black figure lying prostrate beside a blighted tree (see Plate 1). Erdman comments:

> Blake draws a picture . . . stretching across the page, of a Negro worker smitten into desperate horizontality, wilted like the heat-blasted vegetation among which he has been working with a pickaxe, and barely able to hold his face out of the dirt.[22]

In a dual vision of colonial and patriarchal suppression, then, the picture of the prostrate slave mirrors the image of Oothoon subjected to Theotormon's barbarous gaze: indeed, on the facing page, Oothoon's body lies horizontally, like the slave's, as a punishing eagle descends upon her. Moreover, just as Oothoon's bloody breast stains the clarity of Theotormon's self-mirroring, so the slave's black body – in a visionary retort to Theotormon's obsession with whiteness – interrupts his pious

Plate 1 Blake, *Visions of the Daughters of Albion*, plate 2.
Reproduced by permission of the Trustees of the British Museum.

self-contemplation with an image of colonial violence.

Erdman also argues that Blake's Theotormon is a critical portrait of John Gabriel Stedman, a Captain in the Scots Brigade who, in 1790, completed a book of memoirs published in 1796 as *A Narrative, of a Five Years' Expedition, against the Revolted Negroes of Surinam, in Guiana, on the Wild Coast of South America; from the year 1772 to 1777*. As the title indicates, Stedman was part of a military expedition to Dutch Guiana, dispatched in order to suppress a slave-revolt against the European planters. In his capacity as a professional engraver, Blake produced approximately fourteen plates for Stedman's *Narrative* between 1792 and 1793 – at roughly the same time he was writing and etching *Visions*. Erdman contends that, in *Narrative*, Stedman appears as a deeply divided figure. On the one hand, he is involved in the violent suppression of a slave-rebellion, but on the other meticulously observes and records colonial brutalities – acts of barbarism which he deplores and which, following Stedman's original drawings, Blake depicts in a series of harrowing designs. Erdman remarks:

> In his *Narrative* Stedman demonstrates the dilemma, social and sexual, of the English man of sentiment entangled in the ethical code of property and propriety. A hired soldier in Guiana, Captain Stedman was apologetic about the "Fate" that caused him to be fighting bands of rebel slaves in a Dutch colony: "'Twas *yours* to fall – but *Mine* to feel the wound," we learn from the frontispiece, engraved by Bartolozzi: *Stedman with a Rebel Negro prostrate at his feet*.[23]

In the image to which Erdman here refers, Stedman's gun stands murderously over a dead slave – just as Theotormon's gaze prostrates the exhausted Negro in the design from *Visions*.

Erdman sees Theotormon, the pious thinker aware of Oothoon's suffering in her slavery but unable or unwilling to intervene, as "analogous to the wavering abolitionist who cannot bring himself openly to condemn slavery although he deplores the *trade*."[24] Indeed, Stedman himself, as Goslee reminds us, advocated only the gradual abolition of the British slave-trade, fearing that it would come to be dominated by what he considered to be the more brutal masters of other nations.[25] Thus, as if to restore the violence to Stedman's sentiment,

Theotormon in *Visions* colludes with Bromion's brutality: like the wavering Stedman, he weeps for those laid low by slavery, but reproduces nevertheless the thing he abhors.

In a rewriting of Plato's simile, Theotormon sits at the entrance to a metaphysical cave, listening pacifically to the victims of empire, commerce and repressive theology:[26]

> At entrance Theotormon sits wearing the threshold hard
> With secret tears; beneath him sound like waves on a
> desart shore
> The voice of slaves beneath the sun, and children bought
> with money.
> That shiver in religious caves beneath the burning fires
> Of lust, that belch incessant from the summits of the
> earth
>
> (2.6–10)

Theotormon becomes a demigod of colonial and domestic enslavement, for those suffering under the ideological regime he represents appear "beneath" him, enchained like Oothoon and the prisoners of Plato's cave. Erdman argues, however, that the most significant connection between Theotormon and enslavement is the figure of Oothoon herself. He writes of Stedman's *Narrative*:

> To the torture of female slaves Stedman was particularly sensitive, for he was in love with a beautiful fifteen-year-old slave, Joanna, and in a quandary similar to that of Blake's Theotormon, who loves Oothoon but cannot free her . . . . [H]e was unable to purchase her freedom, and when he thought Joanna was to be sold at auction, he fancied he "saw her tortured, insulted, and bowing under the weight of her chains, calling aloud, but in vain, for my assistance."[27]

Although Stedman married Joanna, she was left by him in slavery on his return to Europe: she insisted that she would be the one to purchase her own freedom and, as a black woman, feared what her fate would be in imperialist Europe. Soon after Stedman's departure she died, apparently from poisoning.

As both colonial soldier and deplorer of atrocities, Stedman is a contradictory figure, and the links between certain motifs in *Visions* and *Narrative* make this point starkly. One of Blake's engravings for Stedman is entitled *Family of Negro Slaves from Poango* (see Plate 2). The design shows a man carrying a basket of fish, and a woman some fruit, while the latter is burdened in turn by her two children (one is on her back, one grasps her garment); she is pregnant, and spins yarn as she walks. In the woman's carrying, labouring and mothering (she smokes a pipe, too), there is an element of overladen grotesquerie; her staggering figure is in sharp contrast to the elegant poise of the man, who appears to carry his burden with ease. In the context of *Narrative*, the design (according to Stedman) is of a healthy and contented slave-family, yet Blake seems to undercut this idealized reading with a grim irony. Moreover, in a sharper irony noted by Erdman, Blake had the task of engraving Stedman's initials on the man's right breast. In *Narrative*, Stedman refers to the "J.G.S. in a cypher" stamped on the man's body "by which his owner [i.e. Stedman] may ascertain his property."[28] As Erdman points out, Bromion himself declares in *Visions* (with, in this case, no trace of scruple): "Stampt with my signet are the swarthy children of the sun."

In his refiguring of Stedman's story in *Visions* and the designs to *Narrative*, Blake casts an ironic shadow over the Captain's enlightened sentiments. Just as *Visions* re-introduces brutality into Theotormon's piety, so the designs to *Narrative* emphasize Stedman's complicity in the system he denounces. One of Blake's most striking engravings for *Narrative* is the emblem with which Stedman ends his text, *Europe supported by Africa & America* (see Plate 3). Stedman describes the design:

> I will close the scene with an emblematical picture of *Europe supported by Africa and America*, accompanied by an ardent wish that in the friendly manner as they are represented, they may henceforth and to all eternity be the props of each other.[29]

Erdman's reading of this scene, in which a female Europe is flanked by African and Amerindian female figures and each embraces the other, is that it undercuts the image of harmony it presents. He points to the fact that, while Europe wears pearls, the other two wear slave-bracelets, and that an irony inhabits their sisterly pose; for Europe "*supported* by"[30] Africa and America suggests a relationship of oppression rather than mutuality, of subordination rather than sisterhood. "Support"

Plate 2 Blake, *Family of Negro Slaves from Poango* (design for Stedman's *Narrative*). Reproduced by permission of Oxford University Press.

Plate 3 Blake, *Europe supported by Africa & America* (design for Stedman's *Narrative*). Reproduced by permission of Oxford University Press.

becomes exploitation not equity. Further to Erdman's point, we might note that the hemp which the figures hold between them both binds together in unity and suggests the possibility that, contrary to appearances, those darker sisters who "support" Europe are in fact bound by Europe's power; for it is Europe, not Africa or America, who holds the rope in her hands. While the arrangement of Stedman's figures suggests an egalitarian trinity of graces, Europe's pivotal and aestheticized posture re-emphasizes the fact of her domination. Stedman's sentiments are, in this respect, exposed to the contradiction that inhabits them, for the image of sisterly inclusiveness that the emblem advances is in danger of turning into a vision of hierarchy. The vision of enlightenment becomes that of enslavement. Blake's re-insertion of the dynamics of enslavement into the image thus compromises Stedman's vision of an emancipated community of continents in which subjection is swallowed up in harmony.

If a gesture of exclusion haunts Stedman's harmonious triad (Europe embraces her sisters but enslaves them), a similarly violent logic is at work in Theotormon's relationship to Oothoon. For Theotormon's love, as Oothoon discovers, is inseparable from his self-love, and she herself becomes a mere cipher through which Theotormon accumulates his own value. Moreover, if Theotormon uses Oothoon to ground and augment his narcissism, he also dreams of banishing her from the purity of his self-reflection: he incorporates her only, in the end, to erase her. Part of Oothoon's plight in *Visions*, indeed, is that she is more or less helplessly bound to Theotormon's dreams of self-reflection. Quite literally, she is enslaved to his specularity. She laments:

Silent I hover all the night, and all day could be silent.
If Theotormon once would turn his loved eyes upon me;
How can I be defild when I reflect thy image pure?
Sweetest the fruit that the worm feeds on. & the soul
    prey'd on by woe
The new wash'd lamb ting'd with the village smoke &
    the bright swan
By the red earth of our immortal river: I bathe my
    wings.
And I am white and pure to hover round Theotormons
    breast.

(3.14–20)

If Oothoon seems reduced, here, to a mere "reflection" of Theotormon, her language nevertheless puts in question the subjection under which she labours. While her words seem to enslave her to Theotormon's tyrannous self-image, they also work to deconstruct the patriarchal narcissism that produces it. For example, Oothoon's declaration that she "all day could be silent./If Theotormon once would turn his loved eyes upon me" is ideologically ambivalent: it can be either a plea to Theotormon that he look down upon her in mercy or a demand that he acknowledge her in her difference. In the first reading, Theotormon's ideological world is reproduced; in the second, it is critically overturned. Either way, it seems that Oothoon is on the "margin" of Theotormon's universe, neither simply abject slave to his narcissism nor autonomous being confidently beyond his patriarchal grasp. Indeed, Oothoon is said to "hover" round Theotormon's breast like a fitful spirit, at once within and without his language and ideology. On one level, her assertion that "I am white and pure to hover round Theotormons breast" disturbs the borders of his world, revising his language of purity beyond all recognition; yet it also falls back within the orbit of that language, for Oothoon problematically embraces Theotormon's discourse of punishment and purification: as she says, she is fed on by the worm, preyed on by woe, washed by waters and cleansed by the immortal river.

Theotormon's discourse of defilement constantly shadows Oothoon's claims to purity; but the purity of Theotormon's self-image is undermined by Oothoon's language, too. For Oothoon's anguished cry, "How can I be defild when I reflect thy image pure?" splits into two opposed readings: it subordinates her to the purity of Theotormon's image, but also subverts that image through a series of ironic metaphors. For Oothoon describes herself less as pure than *marked*: she is dark like the fruit that the worm feeds on, clouded like the unhappy soul, "ting'd" with smoke from the fire, and "red" from the earth that gives her life. Oothoon's colours align her more with Europe's darker sisters, Africa and America, than with the white-skinned daughters of Albion. Her language takes on a colonial as well as sexual dimension, and *re-invents* Theotormon's "image pure" rather than simply reflecting it.

However, this is where Theotormon's violence irrupts. For if, according to her own enlightened logic, Oothoon is able to "reflect" Theotormon's image *swarthily as well as clearly*, this is exactly what Theotormon denies. As hierarchy haunts the relationship between Europe and her sisters in the Stedman design, so Theotormon aims to subject Oothoon to the dominance of his own image, enslaving and banishing her beyond the borders of his narcissism. In this sense, Oothoon "reflects" Theotormon's image in another way: she reflects back to him her own exclusion from his imperious gaze, imaging to him her violent effacement from his world.

A composite visionary daughter of America, Africa and Europe, Oothoon projects herself and her sisters beyond Theotormon's and Urizen's patriarchal and colonial worlds – into a utopian space where "every thing that lives is holy!" (8.10). However, as we have seen, a brutal exclusion troubles Oothoon's visions of emancipation, for her generous reflection of Theotormon produces not enlightenment but her own erasure. As the politics of patriarchy shadows Wollstonecraft's arguments for rational enlightenment in *Vindication*, so a politics of exclusion tracks Oothoon in *Visions*. Paradoxically, nevertheless, it is the *contradictory* nature of Oothoon's visions that most powerfully dramatizes their political significance, for her speeches meditate the limits as well as the possibilities of their own utopian prospects. At the poem's end, Oothoon castigates Urizen – the "Father of Jealousy" (7.12), architect of exclusion – for his patriarchal prohibitions, affirming instead the "mild beam" of a universal enlightenment that includes *everything* in its illuminations. Yet, almost against itself, Oothoon's language dramatizes the ideological limits of its own generously inclusive vision:

> Does the sun walk in glorious raiment. on the secret
>   floor
>
> Where the cold miser spreads his gold? or does the
>   bright cloud drop
> On his stone threshold? does his eye behold the beam
>   that brings
> Expansion to the eye of pity? or will he bind himself
> Beside the ox to thy hard furrow? does not that mild
>   beam blot
> The bat, the owl, the glowing tyger, and the king of
>   night.
>
>   (7.30–8.5)

Oothoon's oracular language veers between affirmation of its all-inclusive vision – an enlightenment which *knows no bounds* – and recognition of ideological shadows which eclipse the universality of its aims. At first sight, Oothoon's questions about the "miser" seem merely rhetorical, as if to say: "the generous sun cannot, by definition, walk upon the miser's floor, for the miser closes his house and shuts out the illumination of the sun's rays." The miser's eye does not behold the beam which brings expansion to the eye of pity. Yet when one reaches the words, "will he bind himself/ . . . to thy hard furrow?" it seems that the "he" could refer either to the personified "sun" or the miser, and this possibility reshapes the sense of the preceding lines. If the sun is so generous that it cannot be bound to the space of Urizen's "hard furrow," then its largesse seems to reach even to the miser's mean coffers, benignly illuminating his dark house with its prodigal lights. On one reading, then, the sun's "beam" enlightens even the darkest spaces; but on another, it fails to comprehend everything within its vision. In this sense, the possibility of vision as universal enlightenment seems to be affirmed and denied at once.

The ambiguous power of enlightenment re-appears, moreover, in the lines: "does not that mild beam blot/The bat, the owl, the glowing tyger, and the king of night." The range of this question embraces two contrary possibilities. The sun's "mild beam" reaches into the shades of night, "blotting" its creatures with radiance, illuminating everything. Against this, however, the sun *erases* the creatures of night, and blots them "out" as well as "in." Oothoon's affirmation of the inclusive potential of vision is radically divided: her celebratory cry that "every thing that lives is holy!" dreams of an incorporation of all things under the visionary sun, even as her language refutes its own affirmations, re-introducing unvisionary shades of exclusion. In this sense, Oothoon's own vision of inclusion repeats the gesture of effacement that it was designed to overcome; and, as Oothoon was effaced under Theotormon's gaze, the sun's enlightenment erases the life of the night. Like reason's light in Wollstonecraft, the sun's visionary radiance casts shadows that compromise its benevolent powers of incorporation. Beyond the beams of her own enlightened vision, Oothoon rediscovers – in a re-inscription of irony into utopia – the darkness of a continuing exclusion. *Visions* itself, as it concludes, similarly interrupts

Oothoon's visionary dreams with an image of her remaining exile:

> Thus every morning wails Oothoon. but Theotormon
>   sits
> Upon the margind ocean conversing with shadows dire.
>   (8.11–12)

Despite the darkness in which the poem ends, *Visions* dramatizes the historical uncertainty of its illuminations and its radical potential at the same time. As we have seen, *Visions* scrutinizes the ambiguities that thwart its utopian prospects but, for that same reason, affirms its politics as a discourse of possibility – a language of the "more" – in which vision opens knowledge to contradiction, and ideology to that which, like Oothoon, hovers unstably on its margins.

NOTES

1 W. Blake, *Visions of the Daughters of Albion*, 1.1. All references to the poem are taken from *William Blake: The Complete Poems*, ed. A. Ostriker, Harmondsworth, Penguin, 1977, and appear in the text after citation in parenthesis.
2 This section-heading is adapted from M. Wollstonecraft, *A Vindication of the Rights of Woman*, ed. Miriam Brody, Harmondsworth, Penguin, 1985, 153.
3 A point made by D. Erdman, *Blake: Prophet against Empire*, Princeton, Princeton University Press, 1977, 229.
4 Blake, *The Marriage of Heaven and Hell*, 26.4.
5 Erdman, *Blake*, 233.
6 For discussions of the link between *Visions* and Wollstonecraft's *Vindication* see H.W. Wasser, "Notes on the *Visions of the Daughters of Albion* by William Blake," *Modern Language Quarterly*, 9 (1948) 292–7; N. Hilton, "An Original Story," in N. Hilton and T.A. Vogler, eds, *Unnam'd Forms: Blake and Textuality*, Berkeley, University of California Press, 1986, 69–104; P. Yaeger, *Honey-Mad Women: Emancipatory Strategies in Women's Writing*, New York, Columbia University Press, 1988, 156–61 and N.M. Goslee, "Slavery and Sexual Character: Questioning the Master Trope in Blake's *Visions of the Daughters of Albion*," *English Literary History*, 57 (1990) 101–28.
7 *Vindication*, 104.
8 ibid., 130.
9 ibid., 81.
10 See especially *Vindication*, Chapter 5, Section I, where Wollstonecraft quotes extensively from Rousseau and argues that, while he

depicts women as creatures of desire and deceit, Rousseau's own philosophy falls into the errors with which he charges women, those, that is, of "sensibility." She writes: "But all Rousseau's errors in reasoning arose from sensibility, and sensibility to their charms women are very ready to forgive. When he should have reasoned he became impassioned, and reflection inflamed his imagination instead of enlightening his understanding" (189).

11 ibid., 118.
12 C. Kaplan, "Pandora's Box: Subjectivity, Class and Sexuality in Socialist Feminist Criticism" in G. Greene and C. Kahn, eds, *Making a Difference: Feminist Literary Criticism*, London and New York, Methuen, 1985, 146–76, at 150.
13 M. Jacobus, "The Difference of View," in *Reading Woman: Essays in Feminist Criticism*, London, Methuen, 1986, 27–40, at 32.
14 C. Kaplan, "Wild Nights: Pleasure/Sexuality/Feminism," in *Sea Changes: Essays in Culture and Feminism*, London, Verso, 1986, 31–56, at 35.
15 "The Difference of View," 33.
16 "Pandora's Box," 150.
17 *Vindication*, 257.
18 ibid., 233. See Hilton, "An Original Story," 78–98 for other echoes of *Vindication* in Blake's *Visions*.
19 "Slavery and Sexual Character," 119.
20 ibid., 120.
21 As Hilton, "An Original Story," 91, points out, these lines seem to allude critically to a passage from *Vindication* on the virtues of religion: "Religion, pure source of comfort in this vale of tears! how has thy clear stream been muddied by the dabblers, who have presumptuously endeavoured to confine in one narrow channel, the living waters that ever flow towards God – the sublime ocean of existence! . . . Every earthly affection turns back, at intervals, to prey upon the heart that feeds it; and the purest effusions of benevolence, often rudely damped by man, must mount as a free-will offering to Him who gave them birth, whose bright image they faintly reflect" (*Vindication*, 277).
22 *Blake*, 237. The relationship between Blake and Stedman is considered by G. Keynes, "William Blake and John Gabriel Stedman," in *Blake Studies: Essays in His Life and Work*, Oxford, Clarendon, 1971, 98–104. For a discussion of *Visions* and narratives of slave-revolts, see R. Paulson, *Representations of Revolution (1789–1820)*, New Haven and London, Yale University Press, 1983, 93–4.
23 Erdman, *Blake*, 232.
24 ibid., 228.
25 "Slavery and Sexual Character," 109.
26 For Plato's simile of the cave, see *Republic* VII.
27 *Blake*, 232.
28 J.G. Stedman, *A Narrative, of a Five Years' Expedition against the Revolted Negroes of Surinam*, ed. R. Price and S. Price, Baltimore and London, Johns Hopkins, 1988, 280. For a commentary on

Blake's designs and their relationship to Stedman's text see R.N. Essick, *William Blake's Commercial Book Illustrations: A Catalogue and Study of the Plates Engraved by Blake after Designs by Other Artists*, Oxford, Clarendon, 1991, 71–5.
29 *Narrative*, 394–5.
30 *Blake*, 231.

4

"SILENT REVOLT"
Slavery and the politics of metaphor in *Jane Eyre*
Carl Plasa

Metaphor, in fact, is never an innocent figure of speech.

Alain Robbe-Grillet

There is no private life that has not been determined by a wider public life.

The happiest women, like the happiest nations, have no history.

George Eliot

Oh the horrors of slavery! – How the thought of it pains my heart! But the truth ought to be told of it; and what my eyes have seen I think it is my duty to relate; for few people in England know what slavery is. I have been a slave – I have felt what a slave feels, and I know what a slave knows; and I would have all the good people in England to know it too, that they may break our chains, and set us free.

Mary Prince[1]

THE METAPHORICS OF SLAVERY

Critical debates about the politics of *Jane Eyre* (1847)[2] – is it "radical" or "conservative" or some combination of both? – invariably take place in the context of the questions of gender and sexuality that the novel raises. In what is still perhaps the most influential contribution to these debates, Sandra M. Gilbert and Susan Gubar argue that Charlotte Brontë's text is in large measure an expression of a "rebellious feminism."[3] Jane Eyre's story provides "a pattern for countless others,"[4] being, as they tell us:

> [one] of enclosure and escape, a distinctively female *Bildungsroman* in which the problems of the protagonist as she struggles from the imprisonment of her childhood to an almost unthinkable goal of mature freedom are symptomatic of difficulties which Everywoman in a patriarchal society must meet and overcome . . . . Most important, her confrontation, not with Rochester but with Rochester's mad wife Bertha, is the book's central confrontation, an encounter . . . not with her own sexuality but with her own imprisoned "hunger, rebellion, and rage," a secret dialogue of self and soul on whose outcome . . . the novel's plot, Rochester's fate, and Jane's coming-of-age all depend.[5]

These comments are themselves symptomatic, ironically, of one of the difficulties underlying the analysis in which they occur. The casual troping of Brontë's protagonist as "Everywoman" performs a kind of racial legerdemain by which a female experience of oppression and resistance that is in fact distinctively white and English (and for the most part lower-middle-class) comes silently to occupy the position of being representative of female experience as a "whole": to view the eponymous heroine/narrator of Brontë's novel as somehow universally normative is at the same time for criticism to suggest a certain blindness with regard to forms of subjective experience that are racially and culturally "other."[6]

In the context of *Jane Eyre* such forms are most obviously (if ambiguously) implied by Bertha Mason, the Creole heiress whom Rochester marries, for financial gain, in Jamaica and subsequently transports – following the onset of her "madness" – to England, imprisoning her there in the third-storey attic of Thornfield Hall for some ten years. Precisely *as* a Creole, Bertha's presence in the text is intriguingly equivocal. The term can refer equally to persons born and naturalized in the West Indies of *either* European *or* African descent having, as the *OED* stresses, "no connotation of colour."[7] Yet the inclusion of Bertha within *Jane Eyre* as the uncertain signifier of "otherness" and difference is something that Gilbert and Gubar seem to want to resist. This resistance takes the form of an interpretative strategy that resolutely denies Bertha's *literal* presence as a character within

Brontë's novel, favouring instead a psychofeminist emphasis on her role as the *metaphorical* expression of Jane's own unconscious desires and discontents. Bertha, they write:

> is Jane's truest and darkest double: she is the angry aspect of the orphan child, the ferocious secret self Jane has been trying to repress ever since her days at Gateshead.[8]

While Jane is troped as "Everywoman," Bertha figures, or is figured, here as her "double" or *alter ego*. In this way, the racial and cultural differences which she embodies are effectively erased, along with their ambiguities.[9]

Gilbert and Gubar's reading of the "central confrontation" in *Jane Eyre* along these lines is, it is true, one that Brontë's text openly assists through its fabrication of an entourage of parallels and correspondences between Jane and Bertha from first to last. Yet, as Laura Donaldson has argued, the consequences of such a reading, both methodologically and politically, are highly disconcerting, the effects of what she calls the "Miranda Complex."[10] This term derives from an early exchange in *The Tempest* in which Miranda declines Prospero's invitation to visit the enslaved Caliban by saying "'Tis a villain, sir,/I do not love to look on" (I.ii.311–12).[11] For Donaldson, Miranda's aversion of her gaze from Caliban is replicated in the exemplary failure of Gilbert and Gubar to address questions of slavery, colonialism and race in *Jane Eyre* as in nineteenth-century women's texts in general. Worse still, the very critics who see Bertha as Jane's "secret self" find themselves simultaneously locked into an ironic repetition – at the level of theory – of the workings of patriarchal oppression within the text. Just as Rochester "shuts up" his first wife at Thornfield (both literally and figuratively) so, according to Donaldson:

> Gilbert and Gubar's interpretation of Bertha in *Mad-woman* . . . not only imprisons her within the privatistic cell of Jane's psyche, but also deprives her of any independent textual significance.[12]

The denial to Bertha of an "independent textual significance" produces another irony, since it is precisely the absence of such autonomy "which [Gilbert and Gubar] deplore when it oppresses Anglo-European women."[13] This dilemma is compounded if we recall that one of the epigraphs introducing Gilbert and Gubar's analysis of *Jane Eyre* comes from the work of Jean Rhys, whose *Wide Sargasso Sea* (1966) – standing as revisionary "prequel" to *Jane Eyre*[14] – finally accords to Bertha (renamed in Rhys as Antoinette) that textual independence, as character *and* narrating subject, that is withheld from her by Brontë's latter-day critical readers.[15]

In maintaining a silence over issues of slavery and racial oppression, Gilbert and Gubar – like the generality of white feminist critics of *Jane Eyre* – collude indeed with the text itself and its own evasions of a recent colonial memory. For, despite the pivotal and determinant role of the West Indies in *Jane Eyre* in terms of the narrative and economic fortunes of its major characters, Brontë's text nowhere explicitly refers to the institution of British slavery or the colonialist project with which, for the early Victorian reader, the West Indies would still, in 1847, be strongly associated and against whose distant horizon Jane Eyre lives her metropolitan life.[16]

Yet even as *Jane Eyre* excludes the subject of British colonial slavery at the level of the literal, it is nevertheless widely present as *discourse*, in terms, that is, of the language through which Brontë's heroine characteristically organizes and represents her experience – how, in other words, she comes to understand herself. While *Jane Eyre*'s autobiographical conventions necessarily entail an emphasis on the "personal," the novel also offers a powerful analysis of larger socio-cultural structures in England during the first half of the nineteenth century, focusing upon the aspirations of lower-middle-class women, such as Jane, in particular. This concern with forms of domestic oppression created by gender and class is, paradoxically, the vehicle for the return of the colonial. Like many other nineteenth-century texts (though perhaps more systematically) Brontë's novel precisely formulates its critique of gender- and class-ideology by means of a habitual recourse to a language – principally a metaphorics – of enslavement and mastery.

From this vantage-point it becomes evident that the question of the novel's politics is inseparable from that of its rhetorical operations. The deployment of a metaphorics of slavery as a way of representing forms of domestic oppression is, from one perspective, both a rhetorically powerful and a politically radical manœuvre. Yet from another perspective – that precisely of those who are or have been enslaved, *experienced* the metaphor, as it were – such a strategy can only be viewed as deeply problematic. The unease created by the use of slavery as metaphor, and the need to resist its palliation, are outlined, in the context of American slavery, by Frederick Douglass in the course of a lecture given to a meeting in Newcastle-upon-Tyne on 3 August 1846, the year of *Jane Eyre*'s completion. Defining it as his "duty to direct . . . attention to the character of slavery, as it is in the United States," Douglass goes on to inform the British audience of the urgency of his task:

> I am the more anxious to do this, since I find the subject of slavery identified with many other systems, in such a manner, as in my opinion, to detract to some extent from the horror with which slavery in the United States is so justly contemplated. I have been frequently asked, since coming into this country, "why agitate the question of American slavery in this land; we have slavery here, we are slaves here." I have heard intemperance called slavery, I have heard your military system, and a number of other things called slavery, which were very well calculated to detract from the dreadful horror with which you at a distance contemplate the institution of American slavery.[17]

With their emphasis on the identification of slavery with "many other systems" of oppression and the recognition of how this can "detract from the dreadful horror" with which slavery is more "justly" associated, Douglass's comments precisely illuminate the politically dangerous repercussions ("calculated" or accidental) of the very rhetorical basis on which *Jane Eyre* makes its domestic critique.

The logic of Douglass's argument applies – *mutatis mutandis* – as much to British colonial as to American slavery, one of the differences being, of course, historical – since British slavery in the West Indies had been formally abolished by Act of Parliament with effect from August 1834, well over a decade before *Jane Eyre*'s publication (though full emancipation was not achieved until 1838, following the dissolution of the system of "apprenticeship" which replaced slavery).[18] What needs to be borne in mind, in either context, is the doubleness or reversibility of the slave-metaphor. On the one hand, the articulation of domestic oppression in terms of slavery – colonial or otherwise – is a kind of shock-tactic, designed to move the reader into dramatic awareness of the severity of particular conditions of disempowerment existing "at home." Yet, on the other hand, the simultaneous counter-effect, as Douglass's observations suggest, is to lessen and disguise the true meaning – the literality – of slavery. In these terms, we can see that one of the corollaries to the "doubleness" of the slave-figure is to enmesh the texts in which it operates – and *Jane Eyre* is a significant example – in a certain duplicity: for the purposes of effecting domestic change such texts not only appeal to analogies between forms of oppression that are ultimately incomparable but *in so doing* also falsify and diminish the true nature of that which is the ground of their own efficacy.

As we saw earlier, the large-scale silence of white feminist criticism on the questions of slavery, colonialism and race in *Jane Eyre* is of a piece with the text's own refusal directly to negotiate these issues as they are concretized in the exploitation of African and Creole blacks in the West Indies. Such exclusions – it now appears – are in turn compounded by the figurative logic of Brontë's novel. For at both levels, the literal and the metaphorical, *Jane Eyre* might be said, in Mary Prince's figure, to "put a cloak about the truth":[19] if "few people in England know what slavery is," partial responsibility for this perhaps lies with the workings of metaphor itself.

For these reasons, *Jane Eyre* is a text in which, to modify the terms of this chapter's first epigraph, the guilt of metaphor is liable to be particularly intense. Such proves, indeed, to be the case, as evidenced by the unfolding of Brontë's novel as a double-inscription: not only does it exploit the slave-trope but at the same time it also comments upon and indeed *critiques* its own rhetorical procedures, offering in this way a complex response – or "silent revolt" (141) – to the political problems that they entail.

METAPHORS OF SLAVES AND MASTERS

The first sign of this critique comes in the shape of an allusion to Thackeray offered in the preface to the second edition of Brontë's novel. Thackeray, according to the enthusiastic preface-writer, "Currer Bell," is "the very master of that working corps who would restore to rectitude the warped system of things" – the immediate stimulus for such a judgement being *Vanity Fair* (serialized 1847–8). Yet no sooner is Thackeray figured as "master" than he is implicitly *dis*-figured, since "no commentator . . . has yet found the comparison that suits him, the terms which rightly characterize his talent" (36) a claim that, properly speaking, must embrace the one who makes it, "Currer Bell."

Such a prefatory play of figuration/disfiguration is, in terms of *Jane Eyre* as a whole, a telling one. Positing and then revoking the representation of Thackeray as "master," Brontë's preface marks out for itself a subtle distance from the rhetorical idiom – that precisely of a language of mastery and enslavement – which dominates the novel.

This linguistic self-questioning is underscored in more general terms by the problematic status of the address to Thackeray *as such*. Having dedicated *Jane Eyre*'s second edition to her fellow-author, Brontë comes soon to discover the existence of what she ruefully calls an "unlucky coincidence" between Thackeray's *own* marital situation and Rochester's.[20] The two figures – the real and the fictional – become weirdly compounded. Thus, by a bizarre intersection of fiction and biography, the "disfiguring" of Thackeray's mastery itself implies a questioning of the figurative status comparably accorded throughout the novel to Rochester (he is *Jane's* "master") and hence an unsettling also of that position as "slave" adopted correlatively by Jane herself.

There is one more twist to the doubling of Rochester in Thackeray. Insofar as the latter undergoes a kind of textual disfiguration in the ways indicated, his fate might be said to be a metaphorical version of that literally experienced by Rochester in the form of the physical mutilation – the loss of a hand and the blindness – that he incurs as a result of Bertha's incineration of Thornfield Hall toward the end of *Jane Eyre*. Placed before the narrative but written after it, the preface thus re-enacts the text in the same way that the text contains parallels with the life of the writer to whom it is so unhappily dedicated.

The Thackeray/Rochester relation takes us on to the narrative itself. Having "drawn parallels in silence," the 10-year-old Jane is subsequently provoked into hyperbolic utterance of them, at the end of chapter 1, by the physical violence of John Reed:

> "Wicked and cruel boy!" I said. "You are like a murderer
> – you are like a slave-driver – you are like the Roman
> emperors!"
>
> (43)

The significance of this moment lies not only in the parallels that it advances between domestic oppression and slavery but also in its linkage of the very creation of such parallels (even in the "lesser" form of simile, as opposed to metaphor) with *transgression* – Jane's outburst being, as it is, part of that "moment's mutiny" (44) that leads to her incarceration in the red-room in the following chapter. At a narrative or thematic level, the red-room functions as punishment for female defiance of patriarchy: Mrs Reed offers to "liberate" Jane from its terrors "only on condition of perfect submission and stillness" (49). Yet at the same time Jane's punishment works to dramatize the text's own recognition of the transgressiveness of *its* linguistic actions. It is almost as if the speaking 10-year-old were a kind of preliminary "scapegoat" (47) for her later writing self.

These actions can be seen as particularly problematic in terms of what Thomas Babington Macaulay refers to as the "aristocracy of skin."[21] During her sojourn in the red-room the young Jane is characteristically represented by her older narratorial self as a "rebel" or "revolted slave" (44, 46), the effect of such self-figurations being precisely to mystify or occult, through language, those hierarchies of difference – in the form of race or colour – on which slavery is predicated. Perhaps this is why the "looking-glass" scene in the red-room is also one of failed self-recognition: for the young Jane to grasp "the strange little figure there gazing at [her] with a white face and arms specking the gloom" (46) as her own reflection would also be for the narrative to expose the ways in which its rhetoric works to slight the differences of history.

Yet even as such an exposure is symbolically avoided by Jane's nonself-recognition in the mirror it is effected in another way, since the divisions between the oppressor and the oppressed – the Reeds and Jane – are indeed mapped in terms of racial difference: "I was a discord in Gateshead Hall; I was like nobody there; I had nothing in harmony with Mrs Reed or her children," Jane tells us. She is "a heterogeneous thing . . . a useless thing" (47), forced, as such, to concede the improbability of gaining affection: "how could [Mrs Reed] really like an interloper, *not of her race* . . . an uncongenial alien permanently intruded upon her own family group" (48, emphasis added).[22]

By means of the identification of slavery with racial "otherness" these reflections re-inscribe the specificities of history which *Jane Eyre*'s use of slavery as metaphor implicitly works to obscure. They function, that is, to bring to light – and into question – the political implications of the novel's central rhetorical devices and, as such, are part of the critique to which the text subjects itself.

This is seen more starkly still in Jane's self-description as a "thing" – a linguistic turn giving rise to what might be called a high-friction paradox. On the one hand, the reified status that Jane ascribes to herself is one literally experienced by the enslaved *black* subject through the fact of his or her body being defined as the property of another, the white slave-master. Yet the very condition – slavery – which is synonymous with the negation of black subjectivity precisely affords the figurative materials out of which the novel's *white* narrator comes into possession of her identity. As female autobiography, *Jane Eyre* represents at the level of fiction a form of self-empowerment, as Jane assumes just that position as subject traditionally denied to women by the codes of Victorian patriarchy. The text's enablements remain problematic, however, because of the rhetorical strategies in which they are grounded.

This is a point borne out in another respect, as can be seen by considering the issue of the structure of metaphor. For Eric Cheyfitz the Aristotelian definition is "still basic,"[23] according to which:

> Metaphor consists in giving the thing a name that belongs to something else; the transference being either from genus to species, or from species to genus, or from species to species, or on grounds of analogy.[24]

Metaphor becomes a scene of redistribution wherein a word that is originally (conventionally) the "property" of one thing is assigned to "something else." From this perspective, the very form of metaphor recapitulates the material relations of colonial history as they are articulated in the transference of the enslaved body from its rightful owner to the master. The historically specific referent from which *Jane Eyre* holds back in "literal" terms is thus not only alluded to by the text's figurative language but also appears to inhabit its structures.

The transferences of metaphor (translated by Quintilian as *translatio* or "carrying over")[25] constitute a re-enactment of history in another way which is illuminated by means of Paul

Ricœur's observation, extending Aristotle, that metaphor is "doubly alien."[26] It is, in Patricia Parker's glossing of Ricœur, "a name that belongs elsewhere and one which takes the place of the word which 'belongs.'"[27] In *Jane Eyre* the transferences are from the colonial to the domestic, West Indian slavery to oppression within the metropolis – a movement scrupulously figured, or logged, by the text in Rochester's narrative of his return to Thornfield from Jamaica with the "mad" Bertha: "To England, then, I conveyed her; a fearful voyage I had with such a monster in the vessel" (336). Nevertheless, the above description of metaphor (a word whose origins are "elsewhere" that "takes the place" of one that "belongs") suggests once again how linguistic structure can rehearse colonial history – with *its* usurpations of the native by the foreign.

The notion of metaphor as place-taking provides an apposite perspective from which to view *Jane Eyre* because the events that occur in the novel seem themselves to be largely ordered by a logic of substitution. Mrs Reed "must stand in the stead of a parent" (48) to the orphaned Jane at Gateshead who, given her status as the heterogeneous "interloper" or intrusive "alien," begins *herself* to seem like a strangely metaphorical figure. This impression is one confirmed in the novel's second phase at Lowood school. At the end of chapter 5 Jane's companion at the school, Helen Burns, is unfairly "dismissed in disgrace . . . from a history class, and sent to stand in the middle of the large schoolroom" (84) while at the end of chapter 7 her place has been quite literally taken by Jane, publicly punished by Mr Brocklehurst – equally arbitrarily – for her alleged compulsion to lie by being made to stand upon a stool in "the middle of the room . . . exposed to general view on a pedestal of infamy." Though the narrator tells us that "no language can describe" the "sensations" that this incident instils in her, it is not long before the text resumes its idiom, sliding from simile to metaphor:

> just as they all rose, stifling my breath and constricting my throat, a girl came up and passed me: in passing, she lifted her eyes. What a strange light inspired them! What an extraordinary sensation that ray sent through me! How the new feeling bore me up! It was as if a martyr, a hero, had passed a slave or victim, and imparted strength in the

transit. I mastered the rising hysteria, lifted my head, and took a firm stand on the stool.

(99)

While Helen's otherworldly gaze eventually stabilizes Jane, it is not before it has also shown us *en passant* how something as apparently personal and localized as the self's relations to its own body is typically to be rendered, throughout *Jane Eyre*, in terms of a shifting rhetoric of colonial struggle: the body threatens to make the self the "slave" to a "rising hysteria" and must be "mastered."

The hystericized body can either enslave the self through rage, or be enslaved by it, through spiritual repression. Though it is not only the female but also the male body (St John's) that is prone to the latter effect,[28] the suggestion of the text – in figuring control over the body as "mastery" – is that to lose such control, becoming enslaved to the somatic, is also to be "feminized," occupying what patriarchal ideology defines as the place of a woman.

Similarly, the extended burden of *Jane Eyre* is that to be a woman under patriarchy – whether governess, lover, mistress or wife – is to have the place of a slave. Of the numerous passages that illustrate this point one that is particularly relevant to the concerns of this reading occurs in chapter 24, during the lovers' engagement. Here Jane's evasions of Rochester's sexuality cause him to remind her of its imminent marital assertion:

> "It is your time now, little tyrant, but it will be mine presently; and when once I have fairly seized you, to have and to hold, I'll just – figuratively speaking – attach you to a chain like this" (touching his watch-guard).
>
> (299)

Like Rochester, the text speaks "figuratively," using the slave-idiom as a polemical means by which to mark out the limits of possibility for nineteenth-century women. Rochester's linguistic self-consciousness is momentary and bland however, while that of Brontë's text is sustained and critical, a constant underlining of limits and problems.

The pattern we are tracing, in which relations between the figures at the narrative level of Brontë's novel precisely enact the metaphorical play within it, becomes particularly noticeable

74

during the long central section at Thornfield. Here, for example, Grace Poole recurrently figures as a stand-in, in Jane's bewildered estimation, for Bertha as the agent of domestic violence.[29] Correlatively, the role adopted by Blanche Ingram, particularly with regard to the charade-sequence in chapter 18 where she acts out the "pantomime of a marriage" (212) with Rochester as pretend-groom, has the effect of making her a double stand-in with respect to Bertha and Jane alike since both, in their different ways, are drawn into weddings with Rochester that are nothing more nor less than simulacra (Bertha in the West Indies and Jane at Thornfield, fifteen years later). By the same token Blanche stands in for herself because her position as mock-bride in the charades is a duplication of her status in what passes for the reality beyond them.

The most important example of the workings of the characterological relations in the text as a figuring of metaphor is that between Jane and Bertha. This relation can be defined as a play of reversible substitution. For Gilbert and Gubar Bertha's function is to assume the tasks of a kind of psychic and ultimately suicidal stunt-woman:

> Jane's profound desire to destroy Thornfield, the symbol
> of Rochester's mastery and of her own servitude, will be
> acted out by Bertha, who burns down the house and
> destroys *herself* in the process as if she were an agent of
> Jane's desire as well as her own.[30]

Equally, however, Brontë's novel can be viewed as the drive – finally achieved in the last chapter – to put Jane in Bertha's place as wife to Rochester. Yet the plot-resolution is anti-climactic, a "quiet wedding" indeed, which not even the narratorial nudge of "Reader, I married him" can much enliven (474). As such, the eventual place-taking comes to be *displaced*, ironically marginalized by the earlier scene (in chapter 26) of its *not* taking place.

As the substitution of one woman for another, Rochester's attempted marriage to Jane at this point is evidently arranged on the basis of her *differences* from Bertha. These, in Rochester's account, are considerable. Jane, he tells us, is "something at least human" while Bertha constitutes a "bad, mad, and *embruted* partner!" (320, emphasis added) He drives the point home later:

"That is *my wife*," said he . . . . "And *this* is what I wished
to have . . . this young girl, who stands so grave and quiet
at the mouth of hell, looking collectedly at the gambols of
a demon. I wanted her just as a change after that fierce
ragout . . . . look at the difference! Compare these clear
eyes with the red balls yonder – this face with that mask –
this form with that bulk."

(322)

Insofar as metaphor, the figure of speech that centrally enables
Jane Eyre to articulate its domestic critique, is self-consciously
re-enacted at the level of narrative, the status of Brontë's
heroine as absolutely *other* to Bertha ("the antipodes of the
Creole," 338) might seem to present us with a contradiction.
How can the projected marriage be viewed as a staging of
metaphor when, on the one hand, the substitutions it involves
are marked by radical difference while, on the other hand, those
of the Aristotelian transference demand an analogical ground?
Such an apparent "problem" is, however, exactly why the
suspended union between Jane and Rochester can be seen in the
way proposed. This is so because the "impediment" (317)
placed against the marriage functions, in turn, as the sign of the
text's own silent but nevertheless "pronounced objection"
(323) to the figurative policies that it seeks to implement – the
representation of modes of domestic oppression in terms of
slavery. The charade of marriage in chapter 26 is indeed a
pantomime of metaphor but in a way that precisely discloses
Jane Eyre's anxieties about the dubiety of its own tropological
compulsions.

That the text's revelation of its narrative "mystery" is also a
metaphor for the exposure of rhetorical secrets is underscored
by the language describing Jane's, and the reader's, first introduction proper to Bertha in the recesses of what is both Thornfield's and the novel's "third story": "In the deep shade, at the
farther end of the room, a *figure* ran backwards and forwards"
(320, 321, emphasis added). Narrative and rhetoric come together here as Bertha's movements suggest, by inversion, the
oscillations of the slave-trope itself. The figure of slavery moves
forward from colonial to domestic worlds, in *Jane Eyre*, as a
means of highlighting forms of oppression "at home" even as –
once again – such a movement can only culminate in its self-

reversal, shifting the reader's attention back from the domestic to the colonial context that is the figure's ground. This pattern itself gives rise to a vantage from which a subsequent return to the realm of the domestic can occur, whose own effect is to bring the political dangers of the slave-trope into focus: while being integral to *Jane Eyre*'s ideological critique the language of slavery purchases its effects at the expense of a veiling of the history of colonial oppression that is its literal and culturally specific ground.

REBELLIONS

For Gilbert and Gubar Bertha's destructive impulses – directed as they are against men (Rochester and Richard Mason, her brother) as against marriage and Thornfield itself – enact Jane's own "secret fantasies,"[31] the "fire and violence" (267) of her rage against patriarchal oppression. Yet the third of Bertha's actions (there are five in all)[32] precisely suggests not only the limits of such a reading but also provides a particularly spectacular illustration of the ways in which *Jane Eyre* sets its own linguistic operations in question.

This action involves the tearing of Jane's wedding veil two nights before the scheduled marriage to Rochester discussed above and is recounted in detail in chapter 25. While the veil is, of course, as Adrienne Rich notes, a "symbol of matrimony,"[33] it is also the sign of Rochester's economic power. Purchased from London with "princely extravagance" (308) for a reluctant bride, it consequently functions as an oblique token for slavery, the source from which Rochester's "English gold" (170) – like Jane's inheritance – derives. Thus to read its destruction in solely patriarchal terms is, in a metaphorical sense, critically to mend the veil, covering over the question of colonialism which *Jane Eyre* itself chooses to put aside.

By an obscure cross-cultural coincidence the action literally performed by Bertha in chapter 25 is adopted by Toni Morrison as a metaphor for her own revisionary project of writing as rememory in *Beloved*: "My job," she remarks, "becomes how to rip that veil" behind which the very attempt to "tell the truth" of slavery ironically conceals it.[34] However, in terms of the evasiveness of Brontë's novel toward the truth of British colonial slavery in the West Indies, the moment of Bertha's veil-ripping can be viewed as a model of what the text consistently fails to do, preferring to manipulate colonialism-as-figure rather than represent it directly, in its literality. Indeed, in those moments when the language of enslavement is made culturally specific (as in chapter 24, for example) it is in a way that lures the reader beyond Anglo-European frames of reference, safely transporting the material realities of slave-oppression and rebellion to Oriental contexts (297–8).

However, it is not only that colonialism (literally absent at one level) is transformed by *Jane Eyre* into a consequential presence at another, that of figuration, but that it is *also* figured by Brontë's text. In chapter 17 Jane deems herself to be "purposely excluded" from the "mystery at Thornfield" (195), yet the irony is that in one sense Rochester's "revelation" of his secret only compounds it: as already noted, Bertha's status as a Creole makes the question of her race significantly uncertain.

Nevertheless, the suggestively indeterminate nature of Bertha's racial identity as specified in chapters 26 and 27 seems, at other junctures – equally suggestively – to be less vague. As Susan L. Meyer puts it:

> [Bertha] is clearly imagined as white – or as passing as white – in the novel's retrospective narrative. . . . But when she actually emerges in the course of the action, the narrative associates her with blacks, particularly with the black Jamaican antislavery rebels, the Maroons. In the form in which she becomes visible in the novel, Bertha has *become* black.[35]

In these terms it can be seen that the targets of Bertha's violence are not exclusively patriarchal: a "crime" breaking out, "now in fire and now in blood, at the deadest hours of night" with a "black and scarlet visage" (239, 337), she is also a figure for colonial rebellion, "symbolically enacting precisely the sort of revolt feared by the British colonists in Jamaica" in the years of their dominion prior to the writing of *Jane Eyre*.[36]

The subtext of colonial rebellion not only supplements and disrupts feminist constructions of Bertha as "rebel against patriarchy" but in so doing helps also to reveal the continuing preoccupation of Brontë's novel with the propriety of its own figurative designs. As one confined to and subversive of what is literally a domestic space – Thornfield – Bertha metaphorizes

Jane's own condition "at home," within the space, that is, of the metropolis, England. Conversely, she is a figure *for* the very literality (colonialism) that Jane exploits *as* a figure through which self-representation is enabled: Bertha stands in, in other words, for the "rebel" or "revolted slave" to whom Jane systematically likens herself (and those like her) throughout the novel. However, the moment of their meeting in chapter 25 is implicitly marked by Jane's failure to see the resemblances between Bertha's two roles – as her own patriarchally oppressed double, on the one hand, and as a surrogate for the victims of colonialism, on the other. Jane's statement of her nocturnal encounter with Bertha is given in a series of exchanges with Rochester on the next night. Asking whether Jane saw the face of her intruder, Rochester prompts the following dialogue:

> "Not at first. But presently she took my veil from its place: she held it up, gazed at it long, and then she threw it over her own head, and turned to the mirror. At that moment I saw the reflection of the visage and features quite distinctly in the dark oblong glass."
>
> "And how were they?"
>
> "Fearful and ghastly to me – oh, sir, I never saw a face like it! It was a discoloured face – it was a savage face. I wish I could forget the roll of the red eyes and the fearful blackened inflation of the lineaments!"
>
> "Ghosts are usually pale, Jane."
>
> "This, sir, was purple: the lips were swelled and dark; the brow furrowed: the black eyebrows widely raised over the bloodshot eyes. Shall I tell you of what it reminded me?"
>
> "You may."
>
> "Of the foul German spectre – the vampire."
>
> "Ah! – what did it do?"
>
> "Sir, it removed my veil from its gaunt head, rent it in two parts, and flinging both on the floor, trampled on them."
>
> (311)

As noted above, the division of the veil combines patriarchal with colonial aggressions. Despite both this, however, and the physiognomic stereotyping of Bertha as black, her "savage face" is not revealed, in Jane's account, as what it would be for

Donaldson – the "rem(a)inder of slavery."[37] Instead it is *reveiled* through a Eurocentric association with "the foul German spectre – the vampire": in what amounts to a moment of repressive bathos, Jane precisely fails to see the likeness between Bertha and the "rebel slave" for which she is the hyperbolic or inflated figure. Yet since Bertha is also Jane's double, the failure of recognition is itself twofold – a failure to see the very correspondences between patriarchal and colonial oppression on which, ironically, Jane's text both insists and relies so fully.

Jane's non-apprehension of Bertha as a figure or counter-double for the colonial oppression and rebellion in terms of which she apprehends herself provides another instance of her text's scepticism toward its own rhetorical operations. One of the ironic consequences of this is to suggest the resemblances between Jane and Bertha. Being the signifier of "matrimony" on the one hand and slavery on the other the veil of chapter 25 concomitantly signifies precisely the kind of conjunctions that Brontë's text seeks to establish through metaphor. In rending the veil "from top to bottom in two halves!" (312) Bertha thus aligns herself with the impulses of *Jane Eyre*'s rhetorical self-critique, grounded as it is in a subversive counter-emphasis on the *discrepancies* rather than similarities between the "two parts" – domestic and colonial oppression – of the novel's central figure, the trope of slavery.

With its bafflements and loss of consciousness (312), the encounter with Bertha recalls the events in the red-room of chapter 2, though this time it is a "savage" rather than a "white face" – a "lurid visage" (312) – from which Jane is alienated. It leads us briefly back, equally, to the charade-sequence of chapter 18, introduced in the following:

> Mrs Fairfax was summoned to give information respecting the resources of the house in shawls, dresses, draperies of any kind; and certain wardrobes of the third story were ransacked, and their contents, in the shape of brocaded and hooped petticoats, satin sacques, black modes, lace lappets, &c., were brought down by the abigails; then a selection was made and such things as were chosen were carried to the boudoir within the drawing room.
>
> (211)

Notwithstanding the improbable transvestism of Rochester's

appearance as a gipsy-woman, "almost as black as a crock" (221) in the next chapter, these garments are Bertha's – their removal and appropriation to other uses itself a reminder of the habitual relocation of meaning from literal to figurative in *Jane Eyre* as a whole. In chapter 25, however, Bertha begins *her* charade with a counter-raid on the "suit of wedding raiment" (303) in Jane's wardrobe, sorting out the veil (symbol of marriage and slavery and marriage-*as*-slavery) from the rest.

In the act of Bertha's veil-tearing, as in the larger scene in which it occurs, Brontë's text dramatizes a rejection of the very rhetorical operations it brings into play, giving them what Jane calls "the distinct lie" (312). It is in the context of this kind of textual self-critique that the opening events of chapter 18 (211–14) can be situated.

What most obviously links the two scenes is their common concern with marriage. The first element of the word acted out by Rochester and his company is "Bride!" while the "divining party" is asked to infer the second from a rendering of the Biblical scene at the well in which Eliezer recognizes Rebekah as the future wife to Isaac, his master's son (Genesis xxiv.14 ff). Themselves married together in the "tableau of the whole" the two verbal units spell out Rochester's private meaning, yet in a way that reveals his figurative mode, at this point at least, to be at odds with that of the text at large:

> Amidst this sordid scene, sat a man with his clenched hands resting on his knees, and his eyes bent on the ground. I knew Mr Rochester; though the begrimed face, the disordered dress (his coat hanging loose from one arm, as if it had been almost torn from his back in a scuffle), the desperate and scowling countenance, the rough, bristling hair might well have disguised him. As he moved, a chain clanked; to his wrists were attached fetters.
> "Bridewell!" exclaimed Colonel Dent, and the charade was solved.
>
> (213)

Through the metaphorical pun that turns marriage into a prison (for which "Bridewell" in the nineteenth century is a synonym), Brontë's text appears indeed momentarily to have liberated itself from the confines of its own rhetorical system.

Such an impression is, however, self-undermining. At some

level Rochester is no doubt the victim of the "steps" (159) taken by his own and Bertha's fathers in order to procure his fortune, yet the terms in which he figures this "plight" could hardly be more questionable: even as Rochester theatricalizes himself as "marital prisoner" he stands as Bertha's literal warder, creating for her the material conditions in terms of which he sees himself. The fact subverts the figure.

Structurally, then, the metaphor with which Rochester entertains both himself and the reader (who, apart from the re-membering Jane, is its sole audience) only extends the figurative closure that it seems, in terms of "content," to transcend. His charade rehearses, in other words, the problems built into the emancipatory strategies of the novel as a whole. As if to confirm this point, the ostensible prisoner seems – from "begrimed face" to clanking "chain" and "fetters" – much like a slave in poor disguise, illustrating, as such, the mistakenness of Jane's assumption that the charade is "solved" with "Bridewell!" and hence the manner in which meaning escapes the (Rochesterian) attempt to fix it.[38]

TRANSLATION

The discovery of Bertha's place as prisoner at Thornfield (chapter 26) causes Jane to lose hers. Leaving Rochester she embarks upon the desperate moorland journey that leads to the eventual exhausted arrival at Moor House. In the course of her recuperation, Moor House becomes "more" house, in two senses: Jane gains the Rivers's – St John, Diana and Mary – as her cousins and, through the mutual avuncular link of John Eyre, her fortune also (403–14). This in turn – through John Eyre's Madeiran connection with Richard Mason, a Jamaican wine-maker – indicates, as Meyer notes, that Jane's wealth, like Rochester's, has colonial origins.[39] As throughout, the colonial realities at the "ravished margin" of the text (407) have, in this part, a centrally figurative function, continuing to dictate Jane's constructions of female possibility. Nowhere is the clash of referential margin against figurative centre sharper than in her struggle to persuade St John that he and his sisters should share the "windfall," rather than remain dispersed into hardship. As "governesses in a large, fashionable, south-of-England city" (379), Diana and Mary are envisaged, for example, as "slaving amongst strangers" while Jane is "gorged with gold [she] never earned and [does] not merit!"(413). Similarly, imagining a life as Rochester's mistress in Marseilles turns Jane, at an earlier point, into a "slave in a fool's paradise" (386), just as, later, she can only contemplate working as a missionary with St John in India if her "natural ... feelings" remain "unenslaved" by marriage (433).[40]

St John's missionary ambitions in India indicate *Jane Eyre*'s expansion of its own frame of colonial reference,[41] a broadening of narrative range which is accompanied by another, the incursion into the novel of what Suvendrini Perera calls a "vocabulary of oriental misogyny."[42] Such a vocabulary manifests itself in the form, particularly, of a series of references to the culturally specific practice of suttee – the immolation of Hindu widows on the funeral pyres of their husbands.[43] Despite the obvious differences between *Jane Eyre*'s colonial contexts – or subtexts – the West Indies and India, they nevertheless become precisely interlocked by the ideological purposes to which Brontë's novel puts them.

Urged, in chapter 34, by St John to "give up German and learn Hindustani," Jane soon enough finds herself "poring over the crabbed characters and flourishing tropes of an Indian scribe" (423, 425). Yet the figures she reads thrive equally well in the foreign soil of her own writing, as the trope of suttee – like that of slavery – generates the inscription of the patriarchal and religious oppression of women. In the eyes of St John, Jane's is "a soul that revel[s] in the flame and excitement of sacrifice," (429) prompting, as such, his proposal/ultimatum that she not only support his aims in the role of a "helper amongst Indian women," (429) but do so, moreover, by becoming his wife. Even before she comes to consider the hollow blisses of a domestic relation with St John, the prospect of giving assistance to "Indian women" is figured as suttee, precisely one of the practices that the nineteenth-century missionary sought to abolish:

> if I *do* make the sacrifice he urges, I will make it absolutely: I will throw all on the altar, heart, vitals, the entire victim.
> (430)[44]

Marriage to St John is represented, similarly, as suttee from *within*:

But as his wife – at his side always, and always restrained, and always checked – forced to keep the fire of my nature continually low, to compel it to burn inwardly and never utter a cry, though the imprisoned flame consumed vital after vital – *this* would be unendurable.

(433)[45]

At Moor House Brontë's novel mixes metaphors – suttee with slavery – in terms of marriage as in other respects.[46] The differences between the colonial spaces from which they are drawn – as also between the forms of oppression, the histories and the cultures to which they direct us – should not be overlooked. On the other hand, it is evident that in this section of the novel the language of "oriental misogyny" effectively restates (like Rochester's figuring of marriage-as-prison in chapter 18) the problems inherent to the slave-trope. *Jane Eyre*, that is, co-opts suttee – like slavery – as metaphor into a process of ideological critique "at home" whose liberative aims are compromised by the discursive re-enactment of the very oppressions "out there" that form the ground of their enablement: it is almost as if the text were *translating* the dilemma at its tropological heart into another idiom whose limits, risks and delusions are already implied by the original.

Such an effect is not surprising because Moor House is itself where translation from and into other languages – German, Hindustani – occurs continually. Translation is indeed the concern of Diana and Mary during Jane's first uncanny sight of them:

I had nowhere seen such faces as theirs: and yet, as I gazed on them, I seemed intimate with every lineament. I cannot call them handsome – they were too pale and grave for the word; as they each bent over a book, they looked thoughtful almost to severity. A stand between them supported a second candle and two great volumes, to which they frequently referred, comparing them, seemingly, with the smaller books they held in their hands, like people consulting a dictionary to aid them in their task of translation.

(358)

Nor is the passage here from the strange to the familiar – "I had nowhere seen such faces as theirs; and yet . . . I seemed intimate

84

with every lineament" – entirely unexpected. Diana and Mary not only relate to Jane as her cousins but also because their "task of translation" is one upon which *she* – as a metaphorist – has been engaged throughout the life of her writing. For Quintilian metaphor is *translatio*, as we have seen, like translation a form of "carrying over." The translator strives to transport meaning intact from one language to another while in metaphor it is transferred from one level to another, within the same language – the literal to the figurative. Such a metaphorical movement is also, as Cheyfitz points out, a translation from the "familiar" to the "foreign,"[47] (even as the translation in this particular instance is from foreign to familiar, the German of Schiller's *Die Rauber*[48] to English). Translation, in this light, can be a figure for metaphor in the same way that metaphor can stand in for translation.

A significant example of the former possibility comes in chapter 10, during the transition from Lowood to Thornfield. Having "tired of the routine of eight years in one afternoon" (117) Jane resolves to "get a new place" by advertising her services as a governess in the " – *shire Herald*" (118). Advertisement is concealment, however, the would-be governess styling herself as "J.E." rather than "Jane Eyre," and citing Lowton post office, rather than Lowood, for an address. The act of acronymic substitution is a kind of translation at one remove: "Jane Eyre" is an *alias* for the "I" which names the self even as the letters that replace it – "J.E." – spell out that "I"'s foreign counterpart, the French "Je." Insofar as Jane Eyre's "I" – the self – literally emerges at this point in translation, it enacts a process that in turn provides a figure for *Jane Eyre*'s own self-constitution through metaphor, and *its* translations of the language of slavery from literal to figurative, colonial to domestic settings. Appropriately, the kind of surveillance under which Brontë's novel places itself also marks the transactions carried out by the anxious post-seeker, "J.E.": in the course of literally receiving the reply from Mrs Fairfax that leads her on to Thornfield as a governess, she is also twice given an "inquisitive and mistrustful glance" by the "old dame" who both runs the post office and hands over the "document" in question (119).

Jane Eyre's metaphorical translations are complemented by narrative structure, the series of crossings that take the heroine from place to place: Gateshead to Lowood, Lowood to Thornfield, Thornfield to Moor House, Moor House to Ferndean, as if Jane's life were itself an enactment – or charade – of metaphor. The final removal – from Moor House to Ferndean – also sees her carried across another threshold through the marriage to Rochester which had been originally interrupted in chapter 26.

The earlier débâcle constitutes, as we have seen, a narrative inscription of *Jane Eyre*'s misgivings with regard to its own textual strategies. In this light, as one of the "incongruous unions" (338) to which he refers during the "confession" to Jane in chapter 27, Rochester's marriage to Bertha suggests the interesting possibility that a bad match is itself an apposite figure for a loose metaphor: both involve the joining together of two terms whose similarities cannot offset their differences. In this way the text might be seen as advertising once again a certain discontent with its own characteristic rhetorical gestures. Conversely, Brontë's novel constructs Rochester's relation to Jane (at least in its ideal form) in terms of what Carolyn Williams calls a "rhetoric of romantic congruence."[49] As she notes, such rhetoric is "most graphic" in the proposal scene of chapter 23,[50] as, for example, in the fraught cries of the following:

> "Do you think, because I am poor, obscure, plain, and little, I am soulless and heartless? You think wrong! – I have as much soul as you – and full as much heart! And if God had gifted me with some beauty and much wealth, I should have made it as hard for you to leave me, as it is now for me to leave you. I am not talking to you now through the medium of custom, conventionalities, nor even of mortal flesh: it is my spirit that addresses your spirit; just as if both had passed through the grave, and we stood at God's feet, equal – as we are!"
>
> (281)

As if to authenticate Jane's closing claim Rochester mirrors his terms: "'My bride is here,' he said, . . . 'because my equal is here, and my likeness. Jane, will you marry me?'"(282). Just as the "rhetoric of romantic congruence" is here quite literally a question of the congruence of rhetoric, so the good match is by implication a kind of figuring – displaced into the register of marriage – of the adequation that the text suspects itself to lack at the level of metaphor. The eventual marriage of Jane and Rochester is similarly displaced into the form of a "double

retirement" (39) at Ferndean. On the one hand, such a conclusion can be seen as a realization of the "feminist manifesto"[51]
outlined in chapter 12 where "women feel just as men feel"
(141). Yet, as several critics have observed, such egalitarianism
is distinctly asocial.[52] *Jane Eyre* thus ends with the tacit admission that equality between men and women constitutes a sexual
utopia which indeed has no place in the realms of the socially
real. As such, the novel simultaneously reaches a conclusion with
regard to its own practices at which, from the outset, it seems
already to have arrived, suggesting that the kind of rhetorical
harmony metaphorized in the lovers' "perfect concord" (476)
is a *textual* utopia that has always lain beyond its horizon.

NOTES

1 The sources for the epigraphs to this chapter are as follows: A.
  Robbe-Grillet, "Nature, Humanism and Tragedy," in *Snapshots
  and Towards a New Novel*, trans. B. Wright, London, Calder and
  Boyars, 1965, 75–95, at 78; G. Eliot, *Felix Holt: The Radical*, ed. P.
  Coveney, Harmondsworth, Penguin, 1987, 129, and *The Mill on the
  Floss*, ed. A.S. Byatt, Harmondsworth, Penguin, 1985, 494; M.
  Prince, *The History of Mary Prince, a West Indian Slave*, in, *The
  Classic Slave Narratives*, ed. H.L. Gates, Jr., New York, Mentor,
  1987, 200.
2 C. Brontë, *Jane Eyre*, ed. Q.D. Leavis, Harmondsworth, Penguin,
  1985. This edition is used throughout, cited hereafter by page
  number only in parenthesis.
3 S.M. Gilbert and S. Gubar, *The Madwoman in the Attic: The
  Woman Writer and the Nineteenth-Century Literary Imagination*,
  New Haven and London, Yale University Press, 1979, 338. In this
  respect, Gilbert and Gubar at once repeat – while, of course,
  transvaluing – the contemporary Victorian response to Brontë's
  novel as a "radical" or "subversive" text most strongly formulated
  by E. Rigby in *The Quarterly Review* (December 1848): "We do not
  hesitate to say that the tone of the mind and thought which has
  overthrown authority and violated every code human and divine
  abroad, and fostered Chartism and rebellion at home, is the same
  which has also written Jane Eyre" (cited in *The Brontës: The
  Critical Heritage*, ed. M. Allott, London and Boston, Routledge and
  Kegan Paul, 1974, 109–10). For recent readings that argue that
  Jane Eyre involves a containment rather than affirmation of female
  transgression see B. London, "The Pleasures of Submission: *Jane
  Eyre* and the Production of the Text," *English Literary History* 58
  (1991) 195–213, and K. Sutherland, "*Jane Eyre*'s Literary History:
  The Case for *Mansfield Park*," *ELH* 59 (1992) 409–40.
4 *Madwoman in the Attic*, 338. As is evident from the title of their

project, *Jane Eyre* certainly provides the "pattern" – or paradigm – for the feminist poetics that *Madwoman* itself seeks to formulate: along with Brontë's other novels, it occupies a "central position" in their study, generating "new ways in which all nineteenth-century works by women can be interpreted," ibid., xii. See also 77–9.

5 ibid., 339. The ascription of "hunger, rebellion, and rage" to Brontë is M. Arnold's, made (in relation to the recently published *Villette*) in a letter to J. Forster of 14 April 1853: *Letters of Matthew Arnold 1848–1888*, ed. G.W.E. Russell, 2 vols, London and New York, Macmillan, 1895, I.29.

6 The tendency of "narrowly ... race-blind interpretations" to construct *Jane Eyre* as a feminist epic of self-realization is discussed by P. Boumelha in her *Charlotte Brontë*, Hemel Hempstead, Harvester, 1990, 60. One of the most significant critical attempts to re-inscribe the questions of race and colonialism elided by the kind of analysis pursued by Gilbert and Gubar is made by G.C. Spivak, "Three Women's Texts and a Critique of Imperialism," *Critical Inquiry* 12 (1985) 243–61. See also L. Donaldson's essay-review of both Gilbert and Gubar and Spivak, "The Miranda Complex: Colonialism and the Question of Feminist Reading," *Diacritics* 18 (Autumn 1988) 65–77, and S.L. Meyer, "Colonialism and the Figurative Strategy of *Jane Eyre*," *Victorian Studies* 33 (1990) 247–68.

7 On this point see Meyer, "Colonialism," 252–3.

8 *Madwoman in the Attic*, 360.

9 Yet at the same time they reappear in the linguistic tensions of the very critical formulation that seeks to deny them, Bertha being not only Jane's "truest" but also her "*darkest* double." See also E. Showalter's comment that Bertha's death constitutes for Jane a symbolic destruction of "the *dark* passion of her own psyche," *A Literature of Their Own: British Women Novelists from Brontë to Lessing*, London, Virago, 1978, 122 (emphasis added).

10 See note 6 above.

11 W. Shakespeare, *The Tempest*, ed. F. Kermode, London, Methuen, 1961, 29.

12 "The Miranda Complex," 66.

13 ibid., 68.

14 A term used by E. Baer in her essay on Rhys's rewriting of Bronte, "The Sisterhood of Jane Eyre and Antoinette Cosway," in E. Abel, M. Hirsch and E. Langland, eds, *The Voyage In: Fictions of Female Development*, Hanover and London, University Press of New England, 1983, 132. As Baer informs us (335, n. 6), the term was in fact suggested to her by Gubar in 1981.

15 See Rhys's modest remark in an interview with M. Bernstein that Brontë's Bertha "seemed such a poor ghost, I thought I'd like to write her a life," the London *Observer*, 1 June 1969, 50. The writing of Antoinette's narrative (disrupted by the Rochesterian interpolation that takes up almost all of *Wide Sargasso Sea*'s long second section) is, for Spivak, an ambiguous enterprise. On the one

hand, it can be viewed as itself a startling disruption of the canonical authority enshrined in *Jane Eyre* (described by Rhys as a "reactionary nineteenth century romance," *Jean Rhys: Letters, 1931–1966*, ed. F. Wyndham and D. Melly, London, Deutsch, 1984, 157). Yet, on the other hand, Rhys's recuperation of Antoinette/Bertha's story is inseparable, according to Spivak, from a repetition of the very sort of silence it seeks to oppose. Rhys's novel "marks with uncanny clarity the limits of its own discourse in Christophine, Antoinette's black nurse. . . . She cannot be contained by a novel which rewrites a canonical English text . . . in the interest of the white Creole rather than the native," "Three Women's Texts," 252–3. Spivak could be said, however, to want to have it both ways, since in her reading of *Jane Eyre*, Bertha precisely occupies the position of the "native 'subject,'" ibid., 248, that she is here described as having usurped. This point is succinctly illuminated by Meyer, "Colonialism," 251: "Bertha is either native or not native in the interests of Spivak's critique. Thus it is by sleight of hand that Spivak shows feminism to be inevitably complicitous with imperialism."

16 As Meyer points out, following Q.D. Leavis, "it may not be possible to pinpoint the closing moment of the novel further than within a range of twenty-seven years, between 1819 and 1846." This means that Jane's marriage to Rochester, ten years prior to the writing of her autobiography, occurs either in 1809 or in 1836. Within the calendar of colonialism, it is thus located, at the earliest, either two years after the abolition of the slave-trade by Britain and America in 1807 or, at the latest, two years after the abolition of slavery as such in the British colonies (1834) but also two before the granting of full emancipation, in 1838. Yet despite the considerable discrepancies between them, it is evident that both chronologies place the experiences of the heroine/narrator firmly in the context of British colonial oppression in the West Indies. See Meyer, "Colonialism," 254, and Leavis's edition, 487–9, n. 1.

17 F. Douglass, *The Frederick Douglass Papers*, Series One, *Speeches, Debates and Interviews*, Vol. I: *1841–46*, ed. J.W. Blassingame, New Haven and London, Yale University Press, 1979, 317.

18 See note 16 above. For a detailed account of these events (and the processes leading up to them) see R. Blackburn, *The Overthrow of Colonial Slavery 1776–1848*, London and New York, Verso, 1988, 419–72.

19 *History of Mary Prince*, 214.

20 See Brontë's letter to W.S. Williams, 28 January 1848, in *The Brontës: Their Lives, Friendships and Correspondence*, ed. T.J. Wise and J.A. Symington, 4 vols, Oxford, Blackwell, 1932, II.183. The circumstances of Thackeray's marriage are documented in G.N. Ray, *Thackeray: The Uses of Adversity 1811–1846*, London, Oxford University Press, 1955, 250–77. See also Gilbert and Gubar's comments on Thackeray's marriage, *Madwoman in the Attic*, 680–1, n. 23.

21 *Miscellaneous Writings and Speeches*, London and New York, Longmans, Green and Co., 1889, 487 (cited in Blackburn, *Overthrow*, 448). The context of the phrase is Macaulay's speech on parliamentary reform (2 March 1831). As well as citing the American and French Revolutions as admonitory signs of the dangers involved in ignoring the popular desire for reform, he also invokes "the struggle which the free people of colour in Jamaica are now maintaining" against colonial oppression.

22 Jane is figured in similar terms at Thornfield where she not only engages in what Rochester calls "governessing slavery" (298) but is also looked upon – *qua* governess – as part of an "anathematized race" (206).

23 E. Cheyfitz, *The Poetics of Imperialism: Translation and Colonization from The Tempest to Tarzan*, New York and Oxford, Oxford University Press, 1991, 35.

24 Aristotle, *Poetics*, 1457^b 6–9 (Bywater's translation), as cited in P. Ricœur, *The Rule of Metaphor: Multi-Disciplinary Studies in the Creation of Meaning in Language*, trans. R. Czerny, K. McLaughlin and J. Costello, Toronto and Buffalo, University of Toronto Press, 1977, 13.

25 See Quintilian, *The Institutio Oratoria of Quintilian*, trans. H.E. Butler, 4 vols, Cambridge, Mass., Harvard University Press, 1976, III.viii. 303.

26 *Rule of Metaphor*, 19.

27 P. Parker, *Literary Fat Ladies: Rhetoric, Gender, Property*, London and New York, Methuen, 1987, 36.

28 As for example in his relation to Rosamond Oliver – observed by the narrator in chapter 31: "His chest heaved once, as if his large heart, weary of despotic constriction, had expanded, despite the will, and made a vigorous bound for the attainment of liberty" (390). Against his "large heart"'s struggles for "liberty," St John, we are told, is always "preparing some iron blow of contradiction, or forging a fresh chain to fetter" it, labours of self-enslavement which find apotheosis in the form of his "missionary career" (399, 419).

29 Jane herself is oddly to be discovered, at the end of chapter 15, "standing in a pool!" (182) made by the water she uses to extinguish the fire Bertha lights in an attempt to burn the sleeping Rochester in his bed.

30 *Madwoman in the Attic*, 360.

31 ibid., 361.

32 This count includes Bertha's attempted strangulation of Rochester in chapter 26 (321–2). Consistent with Bertha's marginalization throughout *Jane Eyre* the ambiguous drama of her final moments – setting fire to Thornfield and her own smashing leap to death before the advancing Rochester – is presented at one remove, as a story told to Jane by one of its obscure beholders – Rochester's father's butler (450–3).

33 A. Rich, *On Lies, Secrets and Silence: Selected Prose 1966–1978* London, Virago, 1980, 99.

34 T. Morrison, "The Site of Memory," in W. Zinsser, ed., *Inventing the Truth: The Art and Craft of Memoir*, Boston, Houghton Mifflin, 1987, 103–24, at 110. The immediate source for Morrison's comment is in fact L.M. Child's own veil-figure in the introduction to H.A. Jacobs's *Incidents in the Life of a Slave Girl* (1861). Referring to the sexual ordeals inflicted upon female slaves, Child writes: "This peculiar phase of Slavery has generally been kept veiled; but the public ought to be made acquainted with its monstrous features, and I willingly take the responsibility of presenting them with the veil withdrawn," H.A. Jacobs, *Incidents in the Life of a Slave Girl*, ed. J.F. Yellin, Cambridge, Mass. and London, Harvard University Press, 1987, 4. The allusion to slavery's "monstrous features" looks back to the figurative role of Bertha, as confronted by Jane, in chapter 25, discussed in the text below.

35 "Colonialism," 252.

36 ibid., 255. As J. Walvin notes, an example of just such anticipated violence – particularly disturbing to white colonists in scale – occurs in the "Baptist War" of 1831–2 as "slaves in Jamaica erupted in the latest of that island's seemingly endless slave revolts," *Black Ivory: A History of British Slavery*, London, Harper Collins, 1992, 265. See also 276–8 and Blackburn, *Overthrow*, 432–3. For an interesting account (and recuperation) of the role of black women in shaping the history of slave-resistance in the British colonies see S. Dadzie, "Searching for the Invisible Woman: Slavery and Resistance in Jamaica," *Race & Class: A Journal for Black and Third World Liberation* 32 (Autumn 1990) 21–38.

37 "The Miranda Complex," 66.

38 Rochester's inadvertent likening of himself to a slave is anticipated by his self-description, during an early conversation with Jane in chapter 14, as "a man and a brother" (169) – an oblique reference to the seal of the Slave Emancipation Society manufactured by J. Wedgwood in 1787. On this point see R.J. Dingley, "Rochester as Slave: An Allusion in *Jane Eyre*," *Notes and Queries* 31 (March 1984) 66. It should also be juxtaposed with a passage from Walsh's *Notices of Brazil* cited by T. Pringle in his *Supplement to the History of Mary Prince* in order to illustrate the corrupting effects of slavery upon its practitioners: "'I never walked through the streets of Rio,'" Walsh writes, "'that some house did not present to me *the semblance of a Bridewell*, where the moans and the cries of the sufferers, and the sounds of whips and scourges within, announced to me that corporal punishment was being inflicted. Whenever I remarked this to a friend, I was always answered that the refractory nature of the slave rendered it necessary, and no house could properly be conducted unless it was practised. But this is certainly not the case; and the chastisement is constantly applied in the very wantonness of barbarity, and would not, and dared not, be inflicted on the humblest wretch in society, if he was not a slave, and so put out of the pale of pity.'" (Gates, *Classic Slave Narratives*, 236, emphasis added).

39 "Colonialism," 267.

40 See also, among further instances, Jane's description of the good-night kiss ritually conferred upon her by St John as "a seal affixed to [her] fetters" or, again, the rhetorical question concerning marriage that she directs toward Diana in chapter 35: "Would it not be strange, Di, to be chained for life to a man who regarded one but as a useful tool?" (424, 441).

41 Such an expansion lends support to the argument that Jane Eyre completes the writing of her narrative at the later date of 1846 (rather than 1819) since, as Blackburn notes, "by the 1820s and 1830s a thoroughgoing reorientation of Britain's imperial interests was already well underway" – precisely *toward* the "Orient," in the shape of India, *Overthrow*, 434.

42 S. Perera, "'Fit only for a Seraglio': The Discourse of Oriental Misogyny in *Jane Eyre* and *Vanity Fair*," in *Reaches of Empire: The English Novel from Edgeworth to Dickens*, New York, Columbia University Press, 1991, 79–102.

43 The first direct reference to suttee comes, in fact, while Jane is still at Thornfield. Despite the coercive lyricism of Rochester's serenade ("My love has sworn, with sealing kiss,/With me to live – to die"), its auditrix stubbornly asserts the "right to die" when she pleases rather than "be hurried away in a suttee": she will not be "melted to marrow," as Rochester grudgingly concedes, by the "stanzas crooned in her praise" (301). For a fuller discussion of this particular exchange see Perera, "'Fit only for a Seraglio,'" 87–8, and, on suttee more generally, M. Daly, *Gyn/Ecology: The Meta-ethics of Radical Feminism*, London, The Women's Press, 1979, 113–33. While the use of the term "suttee" (an anglicized version of the Hindu *sati*) is not unproblematic in its implications, it is retained throughout this chapter in accordance with Brontë's text.

44 The motivation behind British colonial attempts to abolish suttee (criminalized in 1829) was far from purely altruistic, a benign concern with female rights and liberation: as Perera puts it, "Throughout the mid-nineteenth century, sati continued to provide justification both for empire and for increased missionary penetration," ("'Fit only for a Seraglio,'" 92).

45 On this point see ibid., 89.

46 As, for example, in terms of Jane's imagination of the silent conflict within St John between desire for Rosamond and Christian vocation: "He seemed to say, with his sad and resolute look, if he did not say it with his lips, 'I love you. . . . If I offered my heart, I believe you would accept it. But that heart is already laid on a sacred altar: the fire is arranged around it. It will soon be no more than a sacrifice consumed'" (393–4).

47 Cheyfitz, *Poetics of Imperialism*, 35–6, 89–90.

48 An appropriate text, whose title – when translated into English, as *The Robbers* – reminds us of the processes by which Rochester comes to acquire his wealth and hence, also, the past from which Jane had sought, at the end of chapter 27, to escape. Hannah's

remark – as she apologizes for having initially misconstrued the destitute Jane as a beggar – produces a similar effect: "I was quite mista'en in my thoughts of you: *but there is so mony cheats goes about*, you mun forgie me" (368, emphasis added).

49 C. Williams, "Closing the Book: The Intertextual End of *Jane Eyre*," in J.J. McGann, ed., *Victorian Connections*, Charlottesville, University Press of Virginia, 1989, 60–87, at 61.

50 ibid., 85, n. 2.

51 Rich's phrase, *On Lies, Secrets and Silence*, 97.

52 See Gilbert and Gubar, *Madwoman in the Attic* 369–71, P. Macpherson, *Reflecting on Jane Eyre*, London and New York, Routledge, 1989, 117, and Sutherland, "*Jane Eyre's* Literary History," 434–5.

5

ANGLO-AMERICAN CONNECTIONS

Elizabeth Gaskell, Harriet Beecher Stowe and the "Iron of slavery"[1]

Elizabeth Jean Sabiston

Mentioning Elizabeth Gaskell (1810–65) and Harriet Beecher Stowe (1811–96) in the same breath may seem like an arbitrary juxtaposition. Perhaps the most obvious common element in their two careers is that both are novelists who, despite tremendous popularity in their own era, have until recently suffered benign critical neglect in ours.[2]

Even when she is incorporated into the canon, Gaskell is often described as a "major-minor" or "minor-major" Victorian novelist, somewhat overshadowed by the four unequivocally major British women novelists of the nineteenth century, Jane Austen, Charlotte and Emily Brontë, and her younger contemporary George Eliot. We tend to forget that the comparison is unfair because the others experimented with the young, flexible form of the novel more daringly than their British male contemporaries; and that Gaskell's substance and technique were far more typical of her era.

Stowe, on the other hand, was certainly not eclipsed during her own time. It is well known that, on being introduced to her, Lincoln is supposed to have said, "So this is the little lady who made this big war."[3] Her *Uncle Tom's Cabin* (1852) is usually cited as the most striking example of a literary work that has changed the course of history. There is, however, always a slight malaise or discomfort when we mention Stowe's triumph. Since the 1950s, both her artistry – in particular, her alleged sentimentality and propagandizing – and her ideology have fallen into disrepute.

In the 1950s *Uncle Tom's Cabin* became an acute source of embarrassment to Civil Rights activists in the United States.[4] As a result of the "consciousness-raising" effected in part by the Supreme Court decision to desegregate the public schools (*Brown v. Board of Education*, 1954), the label "Uncle Tom" carried the accusatory implication of collaborating with the oppressor. Still today, only the few who have read the novel recognize that Stowe's Uncle Tom was by no means an "Uncle Tom" in the 1950s sense: the former was self-sacrificing, while the latter was guileful.[5]

Criticism is coming back to Gaskell, and beginning to do so with Stowe as well.[6] Underlining the importance of a female literary tradition, Ellen Moers mentions some major links between the two writers: not only were they "two of the rare Victorian women writers who were also mothers,"[7] they also knew each other and corresponded, affording a fascinating example of literary networking between women. In an important sense, they create a spiritual network with contemporary women writers, preparing the way for artists who feel capable of seamlessly fusing life and art. Both were aware, however, of the special problems of a woman writer. As Gaskell puts it:

> When a man becomes an author, it is probably merely a change of employment to him. He takes a portion of that time which has hitherto been devoted to some other study or pursuit . . . and another merchant or lawyer, or doctor, steps into his vacant place, and probably does as well as he. But no other can take up the quiet, regular duties of the daughter, the wife, or the mother . . . a woman's principal work in life is hardly left to her own choice; nor can she drop the domestic charges devolving on her as an individual, for the exercise of the most splendid talents that were ever bestowed.[8]

Despite such obstacles, Gaskell was extremely productive. We are told that "in 20 years she produced seven novels, five 'nouvelles' . . . 22 short stories, uncounted short essays (and several long ones), magazine articles, as well as her major work, 'The Life of Charlotte Brontë.'"[9] She accomplished all this without "a room of [her] own."

Stowe herself gives a vivid account of domestic difficulties entailed, in this case, in finding a plumber. In a letter of 1850 she gains eventual rest only in childbirth:

> These negotiations extended from the first of June to the first of July, and at last my sink was completed . . . . Also during this time good Mrs. Mitchell and myself made two sofas, or lounges, a barrel chair, divers bedspreads, pillow cases, pillows, bolsters, mattresses; we painted rooms; we revarnished furniture; we – what *didn't* we do?
>
> Then on came Mr. Stowe; and then came the eighth of July and my little Charley. I was really glad for an excuse to lie in bed, for I was full tired, I can assure you.[10]

There are a number of other curious biographical similarities between the two women. Both turned to writing novels largely as a result of losing a beloved son. Gaskell's only boy, Willie, died of scarlet fever at the age of 10 months, and her husband encouraged her to throw herself into writing. Stowe's sixth child, Charley, died of cholera in 1848 (the later son is named for him) and she took up the pen to describe families separated by slavery, as well as by death. In an 1853 letter to Mrs Follen, she wrote that "much that is in that book ('Uncle Tom') had its root in the awful scenes and bitter sorrows of that summer."[11] Puritan that she was, Stowe determined "to kiss the rod."[12]

Stowe seems to have been the more vigorous of the two. Born to a New England Brahmin family, her father, Reverend Lyman Beecher, was a militant evangelist. Her sister Catherine was a feminist concerned with equal education for women. As George Frisbie Whicher writes, "Any of the Beechers, if cast away on a cannibal island, would have been capable of organizing a church, a school, a temperance movement, and a ladies' aid society before help could arrive" – for the cannibals, presumably![13]

Both women supplemented the family income by their writing, and Moers comments that "there might never have been an *Uncle Tom's Cabin* had the Reverend Calvin Stowe been a better provider for his wife and many babies."[14] Winifred Gérin reports that the Reverend William Gaskell was somewhat sulky when his wife's fame far exceeded his. Without his knowledge, she attempted to make a posthumous provision for her daughters by investing the money earned from writing in property.[15]

Despite their bereavements, hardships, and complaints about the many demands on their time, both were twice the age of

Mary Shelley at their babies' deaths, Moers reminds us, and "both were respectably settled middle-class women, wives of ministers."[16] Gérin recounts how Gaskell, far removed from the *Sturm und Drang* of the Brontës' private lives, simply tumbled off the couch, dead of a heart attack at 55, and characteristically in mid-sentence. Stowe lived to be 85.

In addition to having, for the most part, parallel lives, Gaskell's and Stowe's paths occasionally intersected. The two women had several mutual friends, acquaintances and correspondents. Both had their portraits painted in England by Henry Richmond, in 1852 and 1854 respectively. Charlotte Brontë was an admirer of Stowe and wrote: "I doubt not, Mrs Stowe had felt the iron of slavery enter into her heart, from childhood upwards,"[17] a statement evoking Gaskell's own empathy with factory workers in the Manchester slums of *Mary Barton* (1848) and *North and South* (1855). Furthermore, Gaskell's correspondence reveals that she and Stowe did actually meet during the latter's triumphal tour of Europe. In a letter to Charles Eliot Norton, dated 3 June 1857, following Gaskell's return to smoky Manchester from Italy, she wrote, "Mrs. Stowe comes to us today for one night & tomorrow I shall go for the first time with her."[18]

Despite the well-documented, if unexplored, personal and literary relationship of these two women, no one seems to have noted the remarkable similarity in narrative structure of Stowe's anti-slavery novel, *Uncle Tom's Cabin*, to Gaskell's factory novel, *Mary Barton* (perhaps because American Studies and Victorian scholarship rarely join forces) and, specifically, the reciprocity between the Eliza and George Harris plot of Stowe's novel and the Mary–Jem Wilson plot of *Mary Barton*. Stowe herself detected the analogy – perceived today as essentially false – between the conditions of American slaves and British factory workers but her failure to see its *limits* provides a convincing explanation of some serious gaps in the treatment of slavery in *Uncle Tom's Cabin*.[19]

In the twentieth century Stowe has been accused of lacking any visceral sympathy with, or real knowledge of the condition of slavery. No one, on the other hand, has ever charged Gaskell with lacking compassion for the working classes of Manchester. Indeed, her husband's parish was there, and she assumed many of the duties of his parish visits, giving him time to compose sermons. Many critics have commented that, of all the Victorian novelists, she lived closest to the world she described, unlike Dickens, who tended to treat the working class in an overly sentimental, if not downright maudlin manner, as in *Hard Times* (1854).[20] Living in the Manchester created by Ricardo, Say, Adam Smith and the *laissez-faire* policies of Mancunian economics, Gaskell came soon to cast a sympathetic but realistic eye on the virtues and defects of factory workers and owners, the seamstresses, and even the "fallen women" (*Ruth* 1853). As Gérin writes, "her work was the handmaid of her conscience."[21] In fact, her picture of Manchester life is so accurate that Kathleen Tillotson and others have compared it to Engels' analysis of the city, in which he emphasizes its 60 per cent infant-mortality rate.[22] Tillotson claims that Gaskell was "drenched in her subject"[23] and applies a line from Carlyle's *Past and Present* (1843) to her vision: "sooty Manchester, it too is built upon the infinite abysses!"[24]

Where Gaskell is most often found wanting by modern readers is in her lack of sympathy for trade unions. Like Stowe, she is often labelled resolutely "middle class", burdened with what might be called a certain "small-l liberalism" that makes her uneasy about organized labour. In fairness to Gaskell, we would do well to remember that even such an advanced thinker as George Eliot was later to betray a deep suspicion of the use of systems to reform systems – a suspicion that may have been rooted in a womanly sense of disenfranchisement. Why should a woman intellectual trust an organization to reform political economy, when neither the radical organization nor the government acknowledged her right to full citizenship, in the form of the vote? Nor were many trade unions open to women. This sense of disenfranchisement is also what Charlotte Brontë had in mind in recognizing that Stowe, as a woman, had some cognizance of what it must mean to be a slave. If Gaskell and Stowe leave us with a final "message" that the world would be a better place if only people were nicer to each other, they were merely working on a variation of the theme George Orwell ascribed to their male contemporary Dickens, who never imagined an alternative political system either.

A more serious criticism of both Gaskell and Stowe relates to the *facture* of both their novels, which split around two principal plots. Gaskell originally planned to call her novel *John Barton* and explore the psychology of a good man driven by desperate social conditions, as well as by a certain lack of moral strength, to the commission of a crime of violence. Some readers ask, in fact, how it can be read as a feminist text when the focus is on John, not Mary. I will argue, however, that the Mary–Jem plot is more central and less conventional than has been recognized. Gaskell creates a working-class heroine whom she must make palatable to the middle class, her intended audience for implementing reforms. As we shall see, however, Mary is an active heroine, unlike most female characters in the genteel tradition but like Scott's Jeanie Deans (1818) or, later, George Eliot's Dinah Morris (1859), who also works in a factory when she is not preaching Methodism.

All things are not as they seem. Mary is not really a traditional heroine, and Gaskell's appeal to the middle class is subversive. One detects a similar dire warning to James Baldwin's in *The Fire Next Time* (1963): if not voluntary reform on the part of those in power, then "the fire next time." Gaskell's narrative voice is subtly deceptive. At times cajoling the middle class into sympathy with the workers, it sounds maddeningly naïve, moderate and understated. Yet surely the subtext is a veiled threat, and the author seems conscious that she is stimulating as strong an audience reaction as the rhetorical Carlyle, not by frontal assault, but rearguard action.[25]

An example of such "double-speak" occurs in her preface, when Gaskell states, "I know nothing of Political Economy, or the theories of trade" (38). As Patsy Stoneman suggests, the subtext is not that of a naïve middle class housewife, but of an astute Unitarian social activist who implies that she *wants* to know nothing of Political Economy, because to know it would somehow valorize it, or justify the existing system.[26]

Gaskell subtly undermines her narrator, so that we, as readers or *narrataires* (Gerald Prince's term), sympathize more with the working than the middle class. As in the case of her later novel, *North and South*, the most violent critiques of the middle class are voiced by working-class characters – John Barton in *Mary Barton*, Nicholas Higgins in *North and South*. It is John who makes the Dives/Lazarus comparison, who asks whether God isn't the masters' father too (104), whether the Biblical parable haunts the rich as it does the poor, and says "it's the poor, and the poor only, as does such things for the poor" (45). The tone is far from that of the apparently moderate narrator, notably in her descriptions of the well-intentioned but selfish Carson family, one daughter of which reads Emerson (perhaps 'Self-Reliance' ungenerously interpreted?) while the poor starve to death around them (254).

Yet the dramatic scenes composed of dialogue convey a far more desperate "message" than the narrator's voice. At the same time, that narrator does quietly document the despair of the poor with facts, thereby supporting John Barton's anger. S/he notes, for instance, that Davenport is buried in a pauper's grave covered by "a raised and handsome tombstone; in reality a wooden mockery of stone respectabilities which adorned the burial-ground. . . . But little they recked of this who now gave up their dead" (112–13). Lest we miss the point, Gaskell's own anger is revealed in the factual footnote: "The case, to my certain knowledge, in one churchyard in Manchester. There may be more" (113). She must be aware that the response created in her reader is going to be closer to John's fury than to the narrator's calm benevolence.

A trope for this subtext, the dire warning/Carlylean prophecy of doom, takes the form of the crumpled Valentine from Jem to Mary, on which John Barton has had Mary copy a poem by Samuel Bamford, a radical weaver-poet. John finally abandons language, as well as the love/nurturance implied by the Valentine, for violence when he crushes it into the wadding for the bullet that kills Harry Carson. Moreover, the Valentine both unites and divides three central characters and is expressive of Mary's dilemma, torn between father and true love. Discovered by Esther, the Valentine can be mistakenly used as evidence against Jem, its author, not John its betrayer. What was intended as a verbal and artistic declaration of love is turned into an instrument of hate.

As a two-plot novel, the title of *Uncle Tom's Cabin* also points to the older man as the central figure, persecuted and driven by slavery rather than poverty; but in fact the Eliza and George Harris plot probably occupies more space in the text. It is possible that both John Barton and Uncle Tom lack the articulateness to narrate their own stories, or to attain a full grasp of their significance. Yet in the process Mary, Jem, Eliza and George sound frequently like authorial mouthpieces, somewhat undermining the realism of the novels in which they respectively appear. As Tillotson notes, Mary Barton was probably more "marketable" than her father, and that is why she, of all the working-class characters in the novel, is the only one to speak standard, educated English.[27]

Stowe may actually be more accurate in her treatment of Eliza and George. As mulattoes, they would have been descended from a white plantation owner and a female slave. In the antebellum South, such children were often raised as house- rather than field-servants, and educated with their white half- brothers and -sisters (see, for instance, Faulkner's *Absalom, Absalom!*, 1936). As Franklin Frazier points out in *The Black Bourgeoisie* (1965), after the Civil War the black middle class was naturally recruited from these mulatto house-slaves who were educationally advantaged for upward mobility.

The subtitle of *Mary Barton* foregrounds the social context: "A Tale of Manchester Life." Stowe's subtitle, similarly, "Life Among the Lowly," suggests a focus on the poor and powerless. Gaskell's wedding of writing and social commitment comes out of an impressive tradition of "factory novels" written by women in the Britain of the 1840s and 1850s. Many of these women were wives and daughters of Unitarian ministers. Among the basic tenets of the Unitarian Church were equal education for women, and the notion that the husband does not exercise authority over his wife, but is an equal partner in marriage. Not surprisingly, Unitarians and Quakers were later in the forefront of women's rights movements in both Britain and the United States, as previously they had pioneered factory reform in England and abolitionism in America. Coral Lansbury says of Gaskell's Unitarian background, "to be born a woman and a Unitarian was to be released from much of the prejudice and oppression enjoined upon other women."[28] Gaskell shared this background with Harriet Martineau, Florence Nightingale, and Barbara Bodichon.[29]

Gaskell and Stowe were both aware of the popular analogy between factory workers and slaves. One of the most famous factory novels was *Michael Armstrong, the Factory Boy* (1839–40) by Frances Trollope, mother of Anthony. Frances Trollope and Harriet Martineau also wrote novels about slavery. Indeed, Foster sees Frances Trollope's *The Life and Adventures of Jonathan Jefferson Whitlaw*, written fifteen years earlier, as a possible source for *Uncle Tom's Cabin*. In 1843–4 another

woman writer, Mrs Tonna (known as Charlotte Elizabeth) published a novel called *The Wrongs of Women* about the factory
system in Britain. Aina Rubenius feels that Gaskell was well-
acquainted with and influenced by her work.[30] Stowe not only
read Tonna, as we know, but wrote, in 1844, an introduction to
the American edition of *The Wrongs of Women*.[31] Gaskell
seems not to have read Disraeli's *Sybil, or The Two Nations*
(1845) before writing *Mary Barton*, but had probably read
Tonna (Moers educing the operations of a female literary
tradition from this evidence).

The British public was quick to identify resemblances between
Stowe's moving depiction of the condition of slaves and the
situation of the British working class. Her second novel, *Dred*
(1865), sold 100,000 copies in four weeks and along with *Uncle
Tom's Cabin* was used by the British to build support for the
Reform Bill of 1867, which paved the way for the emancipation
of British labour. Yet it is typically overlooked that Stowe was
herself indebted to, and inspired by the tradition of the British
factory novel.

The nineteenth-century analogy between blacks and the working class breaks down in our day, as Baldwin puts it, because the
black man always wears his badge upon his face. The working
man, on the other hand, if liberated in other ways, can move
upwards socially through education if he polishes his accent and
manners and acquires the tools of capitalism. When Stowe
seems to patronize her Uncle Tom and "favour" her mulattoes
with a "happy ending," she may, in fact, simply have drawn a
mistaken or inexact analogy between slaves and British factory
workers, and underestimated the obstacles to success for former
slaves. By the same token, Chartism scarcely presented a direct
parallel to the flight of slaves, or slave-rebellion, but it may have
been perceived as so doing in the nineteenth century.

Both Gaskell and Stowe see employed and employers, slaves
and masters, as "so bound to each other by common interests"
that it is madness for them to commit violence against each
other. The capitalist does not maltreat his tools or destroy his
own property. For Gaskell, such abuse can arise only out of
ignorance. Stowe, perhaps less sentimentally than one might
expect, recognizes that the relatively benign and conscientious
Shelbys of Kentucky permit the existence of the Simon Legrees
of Mississippi – in a word, that the system itself is evil, far more

so than the individuals caught up in it. Stowe uses as her spokesperson a nameless young man:

> "in my opinion, it is you considerate, humane men, that are responsible for all the brutality and outrage wrought by these wretches; because, if it were not for your sanction and influence, the whole system could not keep foothold for an hour. If there were no planters except such as that one," said he, pointing with his finger to Legree, who stood with his back to them, "the whole thing would go down like a mill-stone. It is your respectability and humanity that licenses and protects his brutality."
>
> (365)

Both women are also sharply perceptive about the links between power and sexual abuse. Gaskell's frame-tale concerns Mary's aunt Esther, the "fallen woman." Mary's mother, the virtuous woman, suffers an equally grievous fate resulting from the complications of a very late pregnancy. Esther, the "pretty woman," serves as a negative role-model to Mary (who resembles her) and keeps her on the "straight and narrow" when she is tempted by Harry Carson, the mill-owner's son. Esther is a kind of *deus* (*dea?*) *ex machina* in the plot. Gaskell does not condemn her melodramatically, or treat her fate with Dickensian bathos; rather, she indicates that only alcohol makes life tolerable for a prostitute with a strong ethical sense. The same can be said for John Barton, who, after his act of violence, takes to drink and drugs. Esther is finally buried in the same grave with John (compare Hester Prynne and Arthur Dimmesdale in *The Scarlet Letter*, 1850), in seeming acknowledgement not only of complicity, but also of his half-conscious sexual attraction to his sister-in-law.

For the slave-woman, virginity was yet more at risk than for the British working-class girl. Eliza is described from the beginning as a "sex object," a possession, "a fine female article." As in Faulkner, the black women are seen as virgin fields ready for the planting. With reference to Bon's quadroon mistress in *Absalom, Absalom!*, who combines the white man's standard of beauty with a supposed African passion and warmth, Faulkner writes, "We, the white men, created them" – that is, a hereditary class of mistresses.[32] Similarly, Stowe's Eliza was "a petted and indulged favorite" (21). As one of the mercenaries capturing fugitive slaves comments, "gals allers is the devil to catch" – because they have the most to lose.

Perhaps the greatest evil of slavery, from Stowe's point of view, as also from that of modern sociology, was the separation of families, which was only made acceptable to whites by the reification of blacks, echoed in one of Stowe's discarded subtitles, "The Man That Was a Thing." As Haley says, echoing the logic of Swift's *A Modest Proposal* (1729), "Tain't, you know, as if it was white folks, that's brought up in the way of 'spectin' to keep their children and wives and all that" (17). In case the reader is in danger of accepting this dehumanization, Cassy, Eliza's real mother, kills her last child to save it from the white world. Stowe also describes in some detail the woman who throws herself from the boat when her baby is stolen from her.

Escape from sexual exploitation precipitates the major action of both plots, though Harry Carson's attempted seduction of Mary Barton is essentially a red herring: he is murdered by her father not for having attempted to seduce his daughter, but for mocking the rag-tag Chartist delegation of which John was a member. In fact, Mary's head is turned only briefly by the owner's son. Ambition alone feeds her attraction to Harry Carson: she "did not favour Mr Carson the less because he was rich and a gentleman" (121). Her innate good sense, bolstered by the warning example of Aunt Esther, almost immediately causes her to reject the temptation. The moment after she refuses Jem's proposal, she realizes that it is he whom she truly loves:

> What were these hollow vanities to her, now she had discovered the passionate secret of her soul? She felt as if she almost hated Mr Carson, who had decoyed her with his baubles. She now saw how vain, how nothing to her, would be all the gaieties and pomps, all joys and pleasure, unless she might share them with Jem; yes, with him she harshly rejected so short a time ago. . . . She had hitherto been walking in grope-light towards a precipice; but in the clear revelation of that past hour, she saw her danger and turned away resolutely, and for ever.
>
> (176–7)

Gaskell refuses to let her heroine become a Cinderella (or a Pamela); indeed, if Mary keeps finally to her class, it is because Jem is more deserving, worthy, and gifted than the idle, thoughtless Harry. Moreover, in Gaskell's England, Harry was only one generation removed from being a factory worker himself, as John Thornton in *North and South* is an ex-worker become mill-owner. Unhappily, the *nouveau riche* Harry seems to have lost all the working-class virtues in his upward move.

Eliza is not even momentarily tempted by a "master" or owner. She is already married to George, who belongs to a neigh-bouring slave-owner and is the father of her son, little Harry. Eliza is sold by Mr Shelby only because, despite his benevolence, he is financially irresponsible and a gambler. Although "good natured and kindly," he had "speculated largely and quite loosely" (19). Stowe suggests that treating human beings as property automatically dehumanizes both master and slave. The Shelbys are implicitly compared to the St. Clares who purchase Uncle Tom. Augustine St. Clare is a kind man, with a spoiled, selfish, petulant wife, Marie, who is narcissistic and hysterical. When he is killed in a duel, his wife sells Uncle Tom down-river. In contrast, in the Shelby ménage, Mrs Shelby is the more liberal and sensible. For Stowe, unlike Gaskell, individual kindness is inadequate to combat a nefarious system. The benevolence which subtends patriarchy is only apparent and evaporates soon enough in case of need: the cash-nexus is primordial.

Shelby tries to turn a blind eye to Eliza's potential fate, but her marketability is based on beauty. As James Baldwin and Margaret Mead have pointed out in *A Rap on Race* (1971), white women, as well as black men and women, were victims of white males – the slave-masters or plantation owners. The white man learned early to divide and conquer, as white and black women, split by status and, more importantly, by white sexual jealousy, were unable to make common cause. When Malcolm X cried, "Give us back our manhood," he was referring to the emasculation, or cuckolding, of black males by the white slave-master. After the Civil War, the emasculation was to continue as black women were often separated from their husbands by poverty, the senseless quirks of the welfare system and the greater availability of jobs, albeit menial, for black women than for black men.

Eliza flees with little Harry to save her marriage from forced separation. She is, moreover, struggling against her own inevit-able dishonour at the hands of white men as yet unknown. Love of George as of their child precipitates her great act of "heroinism": the famous set-piece of "Eliza Crossing the Ice" into free territory. Love for Jem prompts Mary Barton's act of "heroinism": giving her fate into the hands of the rough watermen to reach the ship on which Will Wilson, Jem's cousin and sole defence witness in the murder trial, is due to set sail. Finally, it motivates her even greater heroinism in confessing publicly her love for Jem during the trial, which she has been thus far, privately, unable to do, because of the convention of female reticence. She can admit her love only to save her lover, not to win another proposal. Caught in the Freudian dilemma of having to choose between saving father or lover, she manages to rescue the latter without betraying the former.[33]

The vocations of Mary's and Eliza's young men complete the plot parallelisms. Jem is an engineer in an international firm "who send from out their towns of workshops engines and machinery to the dominions of the Czar and Sultan" (65). He first proposes to Mary when he rises to foreman in the works. Although initially turning him down, she almost immediately regrets her decision. He subsequently makes his fortune as an inventor, though his master owns the patent. Mary comes to learn through her friend Margaret of Jem's rise in the world: "he told me all about his invention for doing away wi' the crank, or somewhat. His master's bought it from him, and ta'en out a patent, and Jem's a gentleman for life wi' the money his master gied him" (189).

In *Uncle Tom's Cabin* George is, similarly, a self-made man, rising by his boot straps during the Industrial Revolution. He invents a hemp-cleaning machine, which "displayed quite as much mechanical genius as Whitney's cotton-gin." Stowe notes the factual basis of this story, that "A machine of this description was really the invention of a young colored man in Kentucky" (22). Black history was not altogether submerged, apparently, in pre-Civil War times. The white man's evaluation of this major contribution, however, reveals his blindness: "a machine for saving work, is it? . . . let a nigger alone for that" (23). Stowe's description of George is patronizing, indeed racist: "From one of the proudest families in Kentucky he had inherited a set of fine European features, and a high, indomitable spirit. From his mother he had received only a slight mulatto tinge." His mother has suffered the fate now threatening his wife: she was "marked out by personal beauty to be the slave of the passions of her possessor, and the mother of children who may never know a father" (123). George's political and religious views bespeak a clever and practical mind at work. This quality – which he shares with Jem – is illustrated when he protests about the supposed Biblical rationale of slavery, "to quote Bible to a fellow in my circumstances is enough to make him give it up altogether" (124). While Stowe, like Gaskell, is herself a minister's daughter and wife, she issues a warning to Christian churches about institutionalized racism and hypocrisy. Similarly, George, as one of the excluded, questions the validity of "knee-jerk" patriotism: "Haven't I heard your Fourth-of-July speeches? Don't you tell us all, once a year, that governments derive their just power from the consent of the governed? Can't a fellow *think*, that hears such things?" (125)

The rebuilding of the extended family, separated in the one instance by the Industrial Revolution and in the other by slavery, is a central theme in both novels. The consequences of its breakdown include physical disabilities and deformities often noted in postcolonial writings such as Rachid Boudjedra's *La Répudiation* (1969). The seamstress Margaret, in Gaskell's novel, is going blind as a consequence of her occupation, and Alice Wilson, the aged white witch, is rapidly losing her hearing. The literal deformities symbolize the spiritual distortions produced in the oppressed, the colonized, the enslaved. Alice expresses a Wordsworthian nostalgia for the countryside, and for the mother from whom she has been separated by time, space and history. In many ways she reflects Mary's own maternal quest. The poor act as parent-surrogates for each other when the old extended family structure is exploded and fragmented into nuclear families by the factory system. Old Job Legh and the other grandfather, Jennings, rescue the infant Margaret from London after the death of her parents. To clinch the point, old Jennings even pretends to be a woman, disguising himself with a chambermaid's cap, to substitute for the child's dead mother (149). Similarly, John Barton and George Wilson, Jem's father, take care of the Davenports when their father dies.

It should be noted that Gaskell identifies strongly with this working-class proclivity for nurturing. She stresses also, especially in the Job Legh/Margaret subplot, their ability to articulate their sufferings and grievances. Margaret in some ways reflects Gaskell's biography, together with her role as artist. Gaskell, like Margaret, was born in London; she was half-orphaned, and taken north to Manchester by her father. Margaret's blindness forces her to make singing, her hobby, a vocation, and she specializes in working-class songs such as "The Oldham Weaver":

Oi'm a poor cotton-weyver, as mony a one knoowas. . . .

We lived upo' nettles, whoile nettles wur good,
An' Waterloo porridge the best o' eawr food.

(72)

Gaskell's work incorporates, often in their entirety, such songs and poems as this (Bamford's "God help the poor!", the text inscribed on the back of the Valentine-clue, is another example). It does so unpatronizingly and signals the author's admiration for the verbal skills and artistry of these compositions. Job Legh, moreover, is a working-class encyclopaedia of information, and there are hints that he is aware all along of John Barton's guilt.

Lord David Cecil accuses Brontë of stretching the long arm of coincidence, in *Jane Eyre*, until it is dislocated.[34] Stowe, however, manages to outdo Brontë in the ingeniousness of her plot coincidences. Madame de Thoux happens to be travelling on the same steamboat as young George Shelby, who has arrived too late to rescue Uncle Tom from Simon Legree, and turns out to be George Harris's sister Emily, while Cassy, escaped from Legree and herself travelling on the boat, is revealed as Eliza's mother. George Shelby is thus able to re-unite a family separated by his father's reckless speculation. In a somewhat similar vein, Gaskell effects a reconciliation between John Barton and the former "exploiter," the mill-owner Carson, just before John's death. Again, however, Stowe may be the more realistic, despite the multiple coincidences. As Herbert G. Gutman has demonstrated, in *The Black Family in Slavery and Freedom, 1750–1925* (1976), black families both before and after slavery "invented" family networks to compensate for the disruption of normal life. Hence, aged "Uncles" and "Aunts" (usually honorific titles only) would supply parental love to the young if their parents were sold, under slavery, or out working, after the Civil War. Rather than destroying black family life, the white man succeeded only in augmenting its value, in any possible form.

The inventiveness of Jem and George finally equips them both to create a new life for their families in Canada. If local attachments are lost in town in *Mary Barton* (158), perhaps the answer is to create a new structure elsewhere. The solution to a lack of fortune in England is to seek it in the "colonies," and Canada becomes a kind of Promised Land for Jem and Mary. Jem's old master, Mr Duncombe, well aware of Jem's innocence but also of the difficulties his chequered past will create for him in England, is asked "to recommend an intelligent man, well acquainted with mechanics, as instrument-maker to the Agricultural College they are establishing at Toronto in Canada" (446). Job Legh, the amateur entomologist, eventually decides to visit them "to try and pick up a few specimens of Canadian insects" (466); Gaskell, as we have seen, constantly underlines the intellectual curiosity of the working class, exemplified both in Jem's inventiveness and Job's scientific hobby.

Edgar F. Wright sees the escape to Canada as an unrealistic Wordsworthian return to nature,[35] but in fact the ending *is* convincing in the sense that Gaskell knowingly focuses on the great period of British emigration to the New World, seen problematically, from the perspective of colonialism, as the land of promise for the working classes.[36] By the same token, George and Eliza, together with their son, can escape the Fugitive Slave Law only by means of the Underground Railroad to Canada. They and the Wilsons are among the earliest of a long line of fugitives, dissidents and poor to choose Canada as a refuge, later to include the Vietnam War draft-resisters and Americans fleeing urban rot. George subsequently spends four years at a French university to complete his education, and ends up going back to Africa to help "his own people." The "solution" is more expeditious and naïve on Stowe's part than we would find acceptable today; she seems to be exiling the issue rather than confronting it. Baldwin and others have felt that such a return to Africa is an evasion: "Negroes are Americans and their destiny is the country's destiny. They have no other experience besides their experience on this continent."[37] Frazier has said that the American black must find a "motive for living under American culture or die."[38] It would be fairer to say, rather, that North American society must recognize the unique contributions of its "native sons" – and "daughters" – to use Baldwin's double-edged term – or die.

The Canadian presence is also felt in *Uncle Tom's Cabin* in another way: the St. Clare family is originally of Acadian stock and has been itself expatriated from Nova Scotia to Louisiana's "Cajun" country (168). Little Eva's full name, Evangeline St. Clare, suggests that she was named after the heroine of Long-fellow's poem "Evangeline" (1847). The one branch of the family, Miss Ophelia's, landed in Vermont, the other in Louis-iana. It is Miss "Feely," the Northern liberal, who must be taught how to feel viscerally, as opposed to intellectually, with the blacks. And Simon Legree, the most villainous, indeed demonic, slave-owner, is also a Northerner.

One plot in each novel, focusing on, respectively, John Barton and Uncle Tom, is so unrelievedly bleak that a conventional romantic subplot is evidently required to lessen the gloom. Arguably, however, the conventional romance is at least equally important because, like the second-generation plot in *Wuthering Heights* (1847), it provides continuum, a means of survival. Unfortunately, Stowe fails to perceive that her real and best survivor is Topsy, black as Uncle Tom, but a female picaro who lives by her wits. She presents the extreme case of a lack of family ties, having been raised by a speculator as if on a chicken farm: "I spect I grow'd. Don't think nobody never made me" (262). She serves as a foil to little Eva, who is all soul and no body. Stowe may not have intended this reading, but Eva's passive religiosity reflects a death wish in the entire St. Clare family, similar to that which Mark Twain was later to parody in Emmeline Granger-ford, in *Huckleberry Finn*,[39] whereas Topsy endures and prevails, by constructing her own surrogate extended family.

It is difficult to arrive at any final position on Stowe's use of racial stereotypes. Certainly, on balance, she is more open than Baldwin suggests. Nevertheless she is guilty of seeing her black characters as "impassioned and imaginative," (40) "not strictly honest" (231) – albeit out of necessity – and as having "pecu-liarly strong" "instinctive affections" (109). Dinah, the cook, is "a self-taught genius" creating order "out of chaos and old night down there" in the cave-like kitchen (239). The image is both positive and negative, connoting as it does the African-American's power of creativity, of bringing light out of dark-ness, in a variation on the Platonic parable. However, Stowe gives with one hand and takes away with the other by implying that this creativity is purely instinctual and domestic.

Alternatively, Stowe allows her sympathetic white drover the comment, "the Lord made 'em men, and it's a hard squeeze getting 'em down into beasts" (121). Discussing heroism, Stowe compares the applauded actions of a hypocritical Hungarian refugee helping others flee from Europe to America to a black man's, and asks why praise is held back "when despairing African fugitives do the same thing" (216).

This is not to suggest that Stowe's depiction of "Life Among the Lowly" is realistic and accurate, merely that she may have further confused the race issue by using a wrong and incompatible model, that of working-class Jem and Mary, for her young couple, George and Eliza, thereby projecting for them a more immediately hopeful future than most blacks could plausibly expect. Whatever her faults on the matter of racial stereotyping, however, Stowe's contribution is genuine and more nuanced or complex than has generally been recognized. It is time for a reassessment of her thinking from a feminist perspective. She was clearly working in an already existing female tradition of social commitment in fiction. Moreover, both she and Gaskell were alert to the analogy between the female condition – passive, receptive, suffering – and the powerlessness of the American slaves and the British factory workers.

Ultimately, both novels have perhaps too small an exit. Each writer posits a solution in human kindness and "brotherhood," neither focusing on political or legal action. Gaskell modestly admits that it would take a Dante to describe the realities of Manchester. If the city did not get a Dante, we may be grateful that at least it found a Gaskell, as slavery found a Stowe. If *Mary Barton* was "the first great factory novel,"[40] Stowe may have been the first to apprehend its connection with other conditions of servitude.

Uncle Tom's Cabin has been called a rich historical document; and Gaskell's novels present a clear-eyed panorama of the Victorian period, its politics, economics and religion. Neither Stowe's text nor *Mary Barton* would withstand close structuralist analysis, and deconstructionists might suggest that the "realism" of both texts represents an attempt to "sell" bourgeois ideology. However, some deconstructionist critics are returning to referentiality. They remind us that the text is, after all, worldly, in and of the world, as well as being a structure of words. A Sartrean, Marxist, deconstructionist or feminist critic would find in both

novels ample material for historico-literary analysis, whether
that material supports or subverts bourgeois ideology.

Neither Gaskell nor Stowe ever pretended to a Jamesian
concern with form and experimental techniques; both are pre-
occupied with social texture, with life as it is lived, and not with
theory. As Gaskell writes at one point, "So much for generalities.
Let us now return to individuals" (223). An almost mythic
journey or quest motif permits both women to bind together all
the elements of their given society at a particular moment in
history. Stowe's contrast between North and South corresponds
in some ways to Gaskell's contrast of the industrial North of
England and the agrarian South, genteel and static, in her later
novel of the same name (*North and South*). The same dualistic
vision informs the contrast of country and city, of worker and
owner, of Dives and Lazarus in *Mary Barton*. In keeping with
the dialectical tendency – the willingness to show the humanity
of characters who, in more melodramatic hands, would be
cardboard villains – both women focus on individual attitudinal
change as the path to social justice:

> But, what can any individual do? Of that, every indi-
> vidual can judge. There is one thing that every individual
> can do, – they can see to it that *they feel right*. An
> atmosphere of sympathetic influence encircles every human
> being; and the man or woman who *feels* strongly, healthily,
> and justly on the great interests of humanity, is a constant
> benefactor to the human race. See, then, to your sympathies
> in this matter!
>
> (472)

Stowe's peroration may belong in the realm of the pious hope,
but she intends to leave it to the reader to complete the action.
Her appeal is directed to all our consciences, as is Gaskell's
summary of the reforms instituted by the repentant Carson:

> Many of the improvements now in practice in the
> system of employment in Manchester, owe their origin to
> short earnest sentences spoken by Mr Carson. Many and
> many yet to be carried into execution, take their birth
> from that stern, thoughtful mind, which submitted to be
> taught by suffering.
>
> (460)

Like the factory workers and the slaves, Gaskell and Stowe emphasize the connectedness of quasi-familial relationships as the chief means of alleviating human suffering.[41] By expanding their compassion from their own families to encompass the entire human race as a family, they are "maternal feminists" whose not-so-naïve solution to the evils of the factory system and slavery is a new version of the "extended family."[42] Both women, while remaining resolutely middle class, nevertheless escape the prison of womanhood – genteel womanhood – by a kind of maternal "heroinism" which transcends that of their creations, Mary and Eliza.

NOTES

1 The title-phrase comes from C. Brontë. See her brief comments on Stowe in E. Gaskell, *The Life of Charlotte Brontë*, ed. A. Shelston, Harmondsworth, Penguin, 1985, 483.

2 Their current "canonical" status depends on one's historical perspective. S. Roe, editor of Indiana University's Key Women Writers series, which includes P. Stoneman's *Elizabeth Gaskell*, Bloomington, Indiana University Press, 1987, asks whether mainstream women writers, among whom she includes Gaskell, can be regarded as feminists. For some feminist critics, mainstream means "malestream". Perhaps, however, some of these mainstream writers have been canonized for the wrong reasons, co-opted by the malestream, when in their own day they may have been subversive. Roe suggests that they too may have been misread, and that it is time for revisionist readings of the canon.

3 Cited in the "Afterword" to H.B. Stowe, *Uncle Tom's Cabin*, ed. J.W. Ward, New York, Signet, 1966, 480. All subsequent references to *Uncle Tom's Cabin* are to this edition and appear in the text in parenthesis.

4 The most famous voice attacking Stowe's "message" is J. Baldwin in his essay "Everybody's Protest Novel," in *Notes of a Native Son*, London, Michael Joseph, 1964, 19–28. Baldwin objected strenuously to Stowe's alleged "racism": her mulatto couple, Eliza and George Harris, are able to escape via the Underground Railroad to Canada because they can pass for white, whereas her "Uncle Tom," African to the core, "jet-black, woolly-haired, illiterate . . . and . . . phenomenally forbearing," (22) cannot escape by disguising himself and is therefore sold down-river to die ultimately at the hands of the archetypally villainous slave-owner, Simon Legree.

5 Moreover, A. Crozier, in *The Novels of Harriet Beecher Stowe*, New York, Oxford University Press, 1969, reminds us that Uncle Tom dies as a result of courage, not cowardice: "Uncle Tom was killed by Simon Legree because he would not inform on his escaped

fellow slaves, Cassy and Emmeline . . . . The reason that Tom is today regarded as a symbol of the cowardly, bootlicking slave is that he forgives Legree" (vii).

6 In her useful historical overview of the criticism Stoneman notes that the eminently sensible, tolerant Gaskell is often deemed irrelevant or marginal by those critics who promote Brontë's *Jane Eyre* as the central document in nineteenth-century women's literature (see S.M. Gilbert and S. Gubar, *The Madwoman in the Attic: The Woman Writer and the Nineteenth-Century Literary Imagination*, New Haven and London, Yale University Press, 1979). Gaskell, she continues, has been "colonized up to a point by Marxists, [Kettle, Lucas, Williams], but almost ignored by feminists" (*Elizabeth Gaskell*, 1). Yet Gaskell may, in fact, have been more politically radical and committed than her more frequently critiqued literary "sisters," such as C. Brontë, whose heroines explore psychological depths but whose resolutions remain individual.

Stoneman does not deal with W. Gérin's fine biography, *Elizabeth Gaskell*, London, Oxford University Press, 1976, from a theoretical standpoint, but actually Gérin affords many fresh insights into Gaskell's life and writings, forcing one to rethink her feminism. A. Rubenius's *The Woman Question in Mrs. Gaskell's Life and Works*, Cambridge, Mass., Harvard University Press, 1950, should also be mentioned as a major contribution to Gaskell scholarship, pioneering a feminist approach in the 1950s. The most recent addition to these studies is Jane Spencer, *Women Writers: Elizabeth Gaskell*, London, Macmillan, 1993. For Stoneman, poststructuralist theory could point the way to a re-evaluation of Gaskell: women writers are by definition alienated and marginalized, since writing is seen as a male prerogative.

R.B. Yeazell examines the linkage between strong heroines and politics in "Why Political Novels Have Heroines: *Sybil*, *Mary Barton*, and *Felix Holt*," *Novel* 18 (1985) 126–44, while J.P. Tompkins's "Sentimental Power: *Uncle Tom's Cabin* and the Politics of Literary History," *Glyph* 8 (1981) 79–102, is symptomatic of a feminist revival of interest in Stowe. Tompkins argues that critical-scholarly neglect of the book stems from the fact that it was a sentimental novel, a subgenre identified with what Hawthorne castigated as that "damned mob of scribbling women," perceived, moreover, as shoring up the existing social order (80–2). Tompkins, however, sees the novel as both conformist and subversive. While she is a persuasive apologist, she completely omits references to the racial stereotyping that distressed Baldwin, as do other feminist defenders of the sentimental text.

7 E. Moers, *Literary Women*, London, The Women's Press, 1980, 96.

8 Cited ibid., 22.

9 B. Gray, "Mrs. Gaskell's Home Town Drab and not the World of the Novels," *Globe and Mail*, 23 October 1976, 2.

10 Cited by Moers, *Literary Women*, 4.

11 Cited by C.H. Foster, *The Rungless Ladder: Harriet Beecher Stowe*

and New England Puritanism, Durham, Duke University Press, 1954, 27.

12 ibid., 26.

13 G.F. Whicher, "Literature and Conflict," R.E. Spiller, W. Thorp, T.H. Johnson, H.S. Canby and R.M. Ludwig, eds, *Literary History of the United States*, New York, Macmillan, 1953, 563–86, at 582.

14 *Literary Women*, 85.

15 Dickens, who admired Gaskell, may have reflected some of her husband's occasional aggravation with her stubbornness: he commented acerbically when she refused to go back to work on *Cranford*, "If I were Mr. G, Oh Heaven how I would beat her!" (Cited in Gérin, *Elizabeth Gaskell*, 126).

16 *Literary Women*, 97.

17 See note 1 above.

18 *Letters of Mrs Gaskell*, ed. J.A.V. Chapple and A. Pollard, Manchester, Manchester University Press, 1966, 450.

19 This is not to deny that there are numerous possible literary influences on Stowe, in addition to those she names herself in the *Key to Uncle Tom's Cabin* – the 1849 autobiography of the Reverend J. Henson as the source for Uncle Tom, and T. Weld's *American Slavery As It Is* (1839) and *Narrative of the Life of Frederick Douglass, An American Slave* (1845) as the source for George Harris (Foster, *Rungless Ladder*, 18). Foster mentions, for instance, Richardson's sentimentality, Defoe's blend of authentic sources with fiction, and Scott's historical accuracy and journey motif (ibid., 14–16). However, the two-plot novel was characteristically Victorian (see J.R. Adams, *Harriet Beecher Stowe: Updated Edition*, Boston, Twayne, 1989, 24–5), and Stowe is recognizably a novelist of her time.

20 See, for instance, S. Gill, "Introduction," *Mary Barton*, Harmondsworth, Penguin, 1985, 13. All subsequent references are to this edition and appear in the text in parenthesis.

21 *Elizabeth Gaskell*, 10.

22 Adams makes a similar claim for Stowe, whose Augustine St. Clare offers, in chapter 19, a statement that might have come from Marx and Engels' recent *Communist Manifesto*: "there is a mustering among the masses, the world over; and there is a *dies irae* coming on, sooner or later. The same thing is working in Europe, in England, in this country." Ironically, Adams notes, Stowe herself did not share his belief, seeing "wage slavery as free choice" (*Harriet Beecher Stowe*, 30). Yet, it is possible that her model, *Mary Barton*, caused her to push the analogy between slaves and factory workers further than she consciously intended.

23 K. Tillotson, *Novels of the Eighteen-Forties*, London, Oxford University Press, 1954, 222.

24 E.L. Duthie in *The Themes of Elizabeth Gaskell*, London, Macmillan, 1980, compares Gaskell's vision to Disraeli's, in *Sybil, or The Two Nations*: "Disraeli showed two worlds: she shows only one, immerses herself in it, becomes one of its inhabitants, speaks its language and

so conveys, as no arguments could have done, the segregation in which its people exist" (66). It is interesting to see Duthie apply the word "segregation" to factory workers as the United States applied it to blacks. C. Lansbury in *Elizabeth Gaskell: The Novel of Social Crisis*, London, Paul Elek, 1975, underlines the success of Gaskell's social activism: "She was not simply the recorder of her times, but the defining voice of a city that would eventually alter the structure of English society" (21). She also highlights Gaskell's experience "as a prison visitor and social worker," who "knew more about prostitution than most writers of the day" (31).

25 In another vein, R. Warhol's "Toward a Theory of the Engaging Narrator: Earnest Interventions in Gaskell, Stowe, and Eliot," *PMLA* 101 (1986) 811–18, argues that the so-called "sentimental," naïve narrative voices of certain mid-nineteenth-century English and American women novelists were, in fact, breaking with a male tradition of "distancing" in order to "engage" the "narratee" (Gerald Prince's *narrataire*, s/he to whom the tale is supposedly told), and thereby "extend the referentiality of their fiction" (817).

26 *Elizabeth Gaskell*, 68–9. As one of my graduate students, Sheila Greene, who is herself a lawyer, remarked, Jem Wilson is finally freed not by the legal system but by a jury of sympathetic individuals.

27 *Novels*, 213–14.

28 *Elizabeth Gaskell*, 11.

29 ibid., 13. Moreover, in Stowe's United States, abolitionism and feminism both had strong historical ties with Unitarianism and with Transcendentalism, itself both a logical extension of, and form of rebellion against the more structured Unitarian church. Despite the common liberal stances of Gaskell and Stowe, the latter, taught by a suspicious father, did feel that Unitarianism was too extreme and, as Crozier puts it, "beyond the pale of the Christian faith" (*Novels*, 118). Stowe belonged to the liberal Northern wing of the Presbyterian church, then torn by dissension with the Southern branch over the Northern anti-slavery stand. Stowe shows a missionary zeal in claiming that "The Lord himself wrote" *Uncle Tom's Cabin* (ibid., 69). A Unitarian would have seen the divine as immanent in all of us, not as pulling strings from above. With these predictable differences, both novelists share a Christian view of the human condition, though Stowe's is more deterministic (Calvinistic).

30 As noted by Moers, *Literary Women*, 26.

31 ibid., 38.

32 W. Faulkner, *Absalom, Absalom!*, New York, Random House, 1951, 115.

33 Lansbury disagrees with most critics that John Barton was ever intended as a novelistic centre, and claims that the original title was *A Manchester Love Story*, thus foregrounding the Mary-Jem plot (*Elizabeth Gaskell*, 22).

34 Cecil, *Victorian Novelists*, Chicago, University of Chicago Press, 1958, 108.

35 E.F. Wright, *Mrs. Gaskell: The Basis for Reassessment*, London, Oxford University Press, 1965, 96.

36 On the complicities of emigration and the ideology of colonial expansionism in *Mary Barton* see Suvendrini Perera, *Reaches of Empire: The English Novel from Edgeworth to Dickens*, New York, Columbia University Press, 1991, 52–7.

37 "Many Thousands Gone," *Notes of a Native Son*, 29–47, at 45.

38 Cited in Baldwin, "Stranger in the Village," ibid., 151–65, at 160.

39 M. Twain, *The Adventures of Huckleberry Finn*, New York, Holt, Rinehart and Winston, 1948. As Huck describes the morbid Emmeline, who is given to writing odes to the dead, "Every time a man died, or a woman died, or a child died, she would be on hand with her 'tribute' before he was cold. She called them tributes. The neighbors said it was the doctor first, then Emmeline, then the undertaker . . ." (97). Initially, Huck mourns Emmeline's death, finally concluding, however, "But I reckoned that with her disposition she was having a better time in the graveyard" (95).

40 Moers, *Literary Women*, 23.

41 Stoneman suggests that the ethics of the working class are based on "caring" or "nurturing," and are therefore essentially "female" (*Elizabeth Gaskell*, 69). She argues that *Mary Barton* is not "a flawed industrial novel," but embodies a working-class female ethic based on the survival of children. However, she sees the ending of the novel as patriarchal: Mary's "role ends with this enablement of her menfolk" (specifically Jem) in the "world of technology," whereas "Mary's life is as private as her mother's" (ibid., 85). I would suggest, rather, that the ending celebrates Mary's active role as the promoter of the ideal community, of the extended family Gaskell envisages. The very expatriation of this particular family suggests a radical break with the "masculine" revenge/violence tradition represented variously by the owners, the desperate strikers, and John Barton himself when he lapses tragically from his earlier role as nurturer of his own family and the wretched Davenports.

42 Some critics, like R. Bodenheimer in "Private Griefs and Public Acts in *Mary Barton*," *Dickens Studies Annual* 9 (1981) 195–216, see the public sphere as threatening for Gaskell, and consider her locked into the private. It seems to me, however, that Gaskell is consciously trying to bridge the gap. As Crozier describes Stowe's themes as well, "The dramatization of the evils of slavery through its destructive effect on families in the novel implies that the rehabilitation of the nation should come about through a recognition of the sacred ties of family love" (*Novels*, 33). Foster notes that "the theme of mothers separated from children" appears with relation to the whites also, to Augustine St. Clare and even Legree (*Rungless Ladder*, 39).

6

"PAINTING BY NUMBERS"
Figuring Frederick Douglass
Betty J. Ring

Language, for the individual consciousness, lies in the borderline between oneself and the other. The word in language is half someone else's. It becomes 'one's own' only when the speaker populates it with his own intention, his own accent, when he appropriates the word, adapting it to his own semantic and expressive intention.

Mikhail Bakhtin[1]

Any reading of an antebellum slave-narrative must negotiate the elements that go to compose the historical context in which it is located. These include, first of all, the effects of slavery as a total *system* and, second, the machinations of the Abolitionist movement, which enabled the liberation of many slaves, along with their stories, while simultaneously imposing constraints upon the speaking/writing self.[2] Though an historically specific document, the slave-narrative also represents, as autobiography, the writing of the self once abject into history. The framework of the Abolitionist movement obliged the writer working within it to adopt its wider political aims even as the movement was in turn partly dependent upon the writer's text. This interplay is made explicit by the "framing" of that text: the slave-narrative was often accompanied by documents attesting to the writer's veracity, supplementing authorship with a different kind of authority. Even as such framings bespeak a lack of power on the part of the slave, they guide the text to freedom by ensuring that it gain a hearing and be recognized as a purveyor of truth. However, the reader sees not only the liberation of the text in this kind of sign-posting, but also the route literally taken by the absconding slave. Above all, such devices show that the political determinants that temper the autobiographical form work to promote a reading of autobiography as the underwriting of the Abolitionists' truth.

The work of Frederick Douglass clearly represents the literal and in some sense "authentic" voice of slavery, rather than a metaphorical play on enslavement. As one of the most widely disseminated of all slave-texts, *Narrative of the Life of Frederick Douglass, An American Slave* (1845)[3] enjoys a status in both literary and historical contexts that is at once exemplary and yet at the same time problematic or, rather, problematic *because* exemplary. Without disputing Douglass's importance it must be emphasized that each of the slave-narratives (estimated at some 6,000) itself has a representative and yet paradoxically exceptional status.[4] Despite various degrees of editorial distortion, these narratives signify the ability to survive bondage and silence, speaking out for the countless slaves who lived and died beyond the writing of history.

This chapter explores the consequences of placing both Douglass and his work at the top of a critical hierarchy. While showing how Douglass is constructed as "representative slave-narrator" according to particular historical and literary criteria, I want to argue that he in fact deconstructs those processes to which he is subject. The crux of the argument rests upon an analysis of Douglass's use of a specific mode of interpretation which I shall call *semantic intervention*. The following reading of Douglass is principally concerned with defining the nature of this intervention and considering how it illuminates both Douglass's text and the problematic of the slave-narrative as a whole.

RHETORICAL FIGURES

Given the curious fact that between 1845 and 1881 Douglass produced three autobiographies, it is evident that the writing of the self into history was always on-going, the text an entity far from self-contained.[5] Within this process priority and authority are not synonymous: *Narrative* has the status of an "original" text, even as its authenticity is called into question by the subsequent re-inscriptions of the second and third versions. A comparison of all three volumes reveals the places where deviations from the *Narrative* occur but also where repetitions fashion emphasis and, thus, a "uniformity" which needs to be recognized as ultimately deceptive, since the moment in which repetition occurs is by definition a differing from rather than duplication of origins.

By reproducing aspects of the first narrative in this way, Douglass selects passages on the basis of their relevance to shifting needs. However, along with this kind of "repetition" come elaborations and extensions. Fragments of the first text are absorbed into the second – the third incorporating both. The chain of intertextual signification subverts the expectations built into the autobiographical genre: the form presupposes an onto-logical development, paralleled by a textual autonomy, rather than the perpetual reworking and expansion of materials.

In what is perhaps *Narrative*'s most telling rhetorical moment, Douglass declares "You have seen how a man was made a slave; you shall see how a slave was made a man" (*N* 294). The linguistic device of chiasmus not only introduces Douglass's physical struggle with Covey, his brutal overseer (an encounter much discussed by critics) but also prefigures it textually. Up to this point the text has described the process of slave-making. What follows is the reverse, a charting of the movement from slavery to freedom which also constitutes a return to a pre-slave condition – the chiasmus beginning and ending, accordingly, with "man." This is not a regression but a revival for Douglass of "a sense of [his] own manhood" (*N* 298). The chiasmus causes the reader to anticipate the process of slave-unmaking and yet simultaneously *enacts* it. In so doing, it also functions as a synecdoche for the text as a whole which itself evidences the unmaking it claims only to show or represent. The auto-biography itself bears witness to a resistance to slavery and assertion of "manhood," being *in se* a dismissal of the argument that the slave is unable to master written language. For this reason the autobiography is a performative text. It describes the progressive return of slave from bondage to freedom but comes also to stand as one of the elements that constitute and em-phasize that liberation. Nor does the writing merely exist as a chronicle of events, since the narrator also constructs and interprets the past through the text. Even as it sets out to describe, it enacts.

In *My Bondage and My Freedom* Douglass places himself against other views by embarking upon his own independent enquiry into the origins of slavery:

I was not very long in finding out the true solution of the matter. It was not *color*, but *crime*, not *God*, but *man*, that afforded the true explanation of the existence of slavery; nor was I long in finding out another important truth, viz: what man can make, man can unmake. The appalling darkness faded away, and I was master of the subject.

(*MB* 90)

Recalling the famous chiasmus discussed above, this comment arises when Douglass comes to understand that human endeavour rather than divine will is the enabling ground of slavery. It is "*man*" (a rubric significantly including master and slave alike) not God who evidently makes and unmakes – the human agency is quite explicit. In contrast, the chiasmus suggests that the process through which the slave becomes a man will be shown or illustrated elsewhere, specifically in Douglass's subsequent description of his clash with Covey. However, in the second quotation power-relations between master and slave are constructed epistemologically: deciphering the processes by which the true origins of slavery are obscured, Douglass becomes "master" of the "subject," thus transforming his own subjected status. Indeed, the self-transformation anticipated here is – once again – proleptically carried out by his text, through the revisionary excision of the very sign for Douglass's oppression ("slave") that features in the earlier passage. These processes offer us another example of semantic intervention in Douglass.

The play of making and unmaking characterizes Douglass's analyses of the relation between man and slave. It also provides a perspective from which we can consider the relation between Douglass and his work, on the one hand, and the ways in which they are critically constructed, on the other. Douglass's status as a pre-eminent nineteenth-century black man is indisputable. Paradoxically, he can be read as either the exception to black history or as the representative coloured man. The former involves a recognition of his achievement as an individual while the latter democratizes the relation between Douglass and his fellow-slaves.

Yet to figure Douglass as a "black Everyman" involves its own paradoxes. In his introduction to *The Classic Slave Narratives* Henry Louis Gates, Jr. observes:

Douglass's rhetorical power convinces us that he is "the"

121

black slave, that he embodies the structures of thoughts and feelings of all black slaves, that he is the resplendent, articulate part that stands for the whole, for the collective black slave community. His superb command of several rhetorical figures – metaphor, irony, synecdoche, apostrophe, and especially chiasmus – enables him to chart with fine precision in only a few pages "how a man was made a slave," as he puts it . . . and "how a slave was made a man."[6]

Whether by accident or intent, this critical vision of Douglass rests upon one of the skills that it ascribes to him. As a "part that stands for the whole" Douglass is turned, curiously, into one of the rhetorical figures – synecdoche – placed under his "superb command." However, the figuring of Douglass as synecdoche only undercuts itself. Even as his abilities make him a representative of his race, his high profile contradicts this status, drawing attention to the difference between Douglass and other ex-slaves: the exception becomes exemplary even as the example becomes, necessarily, exceptional.

PERFORMANCE

The significance of the uniformity of the slave-narrative is not fixed but depends upon the perspective from which it is approached. For Gates the narrative emerges from the "shared pattern" of African/slave-culture, functioning as a "communal utterance, a collective tale, rather than merely an individual's autobiography."[7] Central to the creation and development of an African-American canon, it is read as resonating with many voices whose presence disrupts the autonomy of a single writing self and implies a concern for those excluded from the privilege of telling. Similarly, in *The Slave's Narrative*, a collection of texts and essays which Gates edits with Charles T. Davis, it is argued that the conventions so frequently adopted by the slave-narrator satisfy "the urge of the human will to transcend the very chaos of experience with imposed literary figures and structures."[8] Rather than simply reflecting the polemical demands of Abolitionist discourse the slave-narratives are equally symptomatic of the development of a distinct black literary tradition.

In a different reading of the genre James Olney emphasizes the repetitious nature of the slave-narrative and the constraints upon its form.[9] He identifies elements common to all the narratives as well as the sequence in which they are likely to appear. Olney delineates what he calls a "master outline"[10] which not only illustrates the structure of a particular auto-biographical mode but also becomes a means of identifying and reading the slave-narrative genre. In relation to this master outline, and indeed to other narratives, Douglass's work (like Douglass himself) once again occupies a paradoxical position. As so often *Narrative* is simultaneously "the best example, the exceptional case, and the supreme achievement."[11] It is thus "standard" in a double sense, being both a norm and the measure of the excellence to which all others must aspire.

Of all the slave-narratives (and according to Olney the "greatest" employ the master outline while the less successful can only cast after it) Douglass's text not only masters the form but also, reciprocally, becomes the master-text and standard-bearer for the rest. It is difficult to determine quite whether the master outline as posited by Olney precedes the form of the narrative or whether the narrative – as a distinct genre – produces his blueprint. Those narratives that embody, as well as in some way transcend the constraints of, a master-text are, it is assumed, qualitatively "greater" than those that do not. It can be seen that Olney enacts a critical strategy which, though informative, at the same time duplicates the process by which texts become canonized as "classics." His master outline makes the same claims on behalf of the slave-narrative as does Douglass's own text.

The schematic nature of the slave-text, Olney goes on to suggest, means that it cannot truly be compared with main-stream autobiographical forms. The slave-narrative, he tells us:

> tends to exhibit a highly conventional, rigidly fixed form that bears much the same relationship to autobiography in a full sense as painting by numbers bears to painting as a creative act.[12]

Due to the conditions in which it was produced, the slave-text cannot match the creativity of its autobiographical counterpart, only imitate its form. Indeed, since slave-narrators who deviated from an objective tone could be accused of lying, the value traditionally accorded to invention comes to be reversed. Similarly, the avoidance of creativity – too successful an imitation – undermines the claim to an authentic voice. In this difficult context, negotiating the poles of creation and imitation, the slave-narrator needs to convince the reader of an essential humanity without, also, insulting his or her white audience through the establishment of an overly convincing kinship.

The dangers courted by overstepping generic boundaries are demonstrated by the fate of Harriet Jacobs's *Incidents in the Life of a Slave Girl* (1861). Jacobs's narrative includes a number of elements which seem to draw on novelistic conventions and thus disqualify the tale from the slave-narrative genre. Instead of imitating slave-conventions, *Incidents* draws on other influences, evoking in particular "the style of sentimental fiction."[13] Such deviations from the expected norm, until recently attributed to Jacobs's white editor, Lydia Maria Child, present an unacceptable literary or intertextual resourcefulness on the author's part. Jacobs's case thus illuminates the constraints imposed upon the writing self by the form in which it is compelled to operate – the tension between the bid for self-representation and regulation of the self through generic and political forces.

Such dilemmas are not exclusive to the field of the written text but manifest themselves equally – for Douglass and the *black* voice at least – in the context of wider political debate. As an orator Douglass soon came to be aware that he did not satisfy notions of how an ex-slave should look, act and speak.[14] For some, what was perceived as his "difference" raised questions about his authenticity and invalidated his claim truly to represent the enslaved. Responding to these suspicions, fellow-Abolitionists instructed Douglass quite simply to "be [him]self" (*MB* 362) – that is, to *perform* the slave. The effect of this is to deny the passage from slavery to freedom – Douglass's ontological development – through an insistence upon the continuing presence of "origins" beyond or beneath the act of speaking about slavery. Though the injunction was resisted, it remains an ironic comment on the way in which Douglass was expected to display traits that could be read according to preconceived notions. Any revelations he might choose to make about slavery had to counter prescriptivism as well as ignorance and prejudice. As is the case with Jacobs's autobiographical use of the conventional motifs of the sentimental novel, Douglass himself succeeded all too well at mastering rhetorical modes that were supposedly beyond his reach.

In these respects, he becomes subject to a process of "unmaking" which is twofold. On the one hand the pro-slavers' denial of the possibility of Douglass's past bondage constitutes an erasure of his history. The Abolitionists, on the other hand, tacitly urge a return to that state, thus annulling the self as constituted in the present. While resisting such pressures Douglass also underwent a self-questioning precipitated by the tedium of repeating his experiences through oral narration. Now "reading and thinking" for himself he wishes to utter more than just the facts of his own bondage, to signify more than a "*brand new fact*." This desire is also opposed by the Abolitionists who allow him only to "*narrate* wrongs" rather than denounce them. Deviation from already rehearsed speeches would further compound doubts about authenticity. Instead of engaging in a "philosophy" (*MB* 361–2) Douglass must simply continue to present his own slave-experience through the repetition of facts.

Responding both to the doubts of "free spoken Yankees" and the demands of his Abolitionist associates, Douglass feels compelled, after a lapse of four years, "to write out the leading facts connected with [his] experience in slavery" (*MB* 363). Far from merely transcribing his lectures into written form, Douglass's *Narrative* includes the denunciations and "philosophy" which, because they were forbidden by his associates, helped initiate the written text. The publication of *Narrative* enabled Douglass to circumvent to some considerable degree the censorship imposed by the Abolitionists. With the detailed written account of his early life he was able to defend the right to speak as an ex-slave, with all that it entailed. However, though the text substantiates the claims made by and for the speaking self it also threatens to bring about a literal, rather than purely autobiographical, return to origins. The possibility of an enforced return to slavery was a reality for Douglass who asserts that he would rather die resisting attempts to "secure [him] as a slave" (*MB* 363). Such physical resistance parallels his refusal, discussed above, to act like a slave in order to satisfy a sceptical audience. Douglass's text advertises his fugitive status, forcing him to take evasive action in the shape of exile. The events leading to his exile illustrate Douglass's consistently problematic status. Seeking to

silence doubters and resist censorship, Douglass writes an autobiography that liberates him from these constraints, proves his
authenticity and enables greater autonomy and yet consequently
jeopardizes his freedom (*MB* 365).

REWRITING THE WORD

The problems involved in elevating a single text by pronouncing
it to be exemplary are addressed by Douglass himself – in a
religious rather than secular context – through his questioning of
the authority invested in the Bible, the master-text *par excellence*.
This is not to say that Douglass disputes the veracity of the Bible;
rather, his concern is to challenge the reactionary politics for
which it is invoked as the ultimate legitimation. This he does, as
we shall see, by insisting upon and recovering an alternative
hermeneutic potential in the Bible which displaces pro-slavery
readings. Douglass's participation in the tradition of Biblical
exegesis is not restricted to the realms of contemporary political
debates about slavery: in challenging selective and literal readings
of the Bible, his activities at the same time recall, while they
subvert, the Puritan origins of white American autobiography.[15]

During the antebellum era the Bible, in contrast to the slave-
narrative, was a text whose authenticity could not be questioned
since its Author was synonymous with supreme authority.[16]
Within the pages of *the* Master's narrative justification for
contemporary situations was sought, the pro-slavery stance of
most Christian denominations being endorsed through well-
circulated passages from Scripture.[17] In order to counter these
reactionary interpretations the Abolitionists had to challenge
the literal authority of the Bible with alternative readings which
enabled them to engage with and indeed exploit the dominant
discursive force of the pulpit.

The use of Scriptural and religious discourse was perhaps the
most expeditious strategy available to both pro- and anti-
slavery factions, largely indicating a pragmatic response to the
complexities of a political debate rather than spiritual conviction. The advantages of appropriating an already established
discourse, working within the confines of an existing structure instead of seeking to demolish it from outside, are considerable: not being able to manipulate a dominant discourse
would make it necessary to develop an alternative (possibly

humanist) ideology, thus questioning not only the centrality of Christianity but also the "civilization" that it helped foster.

The problems attendant upon this latter course are suggested by Harriet Beecher Stowe in *Uncle Tom's Cabin* (1852) through the figure of Augustine St. Clare. While Stowe allows room in her text for a dissentient voice, St. Clare's manifest disdain for a politicized hermeneutics is based upon the devaluation of language and religion that he sees as resulting from the processes of interpretation and counter-interpretation. However, the critique offered by St. Clare (of Stowe's text as well as of the more general debate) is undercut by his failure either to speak or to act with conviction. In response to Miss Ophelia's "do you think slavery right or wrong?" he says:

> "I'm not going to have any of your horrid New England directness, cousin. . . . If I answer that question, I know you'll be at me with half a dozen others, each one harder than the last; and I'm not a going to define my position. I am one of the sort that lives by throwing stones at other people's glass houses, but I never mean to put up one for them to stone."[18]

Unable to propose any alternative to the discursive politics he rejects, St. Clare can only redouble the fecklessness of his protest. Stowe's text, which incessantly fuses true Christianity with anti-slavery, raises the possibility of an irreligious, albeit cynical, humanism but quickly shows it to be defective. What is more, it would seem that for Stowe the final word on the matter of slavery does not come from a human (let alone humanist) source.

In later life Stowe is reported to have said of her novel that "God wrote it" and that she herself "merely did his dictation."[19] This eccentric allegation – that God penned *Uncle Tom's Cabin* as a sort of holy post-script (or ghost-script?) – can be read in a number of ways, as either an act of compositional humility or self-aggrandisement or simply again the attempt to evade criticism for a controversial text. Stowe's pronouncement – however deluded – is an attempt to achieve for her fiction the status of the Word, not only eclipsing her own authority but also usurping that of the slave-narrators, whose texts, on other occasions, she had identified as forming the novel's source.[20]

In *My Bondage and My Freedom* Douglass makes his own contribution to the debate surrounding the novel's origins and

BETTY J. RING

particularly the prototype of its central character, Uncle Tom.
Referring to an "Uncle Lawson" who acts (along with a white
Methodist named Hanson and a "good colored man, named
Charles Johnson," *MB* 166) as one of his spiritual guides,
Douglass remarks:

> [he] was, in christian graces, the very counterpart of
> "Uncle Tom." The resemblance is so perfect, that he might
> have been the original of Mrs. Stowe's christian hero.
>
> (*MB* 183)

Although "pious Lawson" proves to be a formative influence,
Douglass's later experiences at the diverse hands of his Master
and overseer cause him to renounce "the slave's religious
creed" and, in a "fallen state," to resist his persecution by
exercising a strength that is physical rather than spiritual:
despite publicly praising Stowe, one of the crucial moments in
Douglass's life comes when his "hands were no longer tied by
. . . religion" (*MB* 241) and he is free to struggle against the
brutality embodied in Covey.

In order to secure his own safety and autonomy Douglass
overturns the idea of a passive Christianity. He does not,
however, dispense altogether with religious discourse, nor opt
for the ill-conceived humanism of a St. Clare. Instead, Douglass
performs numerous hermeneutic actions that work to subvert
the precepts of Christian oppression. He thus appropriates the
power of the Word through a process that is as subtle as Stowe's
invocation of divine authorship is grand.

Throughout his *œuvre* Douglass discriminates between the
religious practices of the Church and its representatives, and
the Word of God as it is written. In the appendix to *Narrative*
he writes:

> I love the pure, peaceable, and impartial Christianity of
> Christ: I therefore hate the corrupt, slaveholding, woman-
> whipping, cradle-plundering, partial and hypocritical
> Christianity of this land. Indeed, I can see no reason, but
> the most deceitful one, for calling the religion of this land
> Christianity. I look upon it as the climax of all misnomers,
> the boldest of all frauds, and the grossest of all libels.
> Never was there a clearer case of "stealing the livery of the
> court of heaven to serve the devil in".
>
> (*N* 326)

128

Anticipating a hostile reception for his text, Douglass re-asserts his Christian credential but by no means retracts – indeed, he augments – his critique of organized religion. He fervently condemns the Christianity of "this land" which, he believes, is antithetical to the "Christianity of Christ." Distinguishing between an original practice and secondary forms of Christianity which feign it, Douglass's reading of Christ – the first Christian – takes precedence over the subsequent distortions and imitations created by erring disciples.

When Douglass engages with Christianity he also participates in a far larger enterprise that extends beyond the horizon of Biblical hermeneutics. The appropriation of language and meaning is vital both to religious and secular discourses. With the early "writing of America" these two discursive modes converge, since the autobiographical tradition is so closely identified with Puritanism. For the Puritans, the quest for independence or "the man alone, seeking self-definition and salvation"[21] was founded upon religious freedom. However, the desire for religious freedom was manifested through a policy that advocated reform of rather than separation from the Church of England. Clearly, then, the idea of spiritual autonomy is closely allied to the founding of white America. Douglass's own hermeneutic acts similarly suggest that a degree of autonomy can be achieved within a pre-existent framework by effecting various reforms. With his insistence upon hermeneutics he recalls the spiritual origins of autobiographical writing, the Puritan ground of the independent nation. From this we may surmise that the search for physical, literary and spiritual independence simultaneously involved the creation of alternative possibilities for writing the self within the American tradition, and the creation of alternative writings of America.

Douglass's predominantly autobiographical work staunchly champions the right of the oppressed to create secular and religious meaning but also challenges Puritan literalism. While the Puritans perceived the Bible as the Word of God and interpreted its maxims literally, Douglass rejects such approaches when used to legitimate the power-relation between masters and slaves. His own hermeneutics thus opposes not only contemporary slave-holding Christians but also the teleological outlook of the early settlers. Fundamentally, Douglass recognizes that any relation between God and the self must always be mediated by language, particularly given the centrality of the Bible.

Douglass's project is based on the act of admitting an alternative black history into the process of interpretation, thereby challenging otherwise reactionary (and exclusive) readings of the Scriptures. By opposing ideological claims made on behalf of the text with plurality Douglass effects a semantic dispersal. Indeed, the coercions of language are attenuated because the very act of participating in the interpretative process is itself a form of empowerment.[22]

Douglass's refiguring of American origins (doubly significant since he in turn is figured, by white readers for particular reasons, as a "representative black") is exemplified in the following extract from *Narrative* in which the literal mode of interpretation and, by extension, American secular and religious traditions, are undermined alike by the passage of history. The sexual oppression and violence that literally perpetuate American slavery function also to subvert origins and overturn teleology:

> one great statesman of the south predicted the downfall of slavery by the inevitable laws of population. Whether this prophecy is ever fulfilled or not, it is nevertheless plain that a very different-looking class of people are springing up at the south, and are now held in slavery, from those originally brought to this country from Africa; and if their increase will do no other good, it will do away the force of the argument, that God cursed Ham, and therefore American slavery is right. If the lineal descendants of Ham are alone to be scripturally enslaved, it is certain that slavery at the south must soon become unscriptural; for thousands are ushered into the world, annually, who, like myself, owe their existence to white fathers, and those fathers most frequently their own masters.
>
> (N 257)

Douglass counters a literal reading of the Biblical passage concerning Ham (Genesis viii. 18–29) by inserting an "other" (and previously excluded) history of slavery and miscegenation into the account. The literalism of the pro-slavery reading is based, according to the counter-interpretation, upon an equally selective interpretation of both the Bible and American history.

130

The process of exclusion is difficult to sustain, however, when the evidence, humanly embodied in Douglass, speaks for itself.[23] The simplicity of the assumption "that God cursed Ham, and therefore American slavery is right" is transformed to the point of absurdity by a history of racial and sexual oppression.

Within Douglass's revisionary reading the role of the white slave-holding patriarch is brought to the fore. The repercussions of masters' violations of female slaves are numerous, producing offspring whose "very existence" disrupts strict definitions of race, and the distinctions that sustain the master–slave relationship. As a direct result of his transgressions the patriarch unwittingly calls into question the accepted method of registering lineage, at once destabilizing marriage, the family and slavery – all institutions over which he considers himself to hold dominion. The slave-children of white masters signal not only the abuses performed under slavery but also its self-defeating nature. Through them the prediction of freedom through propagation to which Douglass refers becomes more nearly fulfilled.

Douglass challenges orthodox definitions of race, family and religion by introducing a slave-genealogy into an order which otherwise refuses to acknowledge the possibility of the white "double relation of master and father" (N 257). Douglass's critique is also an inscription, his interpretation an active intervention in the writing of history. His hermeneutics is a means of carving the names of unacknowledged black descendants – metaphorically speaking – beside those of legitimate heirs, in the pages of the family Bible. This is still more telling since Douglass was himself – as he points out – the son of a white master. In addition, the words "scripturally enslaved" signify both an historically specific moment and also a contemporary reality. Punning on these words, Douglass indicates the way in which the Scriptures have been used to justify the cause of slavery, to enslave.

Douglass's disruption of white American values is often explicit. For example, he compares the privilege of being chosen to work at the Great House Farm to "election to a seat in the American Congress," but adds that:

The competitors for this office sought as diligently to please their overseers, as the office-seekers in the political parties seek to please and deceive the people. The same traits of character might be seen in Colonel Lloyd's slaves, as are seen in the slaves of the political parties.

(N 262)[24]

The master's home, a localized seat of power, is a microcosm for the political system *in toto*. It is in essence corrupt, "associated . . . with greatness" (N 262) for the slaves and yet concealing the fact that enslavement – political and otherwise – is the norm. By juxtaposing ideals of freedom, independence and democracy with slavery Douglass draws attention to the collision of contexts, white with black. However, he does not merely condemn the plantation system through this analogy but also signals the failure of political representation. Those elected to governmental office are reduced to "slaves" even as the representativeness of the system that creates such effects is shown to be illusory.

Elsewhere the gardens of the Great House Farm are transfigured into "a scene of almost Eden-like beauty" (MB 67), offering hungry slave-children the "temptation" of "the hardy apple of the north" alongside "the delicate orange of the south" (N 264). In Baltimore, Douglass's new mistress, Sophia Auld, is divested of her "angelic face," taking on that of "a demon" (N 274) as she succumbs, despite herself, to the corrupting effects of slavery. At a later point, when Douglass is sent away from his master's family to live with Covey "for the sake of . . . training" (N 289) he extends the lapsarian figure by referring to the degenerate overseer as "the snake" that lies "coiled up in the corner of the wood-fence, watching every motion of the slaves" (N 291–2).

When Douglass represents the changes brought about by the acquisition of literacy in Baltimore the terms he uses are similarly Biblical:

> I would at times feel that learning to read had been a curse rather than a blessing. It had given me a view of my wretched condition, without the remedy. It opened my eyes to the horrible pit, but to no ladder upon which to get out. In moments of agony, I envied my fellow-slaves for their stupidity. I have often wished myself a beast. I preferred the condition of the meanest reptile to my own. Any thing, no matter what, to get rid of thinking! It was this everlasting thinking of my condition that tormented me.
>
> (N 279)

Finding the revelations of the master-slave dynamic more un-
bearable than the materiality of his condition, Douglass overturns the conventional assumption that defines oppression in
purely physical terms (also problematizing the identification of
knowledge and power discussed earlier). In *Narrative* closure
and "a degree of freedom" which at the same time is yet a
"severe cross" (*N* 326) are achieved when the author addresses
a white Northern audience at an anti-slavery meeting in Nan-
tucket. However, though figuratively emancipated in terms of
his ability to represent his life in slavery and slavery as an
institution (up to a point at least), Douglass has not at this
juncture been formally manumitted. His narrative purports to
show how a "man was made a slave" and "a slave was made a
man" yet the making and unmaking alike elude the constraint of
a linearity arising from conventional definitions of slavery and
freedom. Progress from bondage through to escape and eventual
manumission involves many intermediary stages in which spiritual, mental and emotional freedoms are gradually procured
and integrated. Chiefly, Douglass sets out to redefine both the
process of incarceration and, similarly, the "pathway ... to
freedom" (*N* 275). Slavery for Douglass is as much to do with
knowledge as with physical bondage.

Although born into slavery, Douglass does not fully understand the slave's abjection until he undergoes the trauma of
witnessing the brutal whipping of his aunt by an overseer. The
incident, which initiates him into the truth of slavery, is conveyed in a language that violently evokes the image of a second
birthing:

> It was the first of a long series of such outrages, of which I
> was doomed to be a witness and a participant. It struck me
> with awful force. It was a blood-stained gate, the entrance
> to the hell of slavery, through which I was about to pass. It
> was a most terrible spectacle. I wish I could commit to
> paper the feelings with which I beheld it.
>
> (*N* 258)

The "terrible spectacle" propels its beholder/participant into
the horror of a world composed of masters and their slaves.
Inverting a familiar theological argument which propounds the
notion that the slave is inherently damned, Douglass identifies
the onset of this condition with slavery itself. In addition,

Douglass's language renders explicit the gendered nature of the power-relation he beholds. Bearing the whip's full force, the female body also supplies the metaphors through which he represents his own atrocious emergence into slavery.[25] At another level "the blood-stained gate" recalls a powerful myth of salvation, that of the Passover and Jewish Exodus even as, in the Biblical context, to cross the threshold of the gate is ironically to be protected and share in the liberation of the tribe of Moses, the chosen. In the scene witnessed by Douglass, the implication, that God's powers of intervention are absent, is strong.

In the absence of God's assistance, Douglass reads the signs made by man through the mediation of the Bible, his own acts of writing and interpreting coming to occupy the place of divine intercession. Though the "blood-stained gate" is the site for sexual mastery, it is also read in terms of ontological and religious significance. Paradoxically, Douglass contends that the incident defies language so that, powerful as it is, the metaphor simply veils a harsher reality.

INTERPRETATIONS

Douglass's high degree of articulacy had always to confront the hegemonic authority of white, and in some cases also ordained, masters. The process of displacing one interpretation by activating another is common in both secular and religious discourse, familiar to literary critics and theologians alike. In a religious context the chief authority upon which to draw is that – once again – of God. However, the crucial factor to bear in mind is not that Douglass makes recourse to the intentional fallacy but that he participates in the production of meaning at all. The nature of his hermeneutic acts links the acquisition of literacy with the subversion of established meanings. Moreover, Douglass's own readings are indissociable, as we shall see, from the physical – they do not exist solely within the world of the text. This is best demonstrated by considering Douglass's struggle for a literacy which, though sometimes perceived by him as "a curse rather than a blessing," is nevertheless instrumental to his liberation.

In *The Poetics of Imperialism*, Eric Cheyfitz states:

Both Prospero and Caliban curse each other in the same language, the language that Prospero through his daughter

134

and disciple Miranda has taught Caliban. But the absolutely crucial difference is that whereas Caliban's curses remain mere figures of speech, Prospero's figures have the power to literalize themselves, to act immediately, if Prospero chooses, as engines of torture in Caliban's flesh.[26]

The relation between Prospero and Caliban provides a powerful model through which to view the master–slave dialectic in Douglass. The difference that elevates the master and disempowers the slave is registered in the individual's relation to language. The master's language has a performative capacity, his words once uttered becoming deeds, as desired.[27] However, notwithstanding the apparent fixity of the master–slave relation it is possible for the slave to bring about, through language – both speech and writing – its subversion.

Douglass's desire for literacy leads to his master's prohibition of it. The master's "own words" are given as follows:

> "If you give a nigger an inch, he will take an ell. A nigger should know nothing but to obey his master – to do as he is told to do. Learning would *spoil* the best nigger in the world. Now," said he, "if you teach that nigger (speaking of myself) how to read, there would be no keeping him. It would forever unfit him to be a slave."
>
> (N 274)

The master's injunction is presented by Douglass as "the first decidedly anti-slavery lecture to which it had been [his] lot to listen" (*MB* 146). Ironically, the heuristic speech that facilitates "a new and special revelation" provides Douglass with just that "learning" it is designed to prevent since it illuminates "the white man's power to enslave the black man" (N 275). Inevitably, Douglass's literacy and his heightened consciousness of the power-structure that its lack conceals enable him to fulfil his owner's worst fears that, once master of the written word, "'he'll be running away with himself'" (*MB* 146).

At one point Douglass acknowledges his master as "author of [his] situation" (*MB* 160) but his disempowerment is significantly alleviated when an understanding of and ability to create written signifiers is gained. Douglass repeatedly underscores the power entailed in the mere act of writing – let alone interpreting – signs. One of the means by which he learns to signify – or inscribe – is by appropriating for his own use the "copy books" belonging to the master's son. In the "ample spaces between the lines" (*MB* 171–2), Douglass practises his writing, learning, in the process, to imitate Master Tommy's hand. Under very different circumstances, such copying is a vital skill since by counterfeiting the slave-master's hand and imitating his idiom the slave may forge his/her pass to freedom. Literacy could quite literally enable freedom, the ability to "run away" with oneself. Later yet Douglass's skill at counterfeiting becomes operative in another medium, that of speech, as he parodies the pro-slavery sermons of the Southern preachers for the benefit of his own audiences.[28] Douglass offers an imitation of the master-discourse which is acceptable because it is understood to be parodic. In so doing he reminds us – by contrast – of his earlier public performances whose authenticity is undermined by the very command of rhetoric which was thought properly to be beyond the slave's scope.

As a child in Baltimore Douglass quickly learnt that mimicry was considered a worthwhile rhetorical gift, an understanding that informs the development of the reading, writing and interpreting self. For Douglass, the secular text that counterpoints the centrality of the Bible is Caleb Bingham's *The Columbian Orator* (1797). His attention was drawn to this text by the white boys who give him reading lessons in exchange for bread.[29] These same boys are the first to hear and (to his satisfaction) be moved by Douglass's anti-slavery sentiments. The white boys with whom Douglass associates use the text to prepare for an "Exhibition" at school and learn, presumably by rote, some of the speeches. *The Columbian Orator* is the first book Douglass purchases for himself and as well as providing valuable new reading material it teaches him the power of formal rhetorical devices. From this seminal volume, Douglass also gains access, he tells us, to

> one of Sheridan's mighty speeches on and in behalf of Catholic emancipation. These were choice documents to me. I read them over and over again with unabated interest. They gave tongue to interesting thoughts of my own soul, which had frequently flashed through my mind, and died away for want of utterance.
>
> (*N* 278)[30]

Douglass appropriates the oratorical power of another which liberates his own utterances and provides a framework for articulating the sense of his oppression.

Additionally, the volume contains a dialogue between a runaway slave and his master. In response to his slave's request, the master grants him the right to set forth his own understanding of slavery, a rhetorical action which precipitates emancipation. This dialogue – impressing upon Douglass the liberative potential of language – prefigures an incident in which Douglass himself comes to occupy a position almost identical to that of the runaway slave.[31] When Douglass flees from Covey and seeks the protection of his master, he too is granted the opportunity to speak for himself. Though moved by the appeal, the master controls his emotion and orders Douglass's return to the overseer. At the most critical moment defence through language fails to protect, let alone free, the self: forced back to Covey, Douglass must call on physical means in order to survive the slave-system.

Yet the boundary between language and action is never entirely stable – not only when Douglass takes on the role of rhetorician but also because his own drive toward literacy always involved a physical dimension. While his master was issuing injunctions against reading, Douglass was retrieving from the gutters of Baltimore the material (in the shape of the Bible) that enabled him to keep up his education. Douglass literally cleanses the text, recycling the sullied pages for his own use:

> I have frequently with these fingers, from the mud and filth of the gutter, raked leaves of the sacred volume. These I have washed and dried, and read the words of heavenly wisdom which they contained with a glad heart, considering myself fortunate to enjoy such privilege.[32]

In contrast to Douglass's reverence for the Scriptures, whose materiality is valued as much as the "heavenly wisdom" which they contain, are the actions of the anonymous book-owners who, in contempt for their property, consign both text and God to the gutter. The physicality of Douglass's relation to the text is mirrored in the metaphor he employs to describe the abuse of the Scriptures carried out, this time, not through neglect but through the malice of distorted reading. The "darkest feature of slavery" for Douglass is precisely the spectacle of those ministers who

> Instead of preaching the Gospel against this tyranny, rebuke, and wrong ... have sought, by all and every means, to *throw in the background* whatever in the Bible could be construed into opposition to slavery, and to *bring forward* that which they could torture into its support.[33]

Even to question such interpretative procedures is to face "the charge of infidelity" (*FDP* 282). Attuned as ever to this danger, Douglass – as in the appendix to *Narrative* – takes pains to distinguish between the Christ-based values he embraces and the hermeneutic warping to which they become prone.

In proposing his own readings of the Bible Douglass understands that *the* text, however much disputed, must be afforded a central position in the political debate about slavery. Through the Bible he gains admission to the dominant discourse, repeating hermeneutic acts with a difference, as we have seen. In so doing he implicitly recognizes that all texts – Biblical or otherwise – are sites of interpretative conflict. Both pro- and anti-slave factions must always employ the same language and for Douglass the participation in the discourse of the pulpit enabled him to revise a text that could emancipate as much as enslave. So vital was Christianity to the cause of anti-slavery that the task before him was less that of being reconciled to a pre-existent ideology than a question of actively working to save God, in order that he, and others, both slaves and ex-slaves, could intervene to save themselves.[34]

In composing *Narrative* for the public Douglass was able, retrospectively, to contemplate the process of signification for himself. In a well-known passage he recalls the experience of listening to the singing of the plantation-slaves:

> I did not, when a slave, understand the deep meaning of those rude and apparently incoherent songs. I was myself within the circle; so that I neither saw nor heard as those without might see and hear. They told a tale of woe which was then altogether beyond my feeble comprehension.
>
> (*N* 263)

Positioned within the signifying circle, Douglass cannot interpret the songs. For the moment at least, the privilege of interpretation rests with those who stand outside the bounds of slavery, lacking access to the tradition of the slave-song and the suffering that fuels its continued articulation. The songs fill Douglass with a sense of human impotence and divine indifference, for they incorporate the testimonies and prayers "to God for deliverance from chains." The voices testify to the failure of language as much as God since the slaves' unanswered laments also suffer misinterpretation. Appropriated by the white listeners to the pro-slavery cause, the "wild notes" are read – as songs – to be signs of contentment. Only through the autobiographical retrospect is Douglass able to move from passive silence to active counter-statement, effecting the kind of challenging interpretative shift that characterizes his reading of the Word.

Douglass's recollection of the slave's songs itself brings the argument full circle by setting up clear parallels between the voices of which he speaks and the text in which he speaks of them: describing "Every tone" as "a testimony against slavery, and a prayer to God for deliverance from chains," (N 263), Douglass might almost be providing a commentary upon the status of his *Narrative*, suggesting it to be a synecdoche for the many voices it contains. Yet at the same time the synecdochic relation between text and chorus is unmade by the fact that the voices are only heard of rather than heard. In this way Douglass's reading of the slave-songs – like his revisionary treatment of Biblical authority – alerts us to the dangers entailed in promoting any one figure, or text, to the status of being "representative."

NOTES

1 M.M. Bakhtin, "Discourse in the Novel," in *The Dialogic Imagination: Four Essays by Mikhail Bakhtin*, ed. M. Holquist, trans. Caryl Emerson and M. Holquist, Austin, University of Texas Press, 1981, 259–422, at 293.

2 For a detailed account of the composition of both pre- and post-Civil War narratives see C.T. Davis and H.L Gates, Jr., eds, *The Slave's Narrative*, Oxford and New York, Oxford University Press, 1985.

3 All references to *Narrative of the Life of Frederick Douglass* are taken from the text as printed in *The Classic Slave Narratives*, ed. H.L. Gates, Jr., New York, Mentor, 1987, and are cited throughout as N followed by page number in parenthesis. *Narrative* is framed by a preface written by W.L. Garrison and a letter to the author

from W. Phillips but closes with Douglass's own appendix. Garrison asserts that Douglass's text is "entirely his own production" (*N* 248) adding that it is "sustained by a cloud of witnesses, whose veracity is unimpeachable" (*N* 251).

4 The 6,000 narratives come to stand in for the lives of countless slaves, sixty million or more of whom died in the Middle Passage alone. Douglass shared, to an extent, the feeling that he was in some way "chosen," acknowledging his status as "the representative of three millions of bleeding slaves," *The Frederick Douglass Papers*, Series One, *Speeches, Debates and Interviews*, Vol. I: *1841–46*, ed. J. Blassingame, New Haven and London, Yale University Press, 1979, 36. Subsequent references to this volume are given as *FDP* followed by page number in parenthesis. For Douglass, the privileged position as spokesman which he came to occupy constituted evidence of God's work as well as being the result of his own agency: "I see points in my humble history which seem marked by the finger of God" (*FDP* 128). In *My Bondage and My Freedom* Douglass believes himself to be chosen to live in Baltimore "as a special interposition of Divine Providence in my favor" but is well aware that such an interpretation of events may "be deemed superstitious and egotistical," *My Bondage and My Freedom*, ed. Philip S. Foner, New York, Dover, 1969, 139. Subsequent references to this text are given as *MB* followed by page number in parenthesis. In his 1855 introduction to *My Bondage*, J. M'Cune Smith is far less restrained when dealing with the nature of Douglass's "special mission." Slavery is accordingly viewed as "schooling; the fearful discipline through which it pleased God to prepare him for the high calling on which he has since entered – the advocacy of emancipation by the people who are not slaves" (*MB* xix). For an account of the history of Douglass's text see H.L. Gates, Jr., "From Wheatley to Douglass: The Politics of Displacement" in E.J. Sundquist, ed., *Frederick Douglass: New Literary and Historical Essays*, Cambridge, Cambridge University Press, 1990, 47–65. Gates suggests that Douglass's canonization has effected "the cultural erasure of a female progenitor" – Wheatley (48).

5 The third of these – following *Narrative* and *My Bondage* – is *The Life and Times of Frederick Douglass* (1881; amended 1892).

6 *Classic Slave Narratives*, xiii.

7 ibid., x.

8 *The Slave's Narrative*, 147.

9 J. Olney, "'I Was Born': Slave Narratives, Their Status as History and as Literature," in Davis and Gates, eds, *The Slave's Narrative*, 148–75.

10 ibid., 152.

11 ibid., 156.

12 ibid., 150.

13 J.F. Yellin, "Text and Contexts of Harriet Jacobs' *Incidents in the Life of a Slave Girl: Written By Herself*," in Davis and Gates, eds, *The Slave's Narrative*, 262–82, at 263. For a discussion of Jacobs's

relation to H.B. Stowe see R.W. Winks, "The Making of a Fugitive Slave Narrative: Josiah Henson and Uncle Tom – A Case Study," ibid., 112–46.

14 At this time Douglass was not legally an "ex-slave" since his manumission did not come until he was purchased by British Abolitionists toward the close of his European travels between 1845 and 1847.

15 On this point see H.A. Baker, Jr., "Autobiographical Acts and the Voice of the Southern Slave," in Davis and Gates, eds, *The Slave's Narrative*, 242–61. Baker states that "egotism, self-consciousness, and a deep and abiding concern with the individual are at the forefront of American intellectual traditions," 242.

16 Yet the Apocrypha, or fourteen books added as an appendix to the Old Testament, are, as their name suggests, of questionable authenticity and during the nineteenth century their status was widely debated. Indeed, Biblical truth was coming under pressure from the work of the Higher Criticism in Germany which thus provides an interesting European counterpart to one aspect of the textual or revisionary project of *Narrative*. In one of his speeches, Douglass says: "The Churches of America were responsible for the existence of slavery. Her ministers held the keys of the dungeon in which the slave was confined. They had the power to open or shut – they had the heart of the nation in their hands – they could mould it to anti-slavery or to pro-slavery, and they had put the pro-slavery impress upon the national instrument which spilled his sister's blood" (*FDP* 143).

17 Douglass uses a number of passages repeatedly in both his autobiographies and his speeches, including Ephesians vi: 5; Colossians iii: 22; Titus ii: 9; Luke xii: 47, and Deuteronomy xxiii: 15. For more on Douglass's complex relation to Christianity and God see D. Gibson, "Faith, Doubt, and Apostasy: Evidence of Things Unseen in Frederick Douglass's *Narrative*," in Sundquist, ed, *Frederick Douglass*, 84–99.

18 H.B. Stowe, *Uncle Tom's Cabin*, Harmondsworth, Penguin, 1987, 280.

19 This is recorded in A. Fields, *The Life and Letters of Harriet Beecher Stowe*, Boston, Houghton Mifflin, 1857, 377. See also T.F. Gossett, *Uncle Tom's Cabin and American Culture*, Southern Methodist University Press, 1985, 93. At a later point Gossett remarks: "To introduce the intentions of God into a political issue is dangerous enough. To introduce them in connection with one's own contribution to the debate is worse," 96.

20 For a full account of these sources see both Winks, "The Making of a Fugitive Slave Narrative," and Yellin, "Text and Contexts."

21 Baker, "Autobiographical Acts," 243.

22 Douglass first "learned that the point from which a thing is viewed is of some importance" (*MB* 47) when, accompanied by his grandmother, he walked the 12 miles to his new home on Colonel Lloyd's plantation. Although still a child Douglass feels "too much

of a man" to let his grandmother carry him the whole distance. His imagination transforms the trees in the forest into assorted "wild beasts" (*MB* 46) but, when he draws closer, he is able to master his fear and achieve an understanding of the significance of perspective to perception.

23 As Douglass puts it, "Genealogical trees do not flourish among slaves. A person of some consequence here in the north, sometimes designated *father*, is literally abolished in slave law and slave practice" (*MB* 34–5). Elsewhere, he directly challenges the racist supposition that any skill he might master is the result of his white paternity by emphasizing instead the fact that his own mother was "the *only* one of all the slaves and colored people in Tuckahoe" who could read. To this he adds: "I am quite willing, and even happy, to attribute any love of letters I possess, and for which I have got – despite of prejudices – only too much credit, *not* to my admitted Anglo-Saxon paternity, but to the native genius of my sable, unprotected, and uncultivated *mother* – a woman, who belonged to a race whose mental endowments it is, at present, fashionable to hold in disparagement and contempt" (*MB* 58).

24 This point is expanded in *My Bondage* when Douglass describes Colonel Lloyd's plantation in a way which suggests that the plantation system, though itself a microcosm for national power-relations, is also *beyond* state-government. It is: "a little nation of its own, having its own language, its own rules, regulations and customs. The laws and institutions of the state, apparently touch it nowhere. The troubles arising here, are not settled by the civil power of the state. The overseer is generally accuser, judge, jury, advocate and executioner. The criminal is always dumb. The overseer attends to all sides of a case" (*MB* 64).

25 For an illuminating response to the place of the female slave in Douglass's work see J. Franchot, "The Punishment of Esther: Frederick Douglass and the Construction of the Feminine," in Sundquist, ed., *Frederick Douglass*, 141–65.

26 E. Cheyfitz, *The Poetics of Imperialism: Translation and Coloniz-ation from The Tempest to Tarzan*, New York and Oxford, Oxford University Press, 1991, 33.

27 Though legally impotent, the slave's word was perhaps able to wield a degree of damaging social power. The publication of Douglass's texts obviously exposes those individuals who have abused him to public scrutiny. Perhaps this is why, along with the need for exactitude, Douglass both names and also precisely locates the culprits. At one point in *My Bondage* he takes the opportunity to "immortalize another of [his] neighbors, by calling him by name, and putting him in print. He did not think that a 'chiel' was near, 'taking notes,' and will, doubtless, feel quite angry at having his character touched off in the ragged style of a slave's pen" (*MB* 259).

28 In a speech delivered in Boston on 28 January 1842 Douglass further differentiates between the Christianity of Christ and its practice: "But what a *mockery* of His religion is preached at the

South! I have been called upon to describe the style in which it is set forth. And I find our ministers there learn to do it at Northern colleges. I used to know they went somewhere I did not know where, and came back ministers; and this is the way they would preach. They would take a text . . . and this is the way they would apply it . . ." (*FDP* 16–17). Douglass then cites portions of Scripture and imitates the interpretations that Southern ministers give to them.

29 For Douglass there seems to be an inextricable connection between literacy and labour, a fact which further underlines the physicality of his endeavour. Not only does he exchange bread for lessons with the white boys but later learns the rudiments of writing by studying the markings left on the timbers used by the shipyard carpenters (*MB* 170–1).

30 Although Sheridan appears to express Douglass's own need for a declaration of universal human rights Douglass later rejects the analogy, frequently made by audiences during his lecture-tour of Ireland, between slaves and Irish Catholics (*FDP* 76, 317, 342).

31 See also Ephesians for a letter written by Paul to a slave's master. This story, of Paul returning the runaway slave, was often cited as an example of the Christian justification of slavery. The judgement of Paul is countered in Deuteronomy xxiii. 15: "Thou shalt not deliver unto his master the servant which is escaped from his master unto thee."

32 *FDP* 127.

33 *FDP* 282, emphasis added. Douglass goes on to quote from James iii: 17, declaring his love for the "wisdom of God, which is first pure, then peaceable, gentle, and easy to be entreated, full of mercy and good fruits, without partiality and without hypocrisy." The tenets of this quotation are woven into Douglass's appendix to *Narrative* in which he defends himself by renouncing the "slave-holding . . . Christianity of this land" (*N* 326). As D. Gibson wryly notes, "ordinarily, appendixes are taken out for reasons of health – not put in," "Faith, Doubt, and Apostasy," 87.

34 As Cheyfitz, *Poetics of Imperialism*, 32, remarks: "The slaves were not converting themselves to God, but were converting themselves to each other. As a result, slaves converted God to their new identity and community in the New World and made God active in their struggle for freedom." Gibson notes that "By 1845, when Douglass was writing the *Narrative*, not one of the major denominations other than the Quakers held a strong antislavery position," "Faith, Doubt and Apostasy," 88.

7

PERILOUS PASSAGES IN HARRIET JACOBS'S *INCIDENTS IN THE LIFE OF A SLAVE GIRL*

Jon Hauss

The tenth chapter of Harriet Ann Jacobs's *Incidents in the Life of a Slave Girl* (1861)[1] unveils a range of slave-experiences belonging, in Lydia Maria Child's prefatory phrase, "to a class which some call delicate subjects, and others indelicate" (4). The chapter relates both the narrator's subjection to the slave-master's sexual aggression and her resistance to him – through a secretive, confiding and eventually sexual relationship with another white townsman, who has expressed "sympathy, and a wish to aid" her (54). The chapter's title, "A Perilous Passage in the Slave Girl's Life," carries a number of significances both within this episode and for the narrative as a whole.

While "Perilous Passage" names, in the first instance, that risk-laden experiential passage which Linda Brent, Jacobs's pseudo-nymous narrator, must undergo, it also signifies her dangerous strategy of resistance: a clandestine passage of confidences, a surreptitious opening of relation, to an apparently sympathetic white other. This second "passage" is represented in *Incidents* as an on-going and shared cultural practice of slave-women – an embattled yet continuous effort to extend underground channels, passageways of solidarity, between otherwise alienated social positions. The slave-girl's act is imperilled, at this point, both by the massive institutional power of the slave-master and, import-antly, by the white townsman's potential failure to comprehend the revelation of her endangered circumstances. In this latter sense, the title ultimately names the literary venture of the chapter (and narrative) itself – a dangerous textual passage which, in an effort to produce a broader network of cross-social understanding and alliance in the antebellum North, must risk either the misconstructions of Northern readers or their condemnation of the slave-narrator's tabooed disclosures.

In its accounts of oppression and resistance alike, *Incidents* opens to Northern readers previously veiled aspects of slave-life. The hundreds of slaves' narratives and anti-slavery fictions issued from the Abolitionist presses during this period regularly inveigh against the distinctively brutal and degraded conditions of slave-life. Yet certain "peculiar phase[s]" (4) of enslavement, particular passages of slave-experience, were excised from these accounts, either by ex-slave writers or by their editors who judged Northern readers unprepared to hear them. Child's prefatory remarks allude specifically to the routinized rape of slave-women by male slave-holders,[2] but they also suggest that intimate negotiation of sexuality, and her own body, into which Brent, like other anonymous slave-girls, is pressed in daily and at first largely isolated efforts of defiance. Those who may call these subjects "delicate" or "indelicate" are, of course, white Northern readers – largely female and middle-class – bound by the assumptions of the nineteenth century's cult of True Womanhood. Such readers may well discount or condemn the stories of a woman who, by her own admission, has "fallen" from the pedestal of the recognizably "feminine," with its four cardinal virtues, as Barbara Welter puts it, of "piety, purity, submissiveness and domesticity."[3] It is for its candid exposition of life-passages from beyond the familiar bounds of white cultic Womanhood that Jacobs's *Incidents* is now chiefly, and quite rightly, recognized.

Nevertheless, *Incidents* is equally remarkable, I will argue, in its foregrounding of that second sort of "passage" – the production, through a strategically revelatory storytelling, of underground passageways of solidarity and resistance. It is really, most simply, a certain kind of language-use among slave-women that Jacobs's text both portrays and enacts, a certain ritual of storytelling designed to produce, affirm and extend networks of subversive community. In "Reflections on the Black Woman's Role in the Community of Slaves," Angela Davis challenges scholars of slavery to recognize slave-women's subversive roles in the antebellum South.[4] The historical instances that Davis cites are largely those of black women's participation in overtly

145

militant movements of revolt, especially those launched by insurgent maroon communities who held forested territories across the old South. Yet, Davis's remarks on slave-women's daily and less visible acts of resistance, in the slave-quarters and elsewhere, are powerfully suggestive, in fact looking forward to much of what can be verified through Jacobs's more recently authenticated text.

It seems especially useful to draw from the increasingly detailed scholarship of recent years on the unique cultural dimensions of slave-life, and to read some of this material back through Davis's focus on slave-women's resistance. In particular, Sterling Stuckey's exploration of slave-life and its cultural legacies provides a rich sense of the broader slave-improvised culture that surrounds and infuses the storytelling scenes in Jacobs's narrative.[5] Stuckey argues that slaves improvised an often hidden culture, within the harrowing conditions of American enslavement, through the synthesis of black African tribal beliefs and practices with selected elements of Euro-American culture, especially evangelical Protestantism. This was the culture informing the "ring shouts," graveyard dances, sorrow songs and storytelling circles, often practised secretly, and under cover of night, beyond the surveillance of masters and overseers. The cultural dream with which these rituals resonate is, for Stuckey, one of a life, across the river Jordan, of interdependence without domination, an encircling human unity located beyond exploitation. In the simpler, more contingent language of Jacobs's narrative, it is the dream of "freedom and a home."[6]

In *Incidents*, slave-women repeatedly form the central matrices through which this cultural dream, and its storytelling practices, are not only sustained within slave-communities, but gradually and strategically circulated beyond them. At each new juncture in this extending process, a similar scene unfolds: the slave-woman appraises a social other to be worthy of her trust, and "tells her story" – broaching a passage for possible cross-social understanding and alliance. The immediate aim of every such incident is the expansion of a subterranean and embattled solidarity against the slave-holder, but the tellers also dream the day in which relationships that are now selective and strategic will become general, opening every interhuman channel. In the "Perilous Passage" chapter, Brent begins, in this fashion, to elaborate an underground network (to free herself and her children) which will come eventually to include a prominent white townsman, a slave-holding woman, numerous local blacks (both slave and free), a white ship-captain and several Philadelphia Abolitionists, whose Northern network of resistance is thereby drawn into concert with Brent's own.

Jacobs's narrative constitutes a quite conscious artistic elaboration of this on-going folk practice. *Incidents* narrates a changeful spectrum of storytelling scenes, re-iteratively meditating upon the dangers and promises, the profound conflicts and sudden fluencies, of transsocial exchange in a divided America. At the same time, Jacobs's "delicate" passages enact this perilous storytelling on a broad public scale, revealing the slave-girl's story to an audience whose life-passages are systemically far-removed from Jacobs's own.[7] Explicitly identifying her audience and aims in a brief preface, Jacobs proposes to "arouse the women of the North to a realizing sense of the condition of two millions of women at the South, still in bondage" (1). That "realizing sense," and the subversive political alliances it may generate, are the central goals of Jacobs's cross-social telling.

The opening passage of Jacobs's text momentarily evokes a slave-child's naïve trust in the warm, seemingly stable community of an extended slave-family, whose subjection to the operations of slavery and the slave-market remains as yet unknown. The brief utopian vision must be understood as more than simply a child's egotistical fantasy of a world without contrariety. In the terms of the narrative as a whole, the opening conjures a shared slave-cultural dream – libidinal in a collective and historical sense. Yet Jacobs's beginning moves swiftly from the slave-girl's first sense of her community as blissfully unendangered, and of her own future as uncircumscribed by the power of others, to the stark apprehension that she is "a piece of merchandise" liable to be wrenched from her home "at any moment" (5). What seems a condition of personal freedom within a nurturing community is revealed as a condition already thoroughly regulated by the machinations of slavery.

Such machinations, alienating members of black families one from another "at any moment," throw their lives and desires into radical conflict with those of the white society that surrounds them. The nonthreatening social world which the child so briefly "trusts," and within which trust in others seems both possible and part of this world's desirability, is recognized within the space of a few lines as a realm in which simple trust proves naïve and self-defeating. The passage ends by recounting how the faith of Brent's grandmother in a slave-mistress's promise is, like the child's trust in her early perceptions, summarily betrayed, ruining the chance of this slave-family purchasing its freedom: "she trusted solely to [her mistress's] honor. The honor of a slaveholder to a slave!"(6). This betrayal closes Jacobs's long first paragraph, initiating an on-going dialectic between the life-giving dream of a world where all passageways of understanding are blown clear and fluent, and the punishing experience of systemic social conflicts everywhere undermining the possibility of such relations.

While the text's opening locates the narrator within the strife-torn conditions of the Southern slave-population, ensuing chapters elaborate the further distinction – crucial to Jacobs – for which the work is now famous, encapsulated in her assertion that: "Slavery is terrible for men; but it is far more terrible for women" (77). The complex referents of this line begin to be examined in those early passages based most closely on the popular seduction novels of the time.[8] Here the slave's conflictual relation with her master, "Dr. Flint," is rendered with a focus on male sexual domination generic to the seduction novel format, but intricated with the power-relations of slavery. It is in these doubled terms that Brent narrates the prolonged sexual battle, "the war of [her] life," (19) with Dr. Flint.

Brent's desires for freedom and a home – which at this stage take the form of "first love" (37) for a free black carpenter who wants to marry her, purchase her freedom and raise a free family – are directly countered by Flint's desires to dominate her sexually and claim as alienable property any "chattels" they may produce. Their "war" is comprised, in part, by a series of strategically shifting verbal relationships. When not imposing himself with "stormy, terrific ways" (which Brent confesses to prefer), Flint imagines that his whispered expression of erotic desires will be seductive; he hopes to "people [Brent's] young mind with . . . images" which will arouse a responsive desire for him (27). Though both tactics fail equally, Flint risks little in his disclosures. He is wary of Brent informing her free grandmother, "Aunt Martha," since the latter wields a certain toughly earned "respectability" in town, where her spreading of this knowledge could cost him in status. Yet he guesses correctly that Brent's sense of shame over this matter, in the face, precisely, of Martha's "respectability," will keep her silent. In an alternation of shame and dread Brent grapples at first unaided with Flint, manœuvring toward the protective presence of Martha whenever possible, but as yet at a loss for ways to conscript others into her struggle.

Though she hesitates to speak freely to her grandmother, Brent finally determines to enlist the aid of a local white woman, a friend of Flint, by "t[elling] her my story." This is Brent's first attempt to escape, through a strategic confidence, her shamed silence, isolation and the harassment these perpetuate. She asks the woman to transmit her story to Flint, in hopes of persuading him to sell Brent to the carpenter. In a scene that will be mirrored repeatedly, the woman "listened with kindly sympathy, and promised to do her utmost to promote my wishes." In this instance, the strategy backfires. The woman carries out her charge, but Flint, true to his name, is impervious to Brent's story.

The prolonged exchange between Brent and Flint that follows underscores the fact that their radically contradictory positions, along Southern society's axes of slavery and patriarchy, militate against any easy verbal resolution of their conflict. Brent's initial efforts to make Flint understand her situation end in a cold linguistic warfare. The "story" itself, passed to Flint in the hope of such resolution, becomes an interpretative battlefield for their opposing desires. Flint calls Brent to his private study where, suppressing an obvious rage over the white woman's intercession, he contemplates from his own interpretative angle, with affected amusement, the tale of Brent's "love-dream" (38). Brent distantly observes Flint's inner-sanctum theatre of power, including his cool dismissal of the significance of the carpenter: that "free nigger." Flint goes so far, in his self-serving response to the story, as to feign concern over Brent's social dignity: "I supposed . . . you felt above the insults of such puppies." Brent responds with a trenchant reversal of the social perspective inscribed in Flint's language: "The man you call a puppy never insulted me, sir." While Brent's response dignifies, and re-humanizes, the carpenter, her "sir" is ringingly hollow, coming, as it does, after the implicit charge that Flint *has* insulted her through his sexual conduct. Brent's cool closing remark on the carpenter – "and he would not love me if he did not believe me to be a virtuous woman" (39) – calls Flint entirely out of his affected nonchalance. Disrupting his tactic of distant interpretative authority, it provokes his first physical violence. The comment not only persists in deflecting the master's interpretative control but also reminds him of Brent's equivalent and sustained deflections of his phallic desires.

The doctor's wife plays an initially uncertain role on the peripheries of this sexual struggle. Brent seems spontaneously moved by the obvious personal degradation experienced by Mrs. Flint, a more or less conscious witness to her husband's increasing obsession with the slave-girl: "I was touched by her grief. . . . She felt that her marriage vows were desecrated, her dignity insulted." Nevertheless, Brent hesitates to approach the slave-mistress with a full disclosure and plea for help, fearing her jealousy. That disclosure is simply extracted, rather, in a crucial scene. After Flint has arranged, on a transparent pretext, for Brent to begin sleeping in his private rooms, Mrs. Flint calls the slave-girl to her own room, in secret, and interrogates her: "kiss this holy book, and swear before God that you tell me the truth. . . . Now . . . look me directly in the face, and tell me all that has passed between your master and you" (33).

The surreptitious face-to-face exchange that follows is palpably freighted with the hope and danger every such scene carries in *Incidents*, and for a moment during Brent's narration, a degree of solidarity seems to have been reached:

> As I went on with my account her color changed frequently, she wept, and sometimes groaned. She spoke in tones so sad, that I was touched by her grief. The tears came to my eyes.
>
> (33)

The slave-mistress fails, however, to transcend the white ways of seeing that press the slave-woman beyond the limits of the recognizably human, into the territories of thing or animal. Suffering her own male-initiated crisis Mrs. Flint is unable to discern, in Brent's tale, the signs of a grief allied and yet distinct. As Brent quickly understands:

> She pitied herself as a martyr; but she was incapable of feeling for the condition of shame and misery in which her unfortunate, helpless slave was placed.
>
> (33)

In the slave-mistress's narcissistic listening, the details of Brent's story are felt only as the pathetic mortifications – the spiritual flagellations – of her own isolated martyrdom.

The following scene accords even more strongly, and strangely, with recent scholarly conclusions that slave-mistresses generally ratified the dehumanization of slave-women, for the meagre social superiority this assured them.[9] In a temporary frustration of her husband's wishes, Mrs. Flint arranges for Brent to sleep in a room adjoining her own:

> There I was an object of her especial care, though not of her especial comfort, for she spent many a sleepless night to watch over me. Sometimes I woke up, and found her bending over me. At other times she whispered in my ear, as though it was her husband who was speaking to me, and listened to hear what I would answer. If she startled me, on such occasions, she would glide stealthily away; and the next morning she would tell me I had been talking in my sleep, and ask who I was talking to. At last, I began to be fearful for my life. It had been often threatened; and you can imagine, better than I can describe, what an unpleasant sensation it must produce to wake up in the dead of night and find a jealous woman bending over you.
>
> (34)

In these occult vigils, the slave-mistress studies with fascination the strangely powerful object luring her husband, this dangerously sensual animal lurking within the properly sacred walls of her home. Flint's prerogatives threaten his wife's home too, of course – like Brent's – though not with radical dispersal. The parallel is clear to the reader yet, again, not to Mrs. Flint. She strives to "understand" Brent, not by opening to any cross-social resonance in Brent's own story, but rather through an objectifying surveillance and extraction of information, hoarding all the privileges of subjectivity to herself. Like Flint's, her "care" for Brent is a venture of linguistic, and phallic, dominion. The slave-mistress seems enviously to mimic Flint's ways of power, within a darkened recess of his presumed phallic domain: forcing Brent to sleep near her bed, creeping herself to Brent in the night, whispering in Brent's ear "as though it was her husband who was speaking." Her "jealous" language yearns for every facet of the slave-master's power, in a passage

151

that uncannily dramatizes the ways in which a social world penetrated by designs of domination encourages the dominated to fantasize their own empowerment only as a replicating domination.

Though Brent's first efforts to tell the self – to a local white woman, to Flint, and to her "jealous mistress" – clearly fail, she does not abandon the impulse to facilitate cross-social pathways. She does, however, begin to cultivate a supplementary, and quite contrary, verbal strategy with which to meet such radical adversaries as Flint. The sudden cynical realism that ends the narrative's opening paragraph, doubling back on the child's trusting illusions, bespeaks a distinct sort of linguistic competence with which Brent supplements that of collectivist storytelling. After the explosive exchange in Flint's study, Brent moves from using language as an expression of her difference to manipulating it in order to conceal, and deceptively to advance, her oppositional desires. In the sense suggested by Henry Louis Gates, Jr. in an important chapter on the complex heritage of African-American "masking," Brent begins to deploy language to "mask": to "say one thing, all the while meaning another."[10] In succeeding relations with Flint, Brent refuses to risk once more the revelation of her own mind and motives. She closes verbally as she has already closed sexually against him, her language now forcing the white other outside the inner circle of her designs. Brent manipulates what for Flint is a familiar hegemonic discourse, but one that, in Brent's usage, disguises and promotes her own counterhegemonic goals.

As she observes much later, her strategies of deception are not spontaneous, but a reaction to the exigencies of her condition: "I like a straightforward course, and am always reluctant to resort to subterfuges. So far as my ways have been crooked, I charge them all upon slavery" (165). When Flint expresses regret for having struck Brent, and announces his intention of moving her to a new plantation in Louisiana (where, as she realizes, he can pursue his desires without the hindrance of his wife or Aunt Martha), Brent answers with an unexpected show of faithful servitude: "I am your daughter's property, and it is in your power to send me, or take me, wherever you please" (41).[11] Brent's remark is surprising, of course, only to a reader who, unlike Flint, has recognized the radical contrariety of Brent's desires, and her uncompromising determination to fulfil them.

Her reply actually convinces Flint who, made easy by Brent's apparent acquiescence to his triumph, temporarily relaxes his aggressions. Brent disarms Flint by shrewdly operating within the discourse most familiar to him. She voices, without evident contest, his own lexicon of white "power" and "property," a hegemonic language appropriate to the social order which secures Flint's prerogatives. The reassuring vision of order affirmed by this dominant language is one that fails, by its very nature, to recognize what Raymond Williams has called the "alternative lives and alternative intentions" necessarily produced within societies of domination.[12] Flint's language is inherently blind to these potentially counterhegemonic ranges of social reality, and it is such blindness that Brent's masking cannily exploits. Her ostensible capitulation masks, as the following lines make clear, a private vow of resistance unimagined by Flint: "However that might be, I was determined that I would never go to Louisiana with him" (41).

Even while she learns a "masking" language, however, Brent continues to gauge and try the underground networks within which a vocabulary of self-revelation may be hazarded. In the crucial "Perilous Passage" chapter, which follows the lesson in the exigencies of masking, the "war" between Flint and Brent has reached a "desperate" stage. Flint's proprietary power closes in on the 15-year-old Brent in the form of a "new plan" to remove her from "the midst of people" to a cabin in "a secluded place, four miles away from the town." Flint's strategy indirectly concedes the power of unofficial networks of information within Edenton. He must remove Brent from this context because "considerable gossip in the neighborhood" (53) about their relations threatens his reputation. This "gossip" – a locally whispered sort of slave's narrative – is circulated chiefly by Aunt Martha, who has astutely inferred Brent's plight.

Before Flint can carry out his plan, Brent makes her bid for resistance within the formative network of awareness in Edenton, through channels first limned by Aunt Martha's whispered tales of her granddaughter:

Among others, it chanced that a white unmarried gentleman [Mr. Sands] had obtained some knowledge of the circumstances in which I was placed. He knew my grandmother, and often spoke to me in the street. He became

153

interested for me, and asked questions about my master, which I answered in part. He expressed a great deal of sympathy, and a wish to aid me.

(54)

The romantic/erotic character of Sands's "interest," as of Brent's slowly responsive "tender feeling," is made clear as the passage continues. Unlike Flint's erotic desire for Brent, however, Sands's involves an explicit concern with hearing her story. Brent's "tender feeling" follows a careful appraisal of Sands's dependability as confidant and ally. She recognizes that Sands – like Flint, a "white . . . gentleman" of the old South – will initially be ignorant of her distinctly embattled predicament. If he is truly to "aid" her, he must be capable of acknowledging and negotiating the profound social distance between them: "I knew," Brent says, "the impassable gulf between us" (54). Nevertheless, Sands persuasively manifests precisely the desire to understand and assist that Brent seeks in every potential confidant(e). She begins to return his attentions, dangerously opening a passage – simultaneously cultural, political and sexual – across this apparently "impassable gulf."

Her strategic aim, as always, is to win some semblance of freedom and a home within the brutal hegemonies of the slave South. Her intricate "calculations of interest" in this episode begin with the surmise that Flint, enraged at her choice of another lover, will sell her, and Sands will then be able to purchase and manumit her, as he has promised. Furthermore, she realizes that children from a union with Flint would almost certainly be separated from her, since Flint "never allowed his offspring by slaves to remain long in sight of himself and his wife" (55). Children from a union with Sands, conversely, would be free and well-supported in a home with Brent.

The eventual outcome of Brent's tactics in this chapter confirms that the opening of subversive passageways with white others, in the midst of an overwhelming white hegemony, is indeed a perilous business. While Flint is, as predicted, greatly incensed by news of Brent's relations with Sands, his revenge is to refuse to sell her, though Sands bids to purchase her at unusually high sums. Whether Sands would have subsequently granted Brent's freedom remains an open question. His later actions in regard to their two children – slaves by law – testify

154

that, while apparently willing to liberate them, he is yet obliviously unhurried about so doing. He simply does not comprehend the perpetual danger they are in as alienable property, despite Brent's constant reminders. Jacobs's fictive names for her Southern male characters here take on their fullest import: where Flint obdurately opposes Jacobs's desires, Sands's well-intentioned responses to them prove shifting and infirm.

Within the "Perilous Passage" chapter, Jacobs continually reminds her readers of their similar *naïveté* regarding the lived conditions of slave-women, and of their similar potential for a failure of understanding in response to the chapter's frank sexual disclosures. Jacobs, in her general attraction to direct address, seems intent on casting her readers suddenly and repeatedly back into their own lived conditions, as particular kinds of people in particular social places, to whom the text in hand confides a profoundly alien experience. As if to ensure this effect, Jacobs's "O, Reader" is often followed by an explicit social typification. Her discussion of the Sands affair is framed by two such invocations. Immediately beforehand is this relatively elaborate address:

> But, O, ye happy women, whose purity has been sheltered from childhood, who have been free to choose the objects of your affection, whose homes are protected by law, do not judge the poor desolate slave girl too severely!
>
> (54)

Immediately afterward, another address emphasizes what these readers are not:

> Pity me, and pardon me, O virtuous reader! You never knew what it is to be a slave; to be entirely unprotected by law or custom; to have the laws reduce you to the condition of a chattel, entirely subject to the will of another.
>
> (55)

The two passages produce sharply contrasting images of the lived conditions of the slave-woman and the Northern middle-class white woman, of narrator and reader. The first emphasizes the privileged position of moral "judge[ment]" in which such readers, despite their own patriarchal subordination, sit. The reader can condemn from the ground of moral "purity" because her "purity" is relatively "sheltered" and "protected by law."

The narrator's "pure principles inculcated by [her] grand-mother" (54) are, contrastingly, "unprotected by law or custom," and in fact "entirely subject to the will of another." These addresses presciently undermine the reader's condemnation of the narrator's fall from True Womanhood, with a quiet commentary on the social privilege underwriting the possibility of such "judge[ment]." Within this context, Jacobs's "O virtuous reader" is charged with the subtle irony that her addressee's putative virtue is itself, after all, only an unrecognized fruit of privilege. The salient presence of these addresses, framing the most "delicate" material of the Sands passage, indicates Jacobs's acute awareness, and thorough appraisal – as writer – of the dangerous exchange initiated by the text.

The closing scene of the chapter, in which Brent and Martha are reconciled after Martha's condemnation of Brent as "a disgrace to [her] dead mother," (56) re-emphasizes the need to overcome divisions within systemically subordinated populations. While earlier passages confront the broad, systemic alienation of white American women from black, this passage focuses down to the insidious spread of caste distinctions among Southern black women themselves. Martha, a rare freedwoman turned small-scale entrepreneuse, cherishes the strongest sense of caste among the black women depicted in *Incidents*. By dint of her independent economic vantage and freedom from the sexual dominion of slave-holders, she can conclude about the sexual conditions of slave-women that "there were . . . plenty of slaves who did not care about character" (58). Her initial rejection of Brent constructs the dead mother as a meagre legitimation of Martha's own status, a minor icon of "respectable" womanhood, from whose gracious realm Brent has fallen. Yet in the closing lines of the chapter, Martha "listen[s] in silence" (57) as Brent recounts her story of sexual self-determination. Their subsequent renewal of bonds, at the chapter's close, recovers the narrative's focus on slave- and ex-slave women as central matrices in the production and reproduction of passageways of solidarity. After the multiple failures of transsocial alliance in preceding scenes, Brent unites in on-going struggle with Martha, who suddenly and dramatically transcends her sense of caste distinction.

Jacobs suggests that Martha's capacity to overcome a positional myopia stems partially from her former labours, before manumission, as infant-nurturer and domestic "factotum" for the Flint family. Martha served her slave-masters as living counterpart to the white fantasy of the emotionally bountiful, corporeally abundant "Mammy." Martha is self-sacrificing mother to four slave-children, but her mothering extends to members of her slave-master's family as well. To these whites, Martha seems "an indispensable personage in the household, officiating in all capacities, from cook and wet nurse to seamstress" (6). Even after manumission, she works, significantly, as a tireless kitchen-labourer, baking breads and cakes for Edenton whites. This encompassingly intimate physical and emotional relation of the slave-mother, to both blacks and whites, produces in her a deeply felt sense of connection with a whole network of others in positions quite different from her own.

Brent herself, of course, in her two children by Sands and the white infants she cares for later in the narrative, experiences "ties to life" (78) similar to those felt by Martha. The narrative's vignettes of Brent lavishing care on infants in arms, who respond in turn with an emotionally redemptive trust, suggest that motherhood provides a crucial generative locus for the opening of relation with one's "fellow-beings," black or white. The following scene pictures Brent with a white infant entrusted to her care: "When [the infant] laughed and crowed in my face, and twined its little tender arms confidingly about my neck . . . my wounded heart was soothed" (170). It is recalled at a later juncture: "the darling little babe . . . thawed my heart, when it was freezing into a cheerless distrust of all my fellow-beings" (190). The "pelting storms of [the] slave-mother's life," (146) to which the narrative makes frequent reference, can from such passages be understood as the product of the slave-mother's deeply felt relation to white infants who are inevitably antagonists and to slave-infants routinely torn from her. Such emotional devastation is, it seems, another range of reference, beyond sexual abuse, inherent to Jacobs's description of the slave-woman's life as "far more terrible."

However, *Incidents* refuses to reduce slave-women's practices of solidarity to a simple product of their designated social labours or to some presumed biological imperative. Rather, these practices are understood as the underground sustainment by slave-women of a cultural dream shared by a broader black community – a dream whose communal emphases are inscribed in the very flesh of slave-women assigned the roles of extended

157

JON HAUSS

mothering. Jean Fagan Yellin underscores Jacobs's commitment
to render Brent's struggle within the context of this "extended
black community" – a commitment distinct from that of male
slave-narrators who standardly represent the escape to freedom
in terms of a lone exceptionalist struggle. As Yellin makes clear,
it is not only Brent's immediate family, but a much larger black
community which, at crucial moments, rejoins the "conspiracy"
to free her and her children.[13]

The relation of Brent's personal struggle to a larger black
cultural community is symbolically figured by her return to "the
burying-ground of the slaves . . . in the woods" (90) beside "the
old meeting house," (91) in order to renew her strength for the
final effort of escape. She returns to what cultural historians have
identified as the secluded sites of slave-ritual, on the margins of
the old plantations, where the liberationist culture of slaves was
kept alive, often under cover of darkness. In Stuckey's treatment
of graveyard, forest and meeting-house practices, ritual invocations of slave- and African ancestors to empower contemporary
struggles for freedom are absolutely central. Stuckey relates that,
on these sites, the griots – who often performed for a wide and
responsive circle of listeners – conjured stories of ancestors to
guide slave-life in the present.[14] Stuckey's chief illustration of this
subterranean culture is the "ring shout," an African-descended,
spirit-conjuring dance performed in the graveyards as an "emblem of spiritual continuity and renaissance."[15] The incessantly
circling dance called the spirits of the dead to revivify the
struggles of the living, imaging in its motion an encompassing
communality, across social time as well as space. The danced
circle united the living and the dead while simultaneously affirming the oneness of the contemporary community.

Brent goes back at dusk to the "nearly obliterated" markers
of her parents' graves, to summon "guidance and support in the
perilous step [she] was about to take":

The graveyard was in the woods, and twilight was coming
on. Nothing broke the death-like stillness . . . . My spirit
was overawed by the solemnity of the scene. For more than
ten years I had frequented this spot, but never had it
seemed so sacred to me as now . . . . I knelt down . . . and
poured forth a prayer.

(90–1)

158

The prayer is addressed to "God." However, in accordance with slave-culture's synthesis of a Euro-Protestant divinity with a reverend black ancestry,[16] the responsive "guidance and support" come from Brent's slave-progenitors. Just as her mother's spirit speaks to her "in many an hour of tribulation . . . sometimes chiding me, sometimes whispering loving words into my wounded heart," (90) so now, in answer to her prayer, Brent "seemed to hear my father's voice . . . bidding me not to tarry till I reached freedom or the grave." Her father's spirit speaks from "the wreck of the old meeting house, where, before Nat Turner's time, the slaves had been allowed to meet for worship" (91). Out of the "death-like stillness" of this scene, Brent's supplication has conjured a liberating ancestral power.

The dilapidation and disuse of the graveyard and meeting house are tangible effects, not only of slave-poverty, but also of the widespread suppression of ritual slave-gatherings following Nat Turner's bloody 1831 revolt in North Carolina. Jacobs's allusion to Turner evokes the full revolutionary power that "old meeting house" rituals were capable of unleashing. Turner, a slave "exhorter" who fused Christian apocalyptic tradition with a "ring shout" vision of inexorable black resurgence, eventually led upwards of eighty slaves down Southampton County roads, slaughtering slave-holders in their homes as they went.[17] Turner's inflammatory vocabulary reverberates beyond Brent's prayer, which implicitly re-animates the decaying "letters" (90) of the grave-markers by calling forth the living language of her buried ancestors, as well as Turner's. The voices of the dead respond to Brent's petition, in a ritual creation of transhistorical links, infusing the cross-social passages of the present with ancestral power.

Paradoxically, this ritual of fluid "continuity" empowers a strategy of escape that seems to involve a closing of all passages. Brent's punishing failure to gain freedom and a home through relations with Sands has already led her to a notable withdrawal from open interplay with whites. Her retreat into guarded schemes finds its analogue in Jacobs's narration itself which, after the Sands episode, operates by suspense, refusing to disclose to readers the nature of "the project I had in view" (90), "the perilous step I was about to take." That project, when finally revealed, becomes in turn a powerful emblem, at the heart of the text, of the self-concealment to which a multipally coercive society drives its oppressed. Brent's nearly seven years' confinement, in a darkened crawl-space above Aunt Martha's cabin, becomes the very type, in the narrative, of Brent's tactical withdrawal from white others. While the dark enclosure plainly evokes the "tomb of slavery" before "glorious resurrection," figured in a number of slaves' narratives,[18] its significance within Jacobs's general concern over the opening of social passages should also be clear. The attic is not a passageway to other spaces, but a "dismal hole" (113, 148). The "perilous step" into it is, at least initially, a step back from the perils of self-disclosure.

This aspect of Brent's confinement extends even to relations with her immediate family. She calculates that once Flint feels he has lost her irretrievably, he will consent to Sands's purchase of Brent and her children. Though Flint indeed sells the children to Sands, he still refuses to sell their mother, forcing her to remain in hiding indefinitely. The children now live at Aunt Martha's, but have no idea of their mother's immediate closeness. In an excruciating image of a home that cannot be a home, Brent subsists for seven years in an intimate physical proximity with her children which is yet, uncannily, a near-perfect isolation. Three feet at its highest point, nine long and seven wide, the lightless and virtually airless crawl-space above her family is described in grim factual detail. Yet the emphasis of Brent's account falls on her inability to speak freely even to those whose futures are directly at stake in her scheme: "I heard the voices of my children . . . . How I longed to speak to them!"(114). Martha and Brent's uncle, Phillip, are complicit in her concealment, but even they are unable openly to communicate with her. They "would seize such opportunities as they could, to mount up there and chat with me at the opening. But of course . . . [i]t must all be done in darkness" (115). As a temporary but chilling result of these benumbing and inactive conditions, her "face and tongue stiffened, and [she] lost the power of speech" (122).

Brent's linguistic schemes, within the garret, defy the threat of an isolated and silent defeat, however. She returns to a use of language as combat, her fortress-like garret becoming the base for a renewed project of "masking." The title of the chapter describing her hiding-space, "The Loophole of Retreat" (chapter 21), suggests that the tiny gap in Southern white hegemony through which Brent has slipped becomes a kind of marksman's aperture through which she subsequently fires a particular weaponry at the "Old Enemy," Flint. In the garret, Brent schools herself more thoroughly in English, reading books by the light of a tiny hole she bores in the street-wall. She writes letters to Flint, subsequently smuggled to New York City by a black sailor who knows of her circumstances and mails the correspondence back to Flint. The plan is to convince Flint that her escape is already accomplished and that continued local searches are pointless. From the page of a New York newspaper, which Brent gets from the sailor, she takes addresses and places to mention in the letters: "It was a piece of the New York Herald; and, for once, the paper that systematically abuses the colored people, was made to render them a service" (128). It is a telling opening to a ruse which, like her earlier masking venture, turns a language dominated by the interests of white power back against those interests.

Here, as elsewhere in the narrative, concealment and masking constitute less a final abandonment of collective strategies than their necessary supplement. In a pivotal scene after Brent's escape from the Flints, before the garret has been prepared, Martha re-initiates the networking process. A local slave-holding woman, sensing Martha's trouble, asks to be taken into confidence: "Perhaps I can do something to help you." Martha studies the white woman uncertainly, but "Something in the expression of her face said 'Trust me!' and [Martha] did trust her," tearfully disclosing "the details of [Brent's] story." Though the woman in fact holds "a number [of slaves] in her own name," she steps outside the governing interests of her social position, "listen[s] attentively" (99) and agrees to conceal Brent in her own home while Martha and Uncle Phillip prepare the garret.

Even as Brent discharges her self-masking letters to Flint, she continues to organize an underground network of allies. The failure of the earlier venture of trust with Sands is, importantly, only partial. He tends to forget what he has promised, consistently misapprehending the full danger to Brent and her children. Ultimately, however, he proves true to his word by manumitting the latter. Brent's relations with Sands come to constitute a crucial link in the larger network orchestrated from the garret, often through secret "letters" with a very different function than those dispatched to Flint. Martha and Phillip aid

Brent in this process, as does the black sailor who eventually arranges, in confidence with a white ship-captain, Brent's passage North, where she is received by a network of Philadelphia Abolitionists, black and white.

Brent's labours of alliance do not end after her escape North, nor after the arrival of her children, manumitted and transported by Sands. Against the still-presiding powers of patriarchy and slavery (the latter continuing to endanger Brent through the agency of the Fugitive Slave Law), Brent persists in her subversive practices. In sudden confidence with the New York woman who later arranges to purchase and free her, Brent tells her story: "She listened with true womanly sympathy, and told me she would do all she could to protect me" (180). The narrative's final Northern episodes continue to dramatize dangerous moments of telling and listening which anticipate the circulating future of Jacobs's text itself.

The anti-slavery literatures of antebellum America rarely disclose the full disjunction between the lived experience of black Southern slaves and white Northern readers. Even Frederick Douglass's *Narrative of the Life of Frederick Douglass* (1845) arguably obscures the radical difference of slave-experience by inscribing the narrated black self with familiar Northern ideals of Romantic exceptionalism, eliding the whole slave-cultural underground enabling Douglass's perilous escape.[19] Harriet Beecher Stowe's *Uncle Tom's Cabin* (1852), certainly the most widely read anti-slavery text of its day, displaces the social and cultural differences of slave-life by stressing the typological sameness of white and black characters and histories. As Jane P. Tompkins has argued, the cultural power Stowe's text held for antebellum white readers rests largely on a strategy of "typological narration" with which Stowe reduces the lives of women, children, and slaves to palimpsests of a single Euro-Protestant Christ-story.[20]

The radically conflictual social world imaged in *Incidents* helps toward an understanding of why these texts work the way they do. Arguably, their emptying out of the most unfamiliar elements of slave-life permitted them to win widespread Northern recognition of black slave-humanity – precisely representing the slave as, for Northerners, recognizably human. Following the crucial but oversimplifying work of such texts, Jacobs's *Incidents* recovers and foregrounds, within the genre of the self-

162

written slave-narrative, an alternative body of cultural beliefs and practices sustained within slave-woman centred networks of resistance to slavery. Jacobs offers the ritual storytelling of slave-women as cultural model for an expanding struggle to produce tentative understanding, and political alliance, across the social and cultural schisms of America. It is a struggle inspired by slave-culture's dream of a finally unbounded circle of human community free of exploitation. Across time as well as space, into a persistently violent present, *Incidents* offers a way of struggle that affirms this dream amid the profound systemic dangers of American racial, economic and sexual hierarchies.

NOTES

1 H.A. Jacobs, *Incidents in the Life of a Slave Girl*, ed. J.F. Yellin, Cambridge, Mass., Harvard University Press, 1987. This edition is used throughout, cited in the text by page number in parenthesis.
2 This is a spectrum of experience within the slave South to which other, chiefly male, slave-narrators make only veiled or symbolic reference. See, for example, F. Douglass's account of his slave-aunt bound, stripped to the waist, and sadistically whipped by the male slave-master in *Narrative of the Life of Frederick Douglass: An American Slave*, New York, Signet, 1968, 25.
3 B. Welter, *Dimity Convictions: The American Woman in the Nineteenth Century*, Athens, Georgia, Ohio University Press, 1976, 12.
4 A. Davis, "Reflections on the Black Woman's Role in the Community of Slaves," in A. Chrisman and N. Hare, eds, *Contemporary Black Thought*, New York, Bobbs-Merrill, 1973, 138–57. Published before Yellin painstakingly established *Incidents*'s authorship and historical veracity, Davis's article makes no reference to Jacobs's text.
5 S. Stuckey, *Slave Culture: Nationalist Theory and the Foundations of Black America*, New York, Oxford University Press, 1987, 10–14.
6 Yellin's phrase, in Jacobs, *Incidents*, xxvi, xxxiv.
7 In this sense, *Incidents* constitutes a crucial early instance of what M. Pryse calls "conjuring": a black woman's storytelling practice with the aim of ratifying some larger community of blacks or women. Pryse argues that "conjuring" is a central structural feature of black American women's writing in the nineteenth and twentieth centuries. She makes passing reference to Jacobs, and I hope to substantiate her claims with this detailed reading. See Pryse's introduction to M. Pryse and H.J. Spillers, eds, *Conjuring: Black Women, Fiction, and Literary Tradition*, Bloomington, Indiana University Press, 1985, 1–24.

8 Versions of which Jacobs probably encountered in the anti-slavery
reading room over the office of Douglass's *North Star* in Rochester.
Yellin's is the best discussion of Jacobs's appropriation and reworking of elements of this genre. See her indispensable introduction to
Jacobs, *Incidents*, xiii–xxxiv.

9 See b. hooks, *Ain't I a Woman? Black Women and Feminism*,
Boston, South End Press, 1982. See also M. Gwin, *Black and White
Women of the Old South: The Peculiar Sisterhood in American
Literature*, Knoxville, University of Tennessee Press, 1985, and
"Green-Eyed Monsters of the Slavocracy: Jealous Mistresses in
Two Slave Narratives," in Pryse and Spillers, *Conjuring*, 39–52.

10 H.L. Gates, Jr., "Dis and Dat: Dialect and the Descent," in *Figures
in Black: Words, Signs, and the "Racial" Self*, New York, Oxford
University Press, 1987, 167–95. For a suggestive early treatment of
slave verbal trickery see G. Osofsky, *Puttin' On Ole Massa: The
Slave Narratives of Henry Bibb, William Wells Brown, and Solomon
Northup*, New York, Harper and Row, 1969.

11 Brent has been bequeathed to Flint's 3-year-old daughter. Until the
latter marries, Flint exercises full proprietary power over Brent.

12 R. Williams, *Politics and Letters: Interviews with New Left Review*,
London, New Left Books, 1979, 252.

13 *Incidents*, xxviii.

14 *Slave Culture*, 14.

15 ibid., 12.

16 E. Genovese, A. Raboteau, Stuckey and others have come to affirm
folklorist and novelist Z.N. Hurston's important 1931 insight that
"The Negro has not been Christianized as extensively as is generally
believed. The great masses are still standing before their pagan
altars and calling old gods by new names." See Hurston, *The
Sanctified Church*, Berkeley, Tuttle Island Press, 1985, 103; Genov-
ese, *Roll, Jordan, Roll: The World the Slaves Made*, New York,
Random House, 1974, 232–55; A. Raboteau, *Slave Religion: The
'Invisible Institution' in the Antebellum South*, New York, Oxford
University Press, 1980, 66–73; Stuckey, *Slave Culture*, 35–6.

17 For details of both the event and Turner's religious iconography,
see H. Aptheker, *Nat Turner's Slave Rebellion*, New York, Grove
Press, 1966, 47–50, 35–8.

18 The phrases come from Douglass's account of his climactic battle
with the overseer, Covey, *Narrative*, 83. For an uncannily "literal"
version of the "grave" from which one "r[ises] up" in freedom, see
H. Brown, *Narrative of Henry Box Brown: Who Escaped from
Slavery Enclosed in a Box 3 Feet long and 2 Wide* in Afro-American
History Series, Collection 7, Delaware, Scholarly Resources Inc.
(undated). I suggest that this prevailing structure in the slave-
narratives should be understood as deriving from slave-culture's
syncretism of the Christ-story with ring-shout traditions of liber-
atory resurgence, and not somehow unilaterally from the slaves'
Christian religious instruction.

19 Douglass's escape from slavery was as thoroughly networked, and

arguably as much indebted to slave-culture's empowering vision of black "renaissance," as Jacobs's. For a brief discussion of the elaborate African-American network elided in Douglass's *Narrative* see M.H. Washington, *Invented Lives: Narratives of Black Women, 1860–1960*, New York, Doubleday, 1987, 8.

20 J.P. Tompkins, "Sentimental Power: *Uncle Tom's Cabin* and the Politics of Literary History," in S. Bercovitch and M. Jehlen, eds, *Ideology and Classic American Literature*, New York, Cambridge University Press, 1986, 267–92.

8

THE IRONY OF IDEALISM
William Faulkner and the South's construction of the mulatto
David Lawrence Rogers

CONFUSING THE ISSUE: HUGHES AND THE INCESTUOUS HYBRID

In 1860 the Southern sociologist Henry Hughes denounced the existence of the mulatto. Revealing the idealism at the heart of the racist attitudes of the white antebellum South, Hughes – in a passage occasionally cited by historians as something of a parody of those attitudes – writes that hybridism "is heinous." This is so, he claims, because it is doubly transgressive:

> Impurity of races is against the law of nature. Mulattoes are monsters. The law of nature is the law of God. The same law which forbids consanguinous amalgamation forbids ethnical amalgamation. Both are incestuous. Amalgamation is incest.[1]

As insightful as this series of virtual nonsequiturs may be for exposing the hysteria that enveloped the discourse of slavery immediately before the Civil War, it nevertheless says little not voiced by other writers of the time.[2] Clearly, the years between 1830 and 1860 had not only seen the white South increasingly identify itself with the institution of slavery and its defence, but had also witnessed the growing institutionalization of racism across the western world as a whole. Ideas of race and ethnic difference, previously more or less matters of personal and community prejudice, began to find expression in scientific journals and become the stuff of scientific debate. Were Africans and Europeans species of the same genus and the perceived differences between them the result of climatic and geographical variations?

166

Or did they represent genuses entirely different from one another, the mixture of which would produce offspring – like any combination of two separate genuses of plants or animals – that were at once sterile, degenerate and degenerating?[3]

Hughes, it seems, leans toward the second of these positions, held also in the South by men such as Josiah C. Nott, the South Carolina physician who practised medicine in Alabama and, with George Gliddon, co-authored the widely read polygenetic tract, *Types of Mankind* (1854). What makes Hughes's expression of the standard arguments so remarkable (and, indeed, so telling for the discourse of slavery *per se*) is the illogical and eventually ironic position to which it leads him. By conflating miscegenation – "ethnical amalgamation" – with incest – "consanguinous amalgamation" – Hughes transforms the hybrid or mulatto from someone who is considered "impure" because he combines qualities that are too different to mix successfully, according to the sanctions of nature and God, to someone whose "impurity" and transgression lie in the blending of traits that are, by contrast, too much *alike*.

The result, we might say, is to confuse the "gender" of the hybrid. No longer appearing to hold two antonyms together as if with the tension of oxymoron, the mulatto of Hughes's tortured logic denies or defers difference, merging the contending parts that compose it rather than simply suspending them and retaining the implied dominance of one part over the other. In this sense "emasculated" because it subverts the hierarchical premises of the patriarchal old South, the regendered or degendered mulatto not only emerges as a precursor to representations of the mulatto as effete which appear after the War and around the turn of the century, but also adumbrates the radically "feminized" figures of recent critical theory. More crucially, it serves to insist more emphatically upon the very world that Hughes considers perversely impure, promoting, in other words, precisely the sort of ethnical mixture and diversity that Hughes wants so desperately to condemn. Such, it might be said, is the irony of idealism.

FURTHER SUBVERTING THE LAW: SLAVERY'S FIGURE OF THE UNWED MOTHER

The term "mulatto" entered the language of the South near the middle of the seventeenth century. Originally derived from the

Latin *mulus* meaning "mule," it appeared first in the Virginia legislature, for instance, in 1666. Strictly speaking, "mulatto" referred only to persons with one European and one African parent. It signified, as Edward Byron Reuter writes in 1918, "the first generation of hybridization between the Negro and the Caucasian races."[4] "Mulatto" ought therefore to have operated, again to cite Reuter, exclusively as "a biological concept" and to have been "unavailable for use except in a technical, biological sense."[5] In practice, however, the term maintained no such delimited or fixed referent. As Reuter notes, in everyday language "mulatto" referred to

> all those members of the Negro race with a visible admixture of white blood. . . . The word is a general term to include all Negroes of mixed ancestry regardless of the degree of intermixture. It includes all persons who are recognized, in the communities in which they live, as being of mixed blood.[6]

The crucial word, here, is "visible," since it reveals how the determination of an individual as mulatto depended not on any inherent trait but solely upon the subjective opinion of a perceiver (who was usually white). Denied any distinct and stable referent, "mulatto" then became virtually synonymous with the word "negro" and both words with the signifier "slave."

As with Hughes, however, a vicious irony attends the South's overdetermined response to the mulatto. The American South was unique insofar as its system of slavery was based upon strictly maintained dichotomies of caste and colour. Indeed, it had no terms for the many gradations between so called "pure" whites and "pure" blacks that marked, for example, the systems of slavery in South America or the West Indies. The very existence of the mulatto blurred such distinctions. If it were to prevent "mulatto-ism" from providing the "negro" with a possible escape-route from slavery, the white South had first to acknowledge the existence of the mulatto as a distinct caste, before proceeding to deny that distinction by absorbing the mulatto into the less ambiguous order of "negroes."[7] This was especially true after the first generation because then the mulatto theoretically posited an ever more radical degree of indeterminacy, his or her colour becoming an increasingly uncertain mixture of white and black; an equivocal, undecidable shade

168

somewhere *within* the middle of the two but never precisely *at* that middle, suggesting as such the world of Darwin and Derrida more than that of Newton or Hume.[8] Yet, by extending the signification of the mulatto so widely that it seemed to lose its most threatening referent, the South only exposed the arbitrariness of its system of signs in general, denying, at the same time, the validity of the idea of a transcendental signified. In other words, the old South's response to the figure of the mulatto undermined the linguistic and theological bases upon which its patriarchal authority relied. (This response, with its strategy of acknowledgement, denial and absorption, supports the view that ethnic hatred depends as much, if not more, upon a fear of seeing the self in the Other as upon the process of constructing the Other as wholly different.)[9]

The irony of this wider cultural subversion surfaces conspicuously in the South's legal discourse. Within this context, the denial of the mulatto required a specific – and crucial – exception to the otherwise exclusively patriarchal code of law: the status of a slave's child had to be dissociated from the father and re-assigned to the mother. Stanley Elkins explains one reason why:

> Had status been defined according to the father's condition
> – as was briefly the case in seventeenth-century Mary-
> land, following the ancient common law – there would
> instantly have arisen the irksome question of what to do
> with the numerous mulatto children born every year of
> white planter-farmers and slave mothers.[10]

The application of patriarchal status to those "numerous mulatto children" (exactly how numerous is still a matter of debate) would have meant, Elkins writes, "the creation of a free mulatto class." In addition to undermining the logic of the system over which the "master" prevailed, such a third caste or class would immediately have deprived him "of so many slaves on the one hand, while burdening him on the other with that many colored children whom he could not own." As a result, this "equivocal" relationship, as Elkins phrases it, was never allowed to "vex the law":[11]

* That "the father of a slave is unknown to our law" was the universal understanding of Southern jurists. It was thus

169

that a father, among slaves, was legally "unknown," a husband without the rights of his bed, the state of marriage defined as "only that concubinage . . . with which alone, perhaps, their condition is compatible," and motherhood clothed in the scant dignity of the breeding function.[12]

With all due respect to Elkins, however, it is the vexation of the law – of nature and God himself – that the shift from father to mother precisely *does* represent, and that vexation is far more structural than any mere disruption of Coke's law code, the standard legal text of the South. Indeed, the figure of this vexation – the unwed mother of the slave – reveals the radical arbitrariness of the South's legal system, just as fully as the signifier "mulatto" underscores the arbitrary nature of its discourse as a whole. Along with that signifier, the shift in legal status implies the collapse of the hegemony of patriarchal law, the absence of any rational, patriarchal God, and the emasculation of patriarchal authority.

This repercussion would occur, of course, even if the figure of slavery's unwed mother were to exist in isolation. It takes on a wider importance, however, when we remember that this peculiarly Southern configuration placed the mother of the slave within the more comprehensive nineteenth-century Anglo-American discourse of seduction and adultery beginning with Richardson's *Clarissa* (1747–8) and including such figures as Gaskell's Ruth, Hawthorne's Hester Prynne and, later, Hardy's Tess. The fictional representations of women as either defiled virgins or unwed or adulterous mothers within this discourse creates a figural guide to the period's increasing disenchantment with absolute, patriarchal authority, its eventual rejection of the discourses of idealism and its corresponding attempts to come to terms with the sort of naturalistic world retrospectively described by William James in one of his lectures to the Boston Institute in 1906. James, whose work advocates a virtual reconciliation with such a world, asserts that "For a hundred and fifty years past"

the progress of science has seemed to mean the enlargement of the material universe and the diminution of man's importance. The result is what one may call the growth of naturalistic or positivistic feeling. Man is no lawgiver to nature, he is an absorber. She it is who stands firm; he it is who must accommodate himself. Let him record truth, inhuman tho it be, and submit to it! The romantic spontaneity and courage are gone. . . . You get, in short, a materialistic universe, in which only the tough-minded find themselves congenially at home.[13]

We might consider the figures of nineteenth-century women cited above – Hardy, at one point, refers to Tess as a "spouseless mother" – as post-Darwinian. The reality they represent is, like Darwin's material world, overfecund and, in essence, "impure." Filled with indeterminacy, chance and mutation, it is a world in which all children are, in a sense, mulattoes and can no longer be said to be made in the image of their F/father. The figure of the unwed slave-mother in the old South, like that of her unwed fictional sisters, therefore symbolizes the crucial shift in perception to which James alludes, not only for the American South, but also for the western world. Like Lovelace's actions in *Clarissa*, however, the attempt by the slave-holding South to deny this world by continuing to assert the authority and power of Law produces simply another, if more compelling (and collective) irony of idealism: the creation of a maternal figure which more radically subverts the role of the Father the more strenuously that role is enforced.

COMING TO TERMS WITH IT ALL: FAULKNER AND THE EPICENE

For a writer so closely identified with the American South, William Faulkner rarely presents the material conditions of slavery. Of all his novels, only *Absalom, Absalom!* (1936) and *The Unvanquished* (1938) have primarily antebellum settings, and *Go Down, Moses* (1942) alone draws an explicit connection between ethnic tensions of the antebellum period and those apparent at the time Faulkner was writing. If there is, then, a decisive way in which Faulkner's fictional world engages with and offers a response to the discourses of slavery, it may well be largely in formal and figural terms, at the level of what Henry Louis Gates, Jr. refers to, in his depiction of the tradition of African-American literature, as a text's "literariness."[14] For Gates, who argues against what he sees as the pre-occupation of African-American critics with representations of the social at the expense of literary form, such literariness provides the crucial means by which successive African-American writers have formally revised the tropes and figures of the "racist texts" against which they have been "forced to react"[15] and, at the same time, have amended the texts of their African-American predecessors. The result, as he describes it, amounts to a sort of deconstruction of past narratives, the marking of previous signs and assumptions so that they can be more conspicuously – and comprehensively – overturned. Gates characterizes this strategy as the rhetorical act of "Signifyin(g)":

> a uniquely black rhetorical concept, entirely textual or linguistic, by which a second statement or figure repeats, or tropes, or reverses the first. Its use as a figure for intertextuality allows us to understand literary revision without recourse to thematic, biographical, or Oedipal slayings at the crossroads; rather, critical signification is tropic and rhetorical. Indeed, the very concept of Signifyin(g) can exist only in the realm of intertextual relation.[16]

Although Gates associates such "critical signification" exclusively with African-American writers, there is nothing to prevent a similar rhetorical strategy of repetition and reversal from emerging in writers who strictly lie beyond the scope of his critical concerns, even if, as with Faulkner, such an emergence might be extremely paradoxical. I am not thinking here of Yoknapatawpha County, Faulkner's much-discussed fictional community in which so many of his novels are set and his characters interact. Rather, my concern is with the ways in which Faulkner progressively transforms central figures and formal acts within the western narrative tradition, undoing the premises of that tradition and deconstructing the oxymoronic bias of the old South's discourses of slavery through an intricate, intratextual relationship of form and figures. As will become evident, this quality of Faulknerian "signifyin(g)" not only suspends the sense of closure we might expect any one novel to display, but also converts each of them into something that, I would argue, we are asked to read as we might a chapter in a larger, more comprehensive text.[17]

With specific regard to the discourses of slavery and its key figures of mulatto and unwed mother, this "signifyin(g)" of

172

Faulkner most pertinently enacts their deconstruction through the central oppositional figures of idealism – the male idealist and his figural counterpart, the virginal woman – from which the antebellum South fashioned its defence against the mulatto. The conditions for their rhetorical overturning emerge initially in Faulkner's first published novel *Soldiers' Pay* (1926), a text which, except for a brief closing reference to a choir of African-American women singing spirituals, hardly makes even the slightest direct allusion to slavery or its configurations. In one sense a Modernist allegory of the loss of perspective brought about – and symbolized – by the First World War, the novel tells the story of Donald Mahon, a pilot who returns home after the War to find conditions so changed that he is unable – or unwilling – to abide them. As pilot, Mahon is associated with blue skies and this, together with the Georgian pronunciation of his surname as "Man" casts him, without subtlety, as the first of many Faulknerian idealists. He is, however, literally – and hence figuratively – effaced or "emasculated," a wartime wound having marked his face with a "dreadful scar."[18] Although his injury is not fatal, Mahon dies rather than adapt to post-war conditions. The occasion of his death, however, allows Faulkner to transfer the role of the idealist to a second returning veteran, private Joe Gilligan. Before his death, Mahon himself signals the formal and figural nature of this shift with his repeated imperative to "Carry on, Joe" (*SP* 283). Yet, as he assumes his new prominence, Gilligan proves to be something of a Jamesian figure, and the first of Faulkner's alternative "men." His names make him both anonymous and diminutive ("Joe" needs no explanation, "Gilligan," derived from the Gaelic *Gille*, suggests "boy"), and his emergence from a place originally on the margins of the novel's formal and figural polarities enables Faulkner to revise the patriarchal premises of idealism and expose the illusion behind its constructions of difference.

As if to complete his troping of the idealist figure, Faulkner also reverses the novel's principal figure of woman. This seemingly parallel inversion occurs not once, however, but twice; the formal position originally allocated to the figure of the virgin becomes finally re-aligned, as we shall see, with a figure comparable to slavery's unwed mother. In the first instance, Faulkner marks and overturns the figural significance of the virgin with Cecily Saunders, the young woman to whom Mahon is engaged before the War. Depicting her as fickle, and as sexually and somatically ambiguous, Faulkner tropes the traditional connotations of her virginity. In so doing, he constructs Cecily as the first of many "epicenes,"[19] all of whom suggest, as Faulkner writes in *The Sound and the Fury* (1929), that virginity is an abstract or negative quality nowhere found in nature.[20] When Cecily proves unable to reconcile herself to the effacement of her fiancé and refuses to marry Mahon as planned, her new role as epicene then passes, as has Mahon's own role, to a second, originally marginal, but now even more revisionary, figure. In this case, that figure is Margaret Powers, whose widowhood crucially shifts the referent of the Faulknerian signifier "epicene" from a merely somatically ambiguous figure to one whose apparently unambiguous condition marks her as materially indeterminate as well.[21]

Faulkner announces this newly designated signification by repeatedly referring to Margaret Powers Mahon, as "Mrs. Mahon," her full name now suggesting that she has taken over the "powers" of "man," as if confirming James. It is, however, Margaret's own self-referential definition of "epicene" and her troping of the formal act of marriage that even more convincingly demonstrate the fact that she represents a new and subsequently paradoxical Faulknerian figure – the *maternalized epicene*. In answer to Gilligan's question about the meaning of Cecily's having been associated with the word "epicene," Margaret explains that "Epicene is something you want and can't get" (*SP* 294). Later, she proves to be just such an unattainable ideal for Gilligan. When Mahon dies, she refuses Gilligan's marriage proposal – but not without offering a counterproposal of her own: that she and Gilligan live together as lovers, as "fellows" (*SP* 309), without getting married. Margaret thus replaces the type of union that – like oxymoron – posits only a ruse of convergence and a fanciful denial of patriarchal authority with one in which all sense of hierarchy has been dissolved – since the relationship between its participants no longer depends upon the sanctions of church and state.

Still too much the idealist (and patriarch), Gilligan cannot accept Margaret's counterproposal. Instead he sees her off alone on her train and then enacts what serves as a virtual ritual for those later Faulknerian figures who also reject the chance to "marry" in the same way. He gets drunk, as if to bolster his flagging spirit and forget his emasculated state. He then picks a fight with another man as if in defence of a woman and to prove he is yet capable of the "courage" and "spontaneity" of James's vision. The proposal scene itself and Margaret's re-inscription of the traditional western trope of marriage nevertheless establish, for Faulkner's rhetorical strategy, the outlines of a revisionary act that subsequently emasculated and anonymous figures must perform if they are to come to terms with that which Gilligan cannot: the formal displacement of the oxymoron by the epicene, that which represents the "natural" as "impure," as is the case with Hughes's incestuous hybrid and the unwed slave-mother of the South's legal discourse.

The first unmistakable sign that Faulkner moves toward such a reconciliation within his novels appears in what is formally and figurally his most paradigmatic text, *Light in August* (1932). Perhaps not simply by coincidence, the novel introduces Faulkner's most prominent mulatto – Joe Christmas – and Lena Grove, his most prototypical figure of the unwed mother as epicene. It transforms the roles of the idealist and the virgin even more elaborately than does *Soldiers' Pay*, shifting each through a progressive series of related figures as if connecting them in a sort of relay – much as over the entire corpus of his novels Faulkner *articulates* his tropic revisions, repeating in subsequent novels forms and figures whose significance depends heavily upon an appreciation of their relationship to less fully realized forerunners.[22] In *Light in August* Faulkner enacts this process by inverting the symbolic role of Christmas, passing it first to Gail Hightower (whose names connote idealism as secular transcendentalism) and finally to Byron Bunch. Bunch may be said to assume not only the mantle of Christmas but of Gilligan as well, thus taking his place as the next in Faulkner's line of anonymous and diminished men, his surname casting him as undistinguished and indistinguishable, as one of the bunch, and making him the nominal inverse of Christmas.

In order to complete his rhetorical strategy, Faulkner mirrors this figural progression of men by repeating his earlier deconstruction of the virgin and the conventional epicene. He signifies this process by setting Christmas in opposition to a succession of female figures culminating in Joanna Burden. As critics have noted, all these women display a sexuality that represents for Christmas, along with his own mulatto status, the condition of

impurity and uncertainty from which he constantly seeks escape
– either by absorbing himself into the caste of the "negro" or
passing himself off as "white."

When the novel begins, Lena Grove, who "wears no wedding
ring,"[23] is already pregnant and in search of the father of her
child. One indication that she replaces Joanna as the last and
most comprehensive female figure within a series linking the
problematic of the unwed mother with that of the mulatto
emerges when Faulkner describes Lena's physical condition as
"a swelling and unmistakable burden" (*LIA* 7). A second, more
compelling, figural link between Lena and Christmas occurs,
however, as part of Faulkner's overall rhetoric of colour.
Initially suggested in his first novel *Elmer* (unpublished until
1983), this rhetoric functions, first of all, as a sign that the shift
in significance of the Faulknerian epicene tropes on the mulatto
and on the South's antebellum strategies of denial and absorption. With it, Faulkner moves the identifying colour of his newly
realized epicene from the unambiguous black of the old South's
"negro" to his own indeterminate colour of "faded blue,"
which, like the mulatto, defies strict codes of difference. The
newly adapted colour of the epicene mixes the two most antithetical colours in Faulkner's fiction (and, indeed, in the discourses of the Civil War South) – the traditional blue of the
idealist, which Faulkner often refers to as "horizon" blue, and
the grey that is invariably associated in Faulkner with death.
"Faded blue" (*LIA* 9) is thus an undecidable or constantly
changing shade. Positioned between polar extremes while never
being located in their precise middle, it cannot generate its own,
new polarity.

The development of this rhetoric of colour, beginning with
Soldiers' Pay, is a further sign that the "meaning" of any single
figure in Faulkner can only be fully appreciated when it is read
intertextually against the backdrop of the western narrative
tradition and intratextually through Faulkner's entire *œuvre*. In
Soldiers' Pay, Margaret Powers Mahon serves to align the
Faulknerian epicene with the conventional black of the South's
Other. Although "white," she is considered "dark," with her
black hair and eyes, and indeed, at one point, is even referred to
by Cecily as that "black, ugly woman" (*SP* 136). Read alone, it
might be possible to link this metaphorical blackness with the
idea of mourning, perhaps even with the text's mourning over

the loss of idealism. However, as part of Faulkner's overall strategy of repetition and revision, Margaret's distinguishing colour clearly signifies something quite different. Just what that is emerges when Faulkner transfers the role of the epicene from Margaret to Dilsey, the figure of the "Black Mammy" in *The Sound and the Fury*. A single mother with children, Dilsey, as a truly "black" figure, allows Faulkner to mark the old South's discourse of denial and assimilation more completely than he does with Margaret. Almost as quickly, however, this figure enables him to overturn that discourse and dispense with its old oxymoronic bias. For with Dilsey the colour of the epicene begins to shift to the more appropriate and progressive faded blue. The first sign of this transformation peeks from under Dilsey's skirt at the beginning of the fourth section of the text:

> The door of the cabin opened and Dilsey emerged once more, this time in a man's felt hat and an army overcoat, beneath the frayed skirts of which her blue gingham dress fell in uneven balloonings, streaming too about her as she crossed the yard and mounted the steps to the kitchen door.
>
> (*TSF* 266)

Thus arrayed, Dilsey not only stands as a figure in whom the shift in the epicene's colour first occurs; she also appears as the one in whom Faulkner first completes the shift in the nature of the epicene itself. Moreover, with her introduction of faded blue, Dilsey emerges as precursor to Lena Grove, Faulkner's most visibly maternalized epicene and full-blown figure of faded blue:

> From beneath a sunbonnet of faded blue, weathered now by other than formal soap and water, she looks up at him [Armstid] quietly and pleasantly: young, pleasant-faced, candid, friendly, and alert. She does not move yet. Beneath the faded garment of that same weathered blue her body is shapeless and immobile. The fan and the bundle lie on her lap. She wears no stockings. Her bare feet rest side by side in the shallow ditch. The pair of dusty, heavy, manlooking shoes beside them are not more inert. In the halted wagon Armstid sits, humped, bleacheyed. He sees that the rim of the fan is bound neatly in the same faded blue as the sunbonnet and the dress.
>
> (*LIA* 9)

Given Lena's formal and figurative significance, it is tempting to conclude that Bunch's dogged success in climbing aboard the truck of the travelling furniture-dealer to join Lena and her newborn child at the novel's end effectively argues for a reconciliation with exactly that which Gilligan has rejected. Lena is an Other whose spouseless motherhood connotes a material world wherein patriarchal law no longer rules and the natural is perverse, the perverse natural. It is, however, equally tempting to claim that in V.K. Ratliff, the final figure of faded blue appearing in the trilogy, *The Hamlet* (1940), *The Town* (1957) and *The Mansion* (1959), Faulkner posits an even more comprehensive, intratextual accommodation with the positivistic world of the epicene. For in Ratliff, we encounter someone in whom all prior emasculated figures and epicenes alike converge. His "brown," suntanned skin suggests, for instance, the parchment colour of Christmas, and his references to himself as an "anonymous scoundrel" and "anonymous underhanded son-of-a-gun"[24] align him with Gilligan and Bunch, and such later figures as the nameless Lance-corporal in *A Fable* (1954). Yet we also see that the constant identification of Ratliff with the faded blue workshirts he makes, washes and sews – and always wears – casts him simultaneously in the line of epicenes beginning with Margaret Powers Mahon. Something of a "trans-positional" figure,[25] Ratliff enables Faulkner finally to undo the discourses of the antebellum South and to erase the last troublesome traces of the oxymoron from his texts. By having the anonymous, diminished man and the figure of the epicene "live together," so to speak, in the single configuration of Ratliff, Faulkner accomplishes both – not in spite of the fact that Ratliff is presented as a bachelor, but, paradoxically, precisely because of it.

PATIENCE, YES PATIENCE – BUT PATIENCE FOR WHAT?

One of the most elaborate and at the same time self-effacing puns in Faulkner involves the notions of sobriety and being "on the wagon" (Faulkner himself, of course, had been an alcoholic). The most consistent rhetorical sign that a character in Faulkner's novels has "sobered up" (still drinks, but with an appropriate sense of moderation, as does the true hunter in *Go Down, Moses*) is his quite literally taking a seat *on a wagon*. This physical act, in other words, constitutes the formal index of the acquisition of an appropriately "sober" perspective, from which characters may reconcile themselves to the apparent "impurity" of the epicene. As a result, physical positioning operates metonymically within the wider and more conspicuous Faulknerian motif of alcohol and formal acts of drinking.[26] For example, Bunch, having earlier hitched a ride in a wagon after his fight with Brown, the father of Lena Grove's child, predictably signals his acceptance of Lena – herself constantly located on a wagon – by climbing on to what is essentially an updated buckboard, the converted truck of the travelling furniture-dealer who narrates the final chapter of *Light in August*. Similarly, Ratliff, whose face is said by Gavin Stevens to be "certainly sober" (*T* 127) is always something of a Lena-esque figure. He first travels his sales route (which Faulkner says is "absolutely rigid" but "flexible . . . within itself")[27] in a mule-driven wagon, thus underlining the association of Faulkner's diminished men with the mulatto and Ratliff's link through Bunch with Christmas. He later drives his own modernized version of this vehicle, the customized truck Faulkner refers to as the first pick-up in Yoknapatawpha County.

Participation within the terms of this formal pun therefore entails fairly consistent implications. To get "on the wagon" requires, in fact, at least two vital qualities or attitudes. The first, as we have seen, involves a willingness to acknowledge and abide a sense of diminution/emasculation, to overcome the desire for mastery and control – to accept rather than attempt to dictate the course of events. The second is the ability to quell the powerful anxieties incited by the indeterminacy of the other, to acknowledge such a condition and yield oneself to its spirit. This, we could say, is to exhibit a quietly dignified patience – admit "fear," in Faulkner's idiom, but never succumb to "fright."

In *Light in August*, Bunch begins to acquire these traits during the events leading up to his final, formal reconciliation with Lena. Having been physically beaten by Brown, for example, in what again amounts to a Faulknerian scene of futile chivalry, he learns (unlike Gilligan) to endure effacement. Lying "quietly among the broken and trampled undergrowth, bleeding quietly about the face" (*LIA* 416), he discovers, moreover, that he no longer feels driven either by compulsive resistance or ceaseless activity and routine. He senses:

no particular pain now, but better than that, he feels no haste, no urgency, to do anything or go anywhere. He just lies bleeding and quiet, knowing that after a while will be time enough to reenter the world and time.

(*LIA* 416)

As if to anticipate the sobriety he eventually identifies with Lena, Bunch then gets his ride into town in a wagon. Having realized previously that he is a "small, nondescript" man "whom no man or woman had ever turned to look at twice anywhere" (*LIA* 379), someone that only "*calls [himself] Byron Bunch today, now, this minute*" (*LIA* 402), Bunch here comes closer to accepting that uncertainty of self which marks his earlier vision of the sleeping form of Hightower:

There was a quality of profound and complete surrender in it. Not of exhaustion, but surrender, as though he had given over and relinquished completely that grip upon that blending of pride and hope and vanity and fear, that strength to cling to either defeat or victory, which is the I-Am, and the relinquishment of which is usually death.

(*LIA* 372)

Christmas achieves a similar quality of "sober" understanding. In a scene foreshadowing Bunch's success (and clearly signifying how the epicene specifically implies a reconciliation with the personal lack of autonomy associated with the mulatto figure), Christmas returns to Mottstown after killing Joanna – in what is, nevertheless, formally and figurally a triumph. Having eluded the Yoknapatawpha County posse by swapping shoes with a "black" woman whose path he crosses (an act that constructs him as a mirror-image of Lena who, by contrast, wears a pair of men's brogans), Christmas has begun to overcome his sense of fear. He no longer feels himself to be "a foreigner to the very immutable laws which earth must obey." As a consequence, he now "walks steadily on," experiencing – like Bunch – "peace and unhaste and quiet" (*LIA* 320). Moreover, again like Bunch but especially Lena, Christmas becomes associated with the figurative site of sobriety. He rides into town in a mule-driven wagon, content to move with the same unconcern for his ultimate destination that Lena has maintained toward her own throughout the novel and to which she attests at its close, when, joined by Bunch, she "look[s] out and watch[es] the telephone poles and fences passing like it was a circus parade" (*LIA* 480). Indeed, not only does the description of Christmas riding into town conjure the image of Lena, but its preponderance of negatives also provides a good indication as to why both figures should be considered epicene:

> He is not sleepy or hungry or even tired. He is *somewhere between and among them, suspended*, swaying to the motion of the wagon without thought, without feeling. He has lost account of time and distance.
>
> (LIA 321, emphasis added)

The actions of Christmas on arriving in Mottstown confirm his acceptance of epicenity – and of himself as mulatto. Still wearing his borrowed "pair of second hand brogans" (*LIA* 331) and looking "like he had set out to get himself caught like a man might set out to get married," (*LIA* 330) he goes first to a "white barbershop" (*LIA* 331) for a shave and haircut. As always in Faulkner, the reference to the Biblical Samson indicates that a figure now suffers the emasculation signified elsewhere in Mahon's scar and Bunch's bleeding face (and routinely implied by the added detail of an injured leg). This figural connection appears explicitly – and again predictably – a few pages before when, in preparation for his return, Christmas cuts his face "three or four times" (*LIA* 318) while trying to shave in a local spring. Once in town, properly shaved and shorn, he "walk[s] the streets in broad daylight" (*LIA* 331) calmly waiting for one of the townspeople to identify him. The rest of the scene not only demonstrates Christmas's negotiation of effacement and uncertainty, but also re-asserts the way in which Faulkner's treatment of the mulatto and the epicene squarely tropes the antebellum South's discourse of denial and absorption:

> He never denied it. He never did anything. He never acted like either a nigger or a white man. That was it. That was what made the folks so mad. For him to be a murderer and all dressed up and walking the town like he dared them to touch him, when he ought to have been skulking and hiding in the woods, muddy and dirty and running. It was like he never even knew he was a murderer, let alone a nigger too.
>
> (LIA 331)

The motif of patient surrender not only appears in subsequent novels but, in *Go Down, Moses*, also provides, with the idiom "to wait," at least one formal and figural sense of coherence that transforms the individual short stories into a novel (or, by suspending the text between the two forms, makes it Faulkner's most epicene). In *Go Down, Moses*, however, Faulkner reveals the potential irony lurking even within this otherwise radical troping of slavery's discourses. As Richard Poirier implies, Ike McCaslin, the character through whom the legacies of slavery and hybridity are most thoroughly explored, learns the wisdom of patience and surrender in his experiences in the wilderness.[28] As a consequence of having been taught by the hybrid Amerindian Sam Fathers to see himself as one with the spirit of the woods, Ike acquires the ability to stem his anxiety, "relinquish to it" (*GDM* 147), when confronted by the figures that manifest an epicene otherness – most visibly, the big buck of his first hunt and Old Ben, the ubiquitous bear which stands as the text's most powerful figuration of the material world. It is for this reason that, as a boy, Ike willingly "emasculates" himself in the bear's presence, laying down all signs of technical advantage – watch, compass, gun – when first tracking Old Ben on his own. For this reason also he shows no trace of anxiety at the end of the "The Bear" when, in search of Boon Hoggenbeck, he nearly steps on an enormous rattlesnake. The snake, "once-bright," is now indistinguishable from the material world of which it is both part and emblem, "dulled now to a monotone concordant too with the wilderness it crawled and lurked." Moreover, in keeping with that world, it is "free of all laws of mass and balance." This claim not only equates the snake with the big buck and Old Ben, but also situates it, as they have been, beyond representation: "something else which had no name, evocative of all knowledge and an old weariness and of pariah-hood and of death" (*GDM* 234–5).

When faced in the next story/chapter, "Delta Autumn," with yet another epicene spirit, this time the figure of an ethnic Other, Ike, however, falls victim to his own success. He turns the lessons of patience and relinquishment into the premises for a reactionary gradualism. Ike transforms the wisdom of Sam Fathers into a proposal for maintaining rather than rejecting the segregated culture of the status quo, in a reversal ringing with the irony of Hughes and mocking the liberalism of Faulkner's time. This last meeting also occurs on a hunting trip. Years have passed, and Ike is an old man. The woods have receded so far that he and the other hunters must drive hundreds of miles by car to reach a suitable camp. On the way, it becomes apparent that Roth Edmonds, Ike's nephew, has had a mistress whom he has now left. The following morning, while the others are in the woods, the mistress appears at Ike's tent as if from nowhere. An unwed mother dressed in men's clothes, she plainly displays the transformations of the Faulknerian epicene, simultaneously fitting into the sequence of spirits that Ike has faced:

> entering, in a man's hat and a man's slicker and rubber boots, carrying the blanket-swaddled bundle on one arm and holding the edge of the unbuttoned raincoat over it with the other hand: and bringing something else, something intangible, an effluvium which he knew he would recognise in a moment because Isham had already told him, warned him, by sending the young negro to the tent to announce the visitor instead of coming himself, the flap falling at last on the young negro and they were alone – the face indistinct and as yet only young and with dark eyes, queerly colourless but not ill and not that of a country woman despite the garments she wore, looking down at him where he sat upright on the cot.
>
> (*GDM* 252–3)

Not only is the mistress an epicene, but, as Ike discovers during their conversation, she is, in his words, "a nigger" (*GDM* 255) – more precisely, a mulatto – and, as if Faulkner were making a specific reference to Hughes, she is Edmonds's relative, grand-niece of Ike's grandfather. Ike, however, cannot tolerate the kind of indeterminacy she represents. He cannot accept, that is, the cultural "impurity" she embodies, the state of ethnic confusion, according to Ike, wherein "*Chinese and African and Aryan and Jew, all breed and spawn together until no man has time to say which one is which nor cares*" (*GDM* 258).

The irony of this rejection is unmistakable. In the first place, only a few pages before, Ike voices almost the exact tropological terms from which Faulkner, beginning with *Soldiers' Pay*, has derived his formal accommodation of uncertainty, including that which is implicit in the sort of radical mix of ethnicity repudiated by Ike. "'I think,'" Ike tells Edmonds:

"that every man and woman, at the instant when it dont even matter whether they marry or not, I think that whether they marry then or afterward or dont never, at that instant the two of them together were God."

(*GDM* 246)

Confronted with the incarnation of this position, however, Ike appears nearly overwhelmed by fright. Physically shaking, he demands that Edmonds's mistress, "Get out of here!" (*GDM* 256). Not only does he advise her to marry; but to "Marry: a man in [her] own race." Such an ethnically homogeneous and "pure" marriage, he tells her, is "the only salvation . . . for a while yet, maybe a long while yet" (*GDM* 257).

By denying the spirit of the epicene and attempting to re-absorb her into the dichotomous social world of slavery, which she herself seemingly invalidates, Ike, of course, transgresses every code he had enacted as hunter. Having once accepted the material signs of the epicene, having, in effect, *become* epicene, he now reverts back to the language of patriarchy and oxymoron. He falls, we could say, "off the wagon." Yet the text refuses to support Ike's regression. Indeed, it comments on his pathetic reversal both formally and figurally. The closing story/chapter, "Go Down, Moses," for instance, makes us sharply aware of the irony of Ike's idealism when it brings the text's final embodiment of the epicene, the mulatto Samuel Worsham Beauchamp, before the figure of Gavin Stevens. Now something of a "spirit" of the woods himself, Beauchamp has been executed for a murder in the North and his body returned to his family in Jefferson. Stevens, conversely, assumes a figural role reminiscent of Gilligan and Bunch: he takes over from Ike who – having proved to be an idealist – is described as though he *himself* were a corpse once his grandniece has left: "his hands crossed on his breast . . . rigid save for the shaking" (*GDM* 257).

Usually depicted as an unadulterated idealist, Stevens is in this case a reformed one. At the end of *Go Down, Moses* we see him as a passenger in a car (a version of the wagon), riding with the local editor at the back of the funeral procession that transports Beauchamp's body to its grave. Before the car reaches the cemetery, however, Stevens switches off the ignition, and the cars ahead of him vanish "rapidly away . . . as though in flight, the light and unrained summer dust spurting from beneath the fleeing wheels" (*GDM* 269). Becalmed now (as if sobered), he is therefore made to seem patient in the presence of the epicene, to "wait" as if in respect and acquiescence before the sign of the same ethnic indeterminacy that Ike refuses.

Appropriately, Faulkner leaves the most explicit damnation of Ike's failure in applying the lessons of the wilderness to the problems of ethnicity to the spouseless mulatto mother with the unnamed child. Before disappearing in a "waft of light and the murmur of the constant rain flow[ing] into the tent" she shames Ike with a question that sums up the stance of the text with regard to his ironic regression: "Old man," she asks him, "have you lived so long and forgotten so much that you dont remember anything you ever knew or felt or even heard about love?" (*GDM* 257).

OXYMORONIC, YET AGAIN? FAULKNER'S PUBLIC STANCE ON INTEGRATION

In September 1956 Faulkner published an open letter in *Ebony* originally – and oddly – entitled "If I Were a Negro." The aim of the letter, addressed to prominent figures in the African-American community, was to explain fully what Faulkner claims he had earlier meant in an article entitled "A Letter to the North," published in *Life* in March of the same year.[29] In the *Life* letter Faulkner advises the leaders of the NAACP to drop their demand for federal-government intervention in the affairs of the South. He asks them not to impose integration upon the region from "outside" (86). For Faulkner, such action was likely to incite conservative elements in the South to counter-violence, possibly even to arms. He therefore cautions African-Americans to "Go slow now. Stop now for a time, a moment. You have the power now; you can afford to withhold for a moment the use of it as a force" (87).

Perhaps not surprisingly, African-American leaders rejected Faulkner's gradualism. Thurgood Marshall, for instance, implied that they had heard such arguments many times before with his rejoinder that "'Go slow' really meant 'Don't go.'"[30] Apparently stung by such reactions and various reports that cited him as saying that "between the United States and Mississippi . . . [he] would choose Mississippi" even at the cost of "shooting down Negroes in the street." (107), Faulkner, in the *Ebony* letter, gives a detailed explanation of what lay behind his contentious phrase. He writes that "By 'Go Slow, pause for a moment', [he] meant, 'Be flexible'" (108), flexibility, for Faulkner, signifying a willingness to understand that one of the best "methods of gaining" equality was quite possibly to make oneself "adaptable to circumstance and locality" (109).

To his credit, Faulkner concedes the problems created by his own argument: "It is easy enough to say glibly, 'If I were a Negro, I would do this or that'" (110). Nevertheless, he explores its possibilities in some detail:

> If I were a Negro in America today . . . I would advise the leaders of my race . . . to send every day to the white school to which he was entitled by his ability and capacity to go, a student of my race, fresh and cleanly dressed, courteous, without threat or violence, to seek admission; when he was refused I would forget about him as an individual, but tomorrow I would send another one, still fresh and clean and courteous, to be refused in his turn, until at last the white man himself must recognise that there will be no peace for him until he himself has solved the dilemma.
>
> (109)

The strategy Faulkner advocates here represents an "undeviating and inflexible course – a course of inflexible and unviolent flexibility." Calling it "Gandhi's way," he exhorts its use not only against the public schools, but "all the public institutions from which we are interdict." He admits that he cannot say "how long 'slow' will take" – but no other method, he argues, will succeed (109). African-Americans, therefore, must develop patience "above all," simultaneously transforming it, however, from a "passive quality" to an "active weapon" (111). They must, that is, be willing and able to adjust

> psychologically, not to an indefinite continuation of a segregated society, but rather to a continuation as long as necessary of that inflexible unflagging flexibility which in the end will make the white man himself sick and tired of fighting it.
>
> (110)

Given what we have seen of the rhetoric of his fiction, it is obvious that in his explanation of this political strategy Faulkner incorporates most of those attitudes that appear in the novels to signal progressive, even radical, stances toward ethnicity and gender and make positive virtues out of relinquishment, surrender, inversion, patience and – most importantly – reconciliation with the spirit of the epicene, the uncertain. Three times in the course of what is only a six-page letter, Faulkner conspicuously refers to his plan in terms of an "inflexible . . . flexibility." Three times, that is, he appears to infuse his gradualism with the subversive energies of his own novels.

Where, then, is the problem? Why does this letter, why *did* this letter (like the one it was designed to correct and explain) still seem to strike the wrong note? Is it that Faulkner – no less than Ike McCaslin – becomes a victim of his own consistency? That flexibility and patience, in spite of the self-conscious textuality of *Go Down, Moses*, form the basis for a Faulknerian ideal? Entrap him in an irony of his own making? However we may answer these questions, one thing is certain. Faulkner never once inverts the lexical order of his crucial phrase: "inflexible . . . flexibility," remains fixed throughout the letter, the spectre of the oxymoron refusing – once again – to disappear.[31]

NOTES

1 H. Hughes, *Treatise of Sociology*, Philadelphia, 1860, 31.
2 For most Southerners, as J. Williamson writes, "To merge white and black would have been the ultimate holocaust, the absolute damnation of Southern civilization. And yet that was precisely what the mulatto, by his very being, represented," *New People: Miscegenation and Mulattoes in the United States*, New York, The Free Press, and London, Collier Macmillan, 1980, 95. Indeed, the old South's aversion to hybridity was made repeatedly in publications such as *Debow's Review* and given pseudoscientific justification in official documents like the one produced by the Freedman's Inquiry Commission of 1864, which claimed that mulattoes were inferior in physical power and health to "pure" individuals, of either colour. See also J.R. Berzon, *Neither White nor Black: The Mulatto Character in American Fiction*, New York, New York University Press, 1978.
3 In the South this debate took shape most vehemently between the monogeneticist J. Bachman, a Lutheran minister, and the polygeneticist Dr S.G. Morton. Morton seemed to have been about to

sway opinion when he died in 1851. The South, however, was never likely to accept polygeneticism completely since it went against the teaching of the Bible.

4 E.B. Reuter, *The Mulatto in the United States: Including a Study of the Role of Mixed-Blood Races throughout the World*, Boston, Richard G. Badger, 1918, 12.

5 ibid.

6 ibid., 11.

7 This point is made by numerous writers on the antebellum South, not least of whom is E. Genovese in his highly influential study *Roll, Jordan, Roll: The World the Slaves Made*, New York, Random House, 1974. "Typically," Genovese writes, "the mulatto, especially the mulatto slave, was 'just another nigger' to the whites" (429). Confirming Reuter's observation, W.D. Jordan writes that the term "*mulatto* is not frequently used in the United States. Americans generally reserve it for biological contexts, because for social purposes a mulatto is termed a *negro*," "American Chiaroscuro: The Status and Definition of Mulattoes in the British Colonies," in L. Foner and E. Genovese, eds, *Slavery in the New World: A Reader in Comparative History*, Englewood Cliffs, Prentice-Hall, 1969, 189–201.

8 The dichotomous world of idealism is depicted, for example, in Newton's *Opticks* (1704) which fixes black in polar opposition to white as a deprivation of the original colour, and Hume's *Essays Moral, Political and Literary* (1752) in which Africans are viewed as inherently inferior because of their complexion.

9 For an excellent argument to this effect see J. Barrell, "Death on the Nile: Fantasy and the Literature of Tourism 1840–1860," in *Essays In Criticism* 41 (1991) 97–127. See also B. Johnson, "Thresholds of Difference: Structures of Address in Zora Neale Hurston," in H.L. Gates, Jr., ed., *"Race," Writing, and Difference*, Chicago and London, University of Chicago Press, 1986, 317–28. "Difference," she writes, "is a misreading of sameness, but it must be represented in order to be erased. The resistance to finding out that the Other is the same springs out of the reluctance to admit that the same is Other . . . . Difference disliked is identity affirmed," 323.

10 S. Elkins, *Slavery: A Problem in American Institutional and Intellectual Life*, Chicago and London, University of Chicago Press, 1968, 55.

11 ibid.

12 ibid.

13 W. James, *Pragmatism and The Meaning of Truth*, introd. A.J. Ayer, Cambridge, Mass. and London, Harvard University Press, 1978, 15.

14 H.L. Gates, Jr., *The Signifying Monkey: A Theory of Afro-American Literary Criticism*, New York and Oxford, Oxford University Press, 1988.

15 H.L. Gates, Jr., *Figures in Black: Words, Signs, and the "Racial" Self*, New York and Oxford, Oxford University Press, 1987, 17.

16 ibid., 49.

17 For fuller analysis of the intratextual quality of Faulkner's fiction and its dramatization of Barthes's distinction between the *text* of a writer and a writer's *work* see A. Bleikasten, *The Ink of Melancholy: Faulkner's Novels from The Sound and the Fury to Light in August*, Bloomington, Indiana University Press, 1990. See also D. Rogers, "Articulating the Flesh: The Paradox of Form and Gender in the Novels of William Faulkner," Diss., Rutgers, The State University of New Jersey, 1991.

18 W. Faulkner, *Soldiers' Pay*, London, Chatto & Windus, 1957, 19 (cited hereafter as *SP* with page number in parenthesis).

19 As for example in the following description of Januarius J. Jones's reflections on Cecily: "Not for maternity, not even for love: a thing for the eye and the mind. Epicene, he thought, feeling her slim bones, the bitter nervousness latent in her flesh" (*SP* 226).

20 W. Faulkner, *The Sound and the Fury*, London, Chatto & Windus, 1959, 115 (cited hereafter as *TSF* with page number in parenthesis).

21 See especially F. Reidel, "Faulkner as Stylist," *South Atlantic Quarterly*, 56 (Autumn 1957) 462–79; S. Chakovsky, "Women in Faulkner's Novels: Author's Attitude and Artistic Function," in D. Fowler and A.J. Abadie, eds, *Faulkner and Women: Faulkner and Yoknapatawpha*, Jackson, University of Mississippi Press, 1986, 58–80; and M. Gresset, *Fascination: Faulkner's Fiction 1919–1936*, adapted from the French by T. West, Durham, N.C., and London, Duke University Press, 1989.

22 For a more complete explanation of this relay-effect, the relationships it creates among those it embraces, and the formal implications it contains for Faulkner see Rogers, "Articulating the Flesh." See Rogers also for a demonstration of the way in which articulation in Faulkner not only implies acts of expression and connection but also suggests the obscurer notion of reconciliation – "to come to terms with."

23 W. Faulkner, *Light in August*, London, Chatto & Windus, 1960, 9 (cited hereafter as *LIA* with page number in parenthesis).

24 W. Faulkner, *The Town*, London, Chatto & Windus, 1958, 294, 293 (cited hereafter as *T* with page number in parenthesis).

25 This term is prompted by A. Jardine, who refers to the need to occupy a "trans-position" amidst our "figurative confusion." In language befitting the rhetorical strategy of Faulkner, she writes, "What is henceforth necessary for any human subject who desires to describe the modern world will be to walk through the mirror, dismantle the frame held together by the Big Dichotomies," *Gynesis: Configurations of Woman and Modernity*, Ithaca and London, Cornell University Press, 1985, 88.

26 For a telling psychoanalytic reading of the scenes of drinking see Gresset, *Fascination*. Gresset draws some questionable conclusions, however, because he does not recognize the formal and figurative extensions of the motif he examines, extensions that, for instance, are further supported by the overtly negative language with which

Faulkner describes the mule in his infamous passage in *Flags in the Dust* (1929). The language of the passage clearly relates the mule to the epicene and each to the need to have patience.

27 W. Faulkner, *The Hamlet*, London, Chatto & Windus, 1979, 55.

28 R. Poirier, *A World Elsewhere: The Place of Style in American Literature*, Oxford, Clarendon Press, 1966, 78–83.

29 These letters are respectively reprinted as, "A Letter to the Leaders in the Negro Race" and "Letter to a Northern Editor" in W. Faulkner, *Essays, Speeches & Public Letters*, ed. J.B. Meriwether, London, Chatto & Windus, 1967, 107–12 and 86–91, and cited hereafter by page number only in parenthesis.

30 Marshall's reputed remark is cited by J. Baldwin in "Faulkner and Desegregation," *Partisan Review*, 23 (1956) 568.

31 If I choose to remain somewhat noncommittal here, it is partly because of my own sense that Faulkner's plan is not simply a sign of his certain failure to appreciate the complete significance of his textual treatment of the epicene. For something of the reason why, see D. Rogers, "Shaking Hands: Gestures Toward Race in William Faulkner's *The Unvanquished*," *Mississippi Quarterly* 43 (1990) 335–48.

9

PROPHESYING BODIES

Calling for a politics of collectivity in Toni Morrison's *Beloved*

April Lidinsky

The hard work of a nonracist sensibility is the boundary crossing, from safe circle into wilderness: the testing of boundary, the consecration of sacrilege.

Patricia J. Williams

The possibility exists for fiction to function in truth, for a fictional discourse to induce effects of truth, and for bringing it about that a true discourse engenders or "manufactures" something that does not as yet exist, that is, "fictions" it. One "fictions" history on the basis of a political reality that makes it true, one "fictions" a politics not yet in existence on the basis of a historical truth.

Michel Foucault[1]

Toni Morrison's *Beloved* (1987) calls us to imagine and seize the power of discourse to transform the political and spiritual "habits"[2] of being that produce our understandings of our "selves." In interconnected stories of slavery's manifestations on the bodies and psyches of women and men during and after the American Civil War, and through invented strategies of resistance, Morrison's characters challenge the "naturalness" of the established discursive, disciplinary techniques that historically have produced not only the enslaved proprietary body as an owned "object," but also the viciously individuated Cartesian "subject," which operates through a similar proprietary model of one's body as simply the property of the self. To pun on a central evangelical trope of the novel, Morrison opens a Clearing for revisioning the body as a fluid site of somatic knowledges

191

and shifting, even collective, identities that overflow rigid indi-
vidualist models of self. The Clearing in the woods of Morrison's
Reconstruction-era Ohio, inspirited by the preacher Baby Suggs,
offers us fertile ground on which to consider the productively –
if unexpectedly – complementary aspects of African Methodist
Episcopal (AME) spirituality and postmodern conceptions of
the "subject." These two discourses conceive of our bodies, our
political collectives and the "history" in which we are embedded,
in visionary ways. Once we understand ourselves as "produced"
in discourse we can, as Judith Butler has argued, imagine
discourses that will produce new selves.[3] Baby Suggs sends out
this Call in the Clearing as much to the reader as to the other
characters in the novel: "She told them that the only grace they
could have was the grace they could imagine. That if they could
not see it, they would not have it."[4]

Baby Suggs and postmodernist theorists "Call" alike for a
conceptual shift from the totalized to the multiplicitous subject,
thus interrogating totalized narratives of history that silence all
but the master voices and neatly sunder past from present. Not
only does Morrison's text give voice to the dedication's "*Sixty
Million and more*" who perished in the Middle Passage, it also
impels us to consider *Beloved* as a "history of the present,"[5] in
which the *effects* of slavery's brutality, like the figure of Beloved
herself, are acknowledged spatially and experientially through
"rememory." In "The Site of Memory" Morrison's explanation
of history's spatial presence in her work complements the
"fictioning" (in the Foucauldian sense of imaginative production) that her characters learn in order to make sense of their
own histories:

> What makes it fiction is the nature of the imaginative act:
> my reliance on the image – on the remains – in addition to
> recollection, to yield up a kind of a truth. By "image," of
> course, I don't mean "symbol"; I simply mean "picture"
> and the *feelings* that accompany the picture.[6]

bell hooks characterizes *Beloved*'s history of emotional and
somatic "feelings" as the "psycho-social history of [slavery's]
impact."[7] Such feelings are also the disremembered effects of
events that are not recorded in conventional history or in
notebooks of "facts" like those kept by schoolteacher, the
brutal master of Sweet Home whose scientific racism most

clearly articulates the M/master narrative of slavery's history. The novel asks how we can make meaning of inexplicable brutality when history has recorded no "facts" to counter schoolteacher's narrative – when, as in the fate of Sethe's husband, Halle, "Nobody knows what happened," (224) because of incommensurable versions of events.[8]

Let me hasten to add that this text's postmodernist formulation of history as necessarily contradictory, fragmented and full of gaps that never can be adequately closed does not constitute a denial of historical events. Similarly, postmodern insights need not relegate history to the realm of a political undecidability, as some critics have insisted.[9] Such insights instead challenge totalizing interpretations of events and demand what Linda Hutcheon calls a "critical revisiting"[10] of history – an act of revisioning characterized by collectivity rather than absolute consensus. Sethe formulates this on-going activity of producing, or fictioning, meaning out of history's disremembered effects in this way: "Her story was bearable because it was [Paul D's] as well – to tell, to refine and tell again" (99).

The spatial aspect of rememory – through which past events live "out there, in the world" for anyone to "bump into," (36) as Sethe puts it – works against the masculinist model of the contained, proprietary self by casting history's effects into the realm of collective responsibility. As Mae Henderson aptly notes: "Rememory . . . is something which possesses (or haunts) one, rather than something which one possesses."[11] For this reason, I question psychoanalytic readings of *Beloved* that situate these rememoried narratives in the realm of repressed primal scenes, which each individual analysand must then reconstitute through a re-enactment of the originary event. Henderson's use of this model, for example, leads her to place the onus of meaning-making on Sethe as an individual, whose "job [it] is to reconstitute the past through personal narrative, or storytelling" in order to "make whole" a history (and so a self) that has been "dismembered."[12] However, this vision of a history of cause-and-effect wholeness overlooks the many gaps (like the story of Halle's death) that the text leaves strikingly open, underlining the impossibility of a totalized narrative. In addition, the concept of an essentially reconstituted originary self overlooks the fluidity of identity in *Beloved*. This is not to say that identity is fragmented instead of whole within the text but rather that for these characters, identity slides between many wholes and many knowledges and experiences which can be "mixed up" (88) and re-imagined through bodily practices.

Baby Suggs Calls her community to move beyond those proprietary models of identity that slavery has literally trained into their bodies. Using the dialogic model of call-and-response prayer, she moves them to "listen" (209) their bodies into new forms of somatic literacy, enabling them to retrain their habits of being, gesture by gesture. The effect of this is to redirect slavery's "vertical" flow of power, which segregates and dichotomizes not just master and slave, but all individuals. Redirecting power "horizontally," or dialogically, enables these characters to be moved – somatically, emotionally, spiritually – to invent shifting collectives of differences. As a white, female, middle-class reader conscious of my own position in slavery's brutal legacy and on the margins of Morrison's text, I want to emphasize that this novel is not dreamy about the ease with which these diverse and shifting collectives may be formed, given the viciousness of enculturated dichotomies of race and gender in particular, but I believe it moves readers, as well, to contest these rigidly limiting lines of identity through a sense of history's presence.[13] The rich possibilities of "fictioning" or inventing a new politics based on empathetic, generous "boundary crossing" (to intertwine the visions of Williams and Foucault) are borne out in *Beloved* in the collectives of what I would call a *postmodern spirituality*, inspired in the rememory of Baby Suggs in the Clearing where she Calls her visionary sermons.

"LISTENING" THE INCARNATIONAL BODY INTO SPEECH

Baby Suggs's central sermon reaches us through rememory, as Sethe enters the Clearing in the woods to "listen to the spaces" (89) where many years ago Baby Suggs preached, danced and sang with the community:

> "Here," [Baby Suggs] said, "in this here place, we flesh; flesh that weeps, laughs; flesh that dances on bare feet in grass. Love it. Love it hard . . . . More than your life-holding womb and your life-giving private parts, hear me now, love your heart. For this is the prize."
>
> (88–9)

The Call to "Love," with its emphasis on fleshly sensation and heartfelt emotion, has led Baby Suggs to be read narrowly by some critics as simply "another Morrisonian earth mother."[14] I would argue instead that this discourse of liberation draws more specifically on the doctrinal tradition of "perfect love" within nineteenth-century Holiness currents of the Methodist and AME Churches, which emphasize, as Jean M. Humez has noted, "spiritual and ecstatic experience and expression as the 'heart' of religion."[15] Perfect love, the conviction of "sanctification" or the state of perfect harmony with God's will, is a concept solely reliant upon inspiration rather than institutionalized church hierarchies. This explains its appeal for the large percentage of women converts who formed many of the Holiness prayer-bands which had spread across parts of the United States by the 1840s, including the Ohio countryside of Baby Suggs's Clearing.[16] Inspired women such as Jarena Lee and Julia Foote – like their fictional incarnation, Baby Suggs – challenged Daniel A. Payne's increasingly masculinist, rational and educated mid-century Methodism[17] by preaching at camp meetings and travelling between pulpits, despite the church's refusal formally to recognize them as preachers.[18] We are told that Baby Suggs, created "her own brand of preaching" (147) after slavery "busted" her body:

> she had nothing left to make a living with but her heart – which she put to work at once. Accepting no title of honor before her name, but allowing a small caress after it ["aby Suggs, holy"], she became an unchurched preacher, one who visited pulpits and opened her great heart to those who could use it. In winter and fall she carried it to AME's and Baptists, Holinesses and Sanctifieds, the Church of the Redeemer and the Redeemed. Uncalled, unrobed, un-anointed, she let her great heart beat in their presence.
>
> (87)

As in her sermon, the primacy of the beating heart, of the flesh, reveals the transformative site of the self not simply as logos, the Word, but also as *soma*, the "flesh that weeps [and] laughs" and that Baby Suggs Calls her people to love, stroke and hold. This pleasurable attention to the body is consistent with the primacy of bodily sensation – the "Word was made flesh" – in incarnational theology, as Sue E. Houchins explains:

195

the *Logos*, the Word – not simply the utterance but the breath/the spirit of the Creator – not only is spoken/ breathed into the world, but also the world is heard in return through the intercession of the incarnational, Christic being. The incarnation, then, is discursive like prayer, like autobiography.[19]

This discursive self, inscribed through the ecstatic body in incarnational theology, blurs "whole" identities into Holiness sites of fluxuating authority. Revisionary spiritual autobiographers like Lee and Foote wrote their selves against very different representations of the subject in influential contemporaneous African-American narratives such as Frederick Douglass's *Narrative of the Life of Frederick Douglass, an American Slave* (1845). Borrowing Benjamin Franklin's powerful cultural trope of the self-made man,[20] Douglass's masculinist representation of the secular subject as *rational* and necessarily literate marginalized these women preachers as much as did Payne's patriarchal sacred subject, which, by the 1850s, had come to be defined by the AME Church's push for a college-educated clergy.[21]

In this spiritual discourse, as in previous writings by women mystics,[22] the authority of the "I" blurs, binding together the voices of speaking subject and Holy Spirit, thus allowing even a woman speaker to lay claim to an "I" that is strategically more authoritative than its secular, masculine counterpart and also less discursively fixed. In *Beloved*, for example, Baby Suggs is empowered to speak the Word by divine authorization, assuming public positions otherwise denied to her by racism and sexism. Henderson uses the phrase "speaking in tongues" to characterize the combination of the sacred speech of glossolalia and the public discourse of heteroglossia – or the "gift of prophecy, and the gift of interpretation."[23] Baby Suggs's very name marks the slippage between these multiple private and public discourses, and the multiple identities they signify. "Baby" is the private, intimate name given her by her husband, and borders on the "presymbolic babble" Henderson associates with Holiness glossolalia.[24] "Baby" also speaks against the "Jenny" inscribed on her "sales ticket," a seminal site of the proprietary M/master discourse which accordingly surnames her "Whitlow." The impositions of this discourse she counters with "Suggs," a name that speaks both privately and publicly, like the act of testimony, since it signifies a contract of marriage recognized in slave-circles but not in the eyes of the law. "Suggs" also operates as a code name in the event of escape, since it can be circulated among communities of ex-slaves, but not posted by slave-catchers operating on the basis of the proprietary "bill-of-sale" (142). Finally, "holy," the "small caress" she accepts after her name in the place of a title of honour, both connotes public recognition of her role as a spiritual leader in the community, and also gestures back to the intimate knowledges implied by the position of Holiness.

The dialogic autobiographical writing of Baby Suggs's multiple subject-positions through her names shares the call-and-response hermeneutics of her Call in the Clearing. Houchins argues that African-American women's spiritual autobiographies use the call-and-response structure of direct audience-address to combine and enact the dialogic forms of autobiography, prayer and exhortations to testimony – forms that hinge on the act of *listening* as much as speech, as in the Pentecost story in which "to worship was to be *heard into selfhood* by God."[25] As the production of Baby Suggs's name illustrates, hearing into selfhood in *Beloved* takes place in the dialogic space of the community, where Baby Suggs "didn't deliver sermons or preach . . . she *called* and the hearing heard" (177). Baby Suggs radicalizes the act of hearing into a process that might be called "listening into selfhood," as exemplified by her appeal to Denver to "listen to [her] body and love it" so that she might Call into speech the somatic languages of "pleasure deep down" (209). Like other nineteenth-century spiritual autobiographers who Called for new acts of interpretative literacy if the prophetic effects of their incarnational experiences were to move their audiences to testify in response, Baby Suggs also Calls her community to respond to a new visual literacy that challenges the monologic, objectifying M/master narrative which inscribes them. External and internal experiences of vision blur into the *visionary* here, enabling the community to imagine, and so to Call into sight or existence their own salvational vision, once again, of grace on earth: "She told them that the only grace they could have was the grace they could imagine. That if they could not see it, they would not have it."

The sensuousness of this vision of grace that Calls for "lov[ing] the flesh" borders upon an eroticism common to spiritual autobiographies like Jarena Lee's, in which she recalls that "Great was the ecstasy of my mind" during a vision of being "stripped" by and "covered" with the "glory of God."[26] However, this rapture is defined much in the manner of Audre Lorde's revision of the erotic as "creative energy empowered," and as the "physical, emotional, and psychic expressions" of the self that bridge the dichotomy between the spiritual and political, challenging the fixed, "rational" knowledges of a "racist, patri-archal" society.[27] This is the same challenge posed by the dialogic experience of Baby Suggs's followers in the Clearing, as Baby moves them to derigidify their senses of self by "mixing up" somatic knowledges and practices, Calling each other to understand and enact new pleasures. After initially Calling the children to laugh, the men to dance and the women to weep, the demarcations soon fold:

> It started that way: laughing children, dancing men, crying women and then *it got mixed up*. Women stopped crying and danced; men sat down and cried; children danced, women laughed, children cried until, exhausted and riven, all and each lay about the Clearing damp and gasping for breath.
>
> (88, emphasis added)

Cornel West argues that the spiritual connection between pleasure and knowledge in ecstatic bodily experience – from the "holy dance" of evangelical conversion to the "ring shout" of West African novitiate rites – also serves to restructure "every-day time."[28] The fluxuating call-and-response practices of ecstatic dancing, weeping and laughing in Baby Suggs's Clearing enable just such a collective revisioning of "everyday time," as concepts of history and memory are not banished to a *temporally* inaccessible past, but, rather, reproduced through the shifting subjectivities of collective flesh that *spatially* body forth re-memory. Sethe explains to her daughter Denver that places – Sweet Home being one – themselves hold memories:

> not just in my rememory, but out there, in the world . . . . The picture is still there and what's more, if you go there – you who never was there – if you go there and stand in the place where it was, it will happen again.
>
> (36)

Clearly, rememory posits a radical shift away from transcendental doctrines that, as Donna Haraway has argued, implicitly promise "a way out of history": "Any transcendentalist move is deadly; it produces death, through the fear of it"[29] – and so Baby Suggs Calls her community to envision their own "grace" here on earth. Just as Beloved's name speaks of both her gravestone and spiritual addresses to the living community ("Dearly beloved, we are gathered here today . . ."), Baby Suggs's activist spirituality dissolves the rigid, defensive boundaries set up by "Sword and shield" (86) Christianity between life and death, past and present, inner and outer somatic experience, and fixed identity-positions. Like the visionary women preachers who provide the context for Baby Suggs's Call in *Beloved*, she herself moves the collective to imagine, envision and create, rather than dismantle, the M/master's house with his own tools of war, to adapt Audre Lorde's famous phrase. The somatic literacies that Baby Suggs listens into collective knowledge in the Clearing turn upon the acquisition of new habits of being, in a strategy of bodily revisioning that weaves together spirituality's attention to the emotion and sensuousness of the "Word made flesh" and postmodernism's interest in the inscripted practices through which identities are performed.

IMAGINING THE POSTMODERN SPIRITUAL BODY

Beloved invites us to consider the connections between the discourses of visionary spirituality explored above and those of postmodernism, on the shared grounds of bodily spatiality where both challenge set notions of knowledge, history and, particularly, identity. Just as incarnational theology blurs the distinction between inner and outer experience of the Word, so postmodern understandings of the self blur the inner/outer opposition through the performance of discourse, focusing, that is, on bodily inscription (rather than internalization) of disciplinary historical forces. This inscription of the law, functions, according to Foucault, through a kind of bodily "dressage." As Butler elaborates Foucault's theories of the effects of disciplinary power on prisoners:

the strategy has been not to enforce a repression of their

desires, but to compel their bodies to signify the prohibitive law as their very essence, style, and necessity. That law is not literally internalized, but incorporated, with the consequence that bodies are produced which signify that law on and through the body.[30]

Slavery in the United States fits somewhat uneasily into Foucault's theories of disciplinary regimes because of its use of *force* as well as disciplinary power.[31] Yet Foucault nevertheless provides a useful frame through which to view the political agency for which Baby Suggs Calls. Such an agency is based upon and operates through the discursive understanding of the body as signifying law and identity in a process of *repetitive* action. This "hold" on the body "at the level of the mechanism itself – movements, gestures, attitudes, rapidity," as Foucault observes, is central to disciplinary systems which rely on a vertical flow of power working through the "partitioning" of bodies, in which "Each individual has his own place; and each place its individual."[32] The effect of such a system of power is not only to "break up collective dispositions"[33] (the same collective identity Baby Suggs Calls for in her sermon), but also to organize and control political space – to establish a system of knowledge that conflates the mastering of bodily gestures with the mastering of that space. It is important that this interpellation of the subject need not be read as deterministic; indeed, as Butler has noted, precisely because "signification is not a founding act, but rather a regulated process of repetition," agency is "located within the possibility of a variation on that repetition."[34] In *Beloved*, political agency on the smallest scale – at the level of habit, of bodily movement, of gesture – effects revolutionary change precisely through the connection to political space, as it is traced from the "mastered" to the "rememoried."

Baby Suggs's own transition from a partitioned, proprietary conception of the body to a spiritual, collective one is charted through the narrative of her passage into freedom, which begins as a movement from object/property to subject. In her first moments of freedom, she experiences the disorientating sensation of subjecthood as *self*-ownership, in Douglass's masculinist model: "[Baby Suggs] saw her hands and thought with a clarity as simple as it was dazzling, 'These hands belong to me. These *my* hands'" (141). However Baby Suggs's proprietary relationship to her body immediately shifts further to what might be called a postmodern, spiritual subject-position, based as it is upon both the flexibility of identity and the spiritual union of somatic and emotive knowledges. As in her Call, the "heart" bears the physical and spiritually metaphoric weight as the centre of knowledge in life and love:

> Next she felt a knocking in her chest and discovered something else new: her own heartbeat. Had it been there all along? This pounding thing? She felt like a fool and began to laugh out loud.
>
> (141)

The process of learning to listen into speech her body's vitality and being Called to respond by laughing irrationally, or "fool-ishly," marks Baby's conversion to a spiritual and political pedagogy centred on unlearning slavery's proprietary gestures and attaining instead the literacies of the "loved" body.

Importantly, the rememory-rich space of the Clearing marks the most striking intersection of the pedagogical re-invention of the political body and the body politic. Sethe remembers there that she "along with the others . . . had claimed herself. Freeing yourself was one thing; claiming ownership of that freed self was another" (95). However, through Baby Suggs's Word, "claiming" becomes not an individual, partitioned act, but an imaginative training for a collective disposition that transforms political space gesture by gesture. The Call clearly traces the retraining of each bodily part, as well as the movement toward political collectivity that each gesture evokes:

> And O my people they do not love your hands. Those they only use, tie, bind, chop off and leave empty. Love your hands! Love them. Raise them up and kiss them. *Touch others with them*. . . . They do not love your neck unnoosed and straight. So love your neck; put a hand on it, grace it, stroke it and hold it up.
>
> (88, emphasis added)

Out of this somatic dialogism, through which Sethe recalls "feeling [others'] fun and sorrow along with her own, which made it better" (95), larger acts of spiritual and political connection take place that unsettle social roles and identity-positions in an echo of the ecstatic "mixing up" of experience during Baby Suggs's Call. The eventual absence of political and social community after the townspeople turn their backs on the women of 124 Bluestone Road is striking to Sethe, who laments:

> No more dancing in the Clearing or happy feeds. No more discussions, stormy or quiet, about the true meaning of the Fugitive Bill, the Settlement Fee, God's Ways and Negro pews . . . and the other weighty issues that held them in chairs, scraping the floorboards or pacing them in agony or exhilaration.
>
> (173)

In this passage, as in the space of the Clearing generally, gender is not a divisive force; rather, it is one of the many different subject-positions, or bodily discourses, that are "mixed up" in various ways, according to how one is able to be somatically moved. While most critics have emphasized the matrilineal connections in *Beloved*,[35] Morrison's text is also richly suggestive with regard to the various effects of slavery's disciplinary tactics on *masculinity*, at the same time exploring ways that the "boundaries" of gender, as Williams might say, can be tested and crossed. I will move on accordingly – briefly – to the figure of Paul D, the Sweet Home man who becomes Sethe's lover after the war. His experience of brutality – and the resistance to it – on a coffle, after schoolteacher sells him from Sweet Home, perhaps best illustrates the disciplinary and gestural *propriety* that produces the bodily discourse of *property* which speaks in turn through an enslaved person until those gestures can be unlearned. Paul D's coffle-experience details, then, the disciplinary model to which all the characters are subjected, and literally traces methods of resistance.

While the actual chains ordering the bodies of the men in the coffle must be categorized in terms of force rather than disciplinary power, the narrator suggests that the "miracle of their obedience" is due less to a physical binding than to the discipline of dressage or training. The repetitive performance of the chain gang announces Paul D's identity as property with equal clarity whether the chain is on or off:

> All forty-six men woke to rifle shot. All forty-six. Three whitemen walked along the trench unlocking the doors [of their cages] one by one. No one stepped through . . . .

another rifle shot signaled the climb out and up to the ground above, where one thousand feet of the best hand-forged chain in Georgia stretched. Each man bent and waited. The first man picked up the end and threaded it through the loop on his leg iron. He stood up then, and, shuffling a little, brought the chain tip to the next prisoner, who did likewise.

(107)

Soldier-like discipline seems, more than rifle shots, to be the "miracle" enabling three white guards to achieve such control that forty-six prisoners mechanically chain themselves at a signal each morning. To use Foucault's terms, this discipline is effected through a vertical organization of power which radically partitions these men (via spaces on the chain by day and separate cages by night) in order to eliminate the possibility of collective identity and agency. For a time, Paul D incorporates the gestural training with such devastating thoroughness that his body seems to lose whatever knowledges it might draw on for resistance or even preservation. His hands and legs that are so "steady" and disciplined while going through the motions of coffle-work are no longer trained for – nor do they seem to contain knowledge of – any other use:

when they shoved him into the box and dropped the cage door down, his hands quit taking instruction. On their own, they traveled. Nothing could stop them or get their attention. They would not hold his penis to urinate or a spoon to scoop lumps of lima beans into his mouth. The miracle of their obedience came with the hammer at dawn.

(107)

From this most concretely realized illustration of the devastating effects of discipline, however, comes an equally concrete example of how a horizontal redirection of power at the level of the gesture can enable precisely the collective disposition that the coffle-masters fear. This redirection begins, just as Baby Suggs preaches, with the men being moved to "listen" to the body's alternative knowledges, since disciplinary partitioning eliminates the possibility of meaningful speech. As in spiritual doctrine, visual literacy takes on new meaning: "The eyes had to tell what there was to tell: 'Help me this mornin; 's bad'; 'I'm a make it'; 'New man'; 'Steady now steady'" (107). Once the men begin "listening each other into speech," according to the spiritual model, collective action becomes a possibility, and not simply for inventing a collective and private glossolalia of "tricking the words [of their songs] so their syllables yielded up other meanings." Through the guidance of Hi Man, who serves as the Baby Suggs figure on the coffle and similarly knows "what was enough, what was too much, when things were over, when the time had come," (108) the men develop yet another discourse of motion and emotion – a series of tugs and pulls with which "They talked through that chain like Sam Morse," thereby transforming the very device that keeps them partitioned into a mechanism for collective agency. This passage crystallizes the politics and Holiness spirituality of Baby's Call for connection: "For one lost, all lost. The chain that held them would save all or none, and Hi Man was the Delivery" (110). This gestural discourse of conflated motion and emotion enables the men to swim simultaneously, blindly, out of the deadly muck which crushes and loosens their cages in a cataclysmic rainstorm, and to escape northward as a collective, their bodies no longer speaking the mastered, proprietary discourse, but instead beginning to articulate new identities.

This gestural retraining demands repetition, however, and Paul D survives the powerful experience of connection without entirely learning to "love" and "listen to" his heart, which remains a "tobacco tin lodged in his chest," (113) perhaps because he is inscripted with specifically masculine cultural discourses of individuation – discourses built on the same proprietorial tropes found in Douglass's culturally central narrative. What makes Sweet Home so exceptional under the Garners, after all, is Garner's willingness to call his slaves "men" – a naming that re-inscribes Garner's own manhood, for it proves to himself he is "tough enough and smart enough to make and call his own niggers men" (11). Yet Garner undermines the nominal power of substituting "men" for "niggers" with the disciplinary logic revealed in his proprietary terms of "making" "his own" men. On this point Paul D reflects, "Is that where the manhood lay? In the naming done by a whiteman who was supposed to know?" "Suppose Garner woke up one morning and changed his mind?" (125, 220) No matter how seemingly noble Garner's intention, his naming and "making" of these men does not challenge their proprietary objectification, nor does it undo the power of ownership central to masculinist models of selfhood like Douglass's. When schoolteacher, as the very letter of the law, takes over the farm after Garner's death, Paul D is renamed or produced as something animal-like, even "less than a chicken" whose freedom taunts him on the farm – a chicken named, with telling mockery, "Mister" (72).

Beloved does, then, explore the specifically gendered trauma of certain effects of slavery's degradation, such as the reification and undermining of cultural concepts of "manhood" at Sweet Home, and the stealing of Sethe's milk by schoolteacher's boys, but the bodily effects of enslavement on both men and women are linked through images of "animality" and "iron," suggesting that Sethe and Paul D must alike unlearn the mechanization of slavery's signifying disciplines of dressage, metallically incorporated into each of them (both figuratively and literally). Like the iron bit schoolteacher forces Paul D to wear, concretizing the horse-like dressage of slavery, Sethe's "iron eyes and backbone to match" (9) are linked to his M/master inscription of her enslaved body as half-consisting of animal characteristics. Paul D must unlearn the sensation of the coffle-irons – incorporated as the "tin" of his heart – as part of the process of redirecting power's flow, just as Sethe must unlearn the choke-hold of the "circle of iron" (101) around her throat that is both the collectively rememoried sensation of the Middle Passage and the somatic effect of Beloved's rage. Instead, Sethe learns to incorporate Baby's Call to "love [her] neck; put a hand on it, grace it" – to "listen" its somatic knowledges into speech through connection, as Paul D learns somatically the language of the numb "ironsmith's" scar on Sethe's back through precisely these spiritually connecting gestures of love and grace:

> He rubbed his cheek on her back and learned that way her sorrow, the roots of it; its wide trunk and intricate branches. Raising his fingers to the hooks of her dress, he knew without seeing them or hearing any sigh that the tears were coming fast.
>
> (17)

Images of liquidity, of somatic movement, mark Paul D's growing ability to produce in 124 a "listening quiet" (15) that summons into speech these fluxuating, nonmechanized bodily

knowledges which, like Baby Suggs's Call, cross gender boundaries through a kind of spiritual "blessing":

> Not even trying, he had become the kind of man who
> could walk into a house and make the women cry . . . .
> There was something blessed in his manner. Women saw
> him and wanted to weep – to tell him that their chest hurt
> and their knees did too. Strong women and wise saw him
> and told him things they only told each other.
>
> (17)

As when he enters 124, a "wave of grief soak[ing] him so
thoroughly he wanted to cry" (9), Paul D's growing ability to
move both others and himself to new somatic knowledges and
connections later becomes such a threat to Beloved's own
connection to Sethe that Beloved "moves" Paul D right back –
blurring inner and outer effects to force him right out of the
house. Similarly, like the "closed portion" of Paul D's head that
"opened like a greased lock" (41), Sethe's own increasing ability
to "listen" her own alternative bodily knowledges into speech is
figured in terms of the mechanized "iron" of her body opening
to spatial rememories. For example, while Sethe initially does
not recognize her daughter in the figure of the adolescent
Beloved, her own body marks this knowledge through a gush of
water whose meaning Sethe must learn to "read" in the manner
of an alternative spiritual discourse. Significantly, her reading
moves first through slavery's readily available discourse of
objectification (figured as animality), and then beyond it to her
own life-affirming birthing experience:

> She never made the outhouse. Right in front of its door
> she had to lift her skirts, and the water she voided was
> endless. Like a horse, she thought, but as it went on and on
> she thought, No, more like flooding the boat when Denver
> was born.
>
> (51)

Later in the "poetic" chapters in which Sethe's subject-positions
blur with those of Beloved, Sethe reads her body's discourse yet
more complexly, as the text merges these "birth" waters with
Beloved's act of drinking:

> I would have known who you were right away because the

cup after cup of water you drank proved and connected to
the fact that you dribbled clear spit on my face the day I
got to 124.

(202)

Whether operating on the small-scale dialogism of Sethe's
gestural readings of her own body's rememories, or on the larger
call-and-response connection between Paul D and Sethe, the
collective identity enabled by the horizontal redirection of
power's flow works discursively, through both new somatic
literacies and the practices of collaborative storytelling. History's presence in their very bodies causes these characters to be
moved – physically and emotionally – not just by a sympathy for
others, but by empathy for the "others in themselves," despite
divisive enculturated lines of identity.[36] Men like Paul D and
Stamp Paid are moved across gender lines to collaborate with
Sethe and Baby on events about which "nobody knows" a
totalising narrative. Similarly, Amy Denver, the runaway
"whitegirl" (8) who midwives Denver's birth, is moved to cross
lines of race in order to mother Sethe and collaborate on class-
based experiences of abuse and creative survival that are
eventually woven into the discursive fabric of 124 through
repeated stories of her nursing and her dreams of buying velvet,
as through the very name carried on by Sethe's second daughter,
Denver. Once gesturally "listened" into eloquence, then, rememory dissolves power's vertical compartmentalization of
knowledge, temporality and identities, evoking Williams's political model based on "the testing of boundary, the consecration
of sacrilege." The challenges to and ramifications of this political
"consecration" lead us toward an analysis of rememory's
"mixing up" of the collectives that become possible through re-
imagined bodies.

ENVISIONING COLLECTIVE POLITICS:
FAMILIES WITHOUT BOUNDARIES

The spatial refigurations of rememory are, as I have argued, also
political insofar as they enable collective identity. As such they
necessarily constitute the means through which Baby Suggs's
Call is felt in this text. This brings us finally to confront the
problem of Baby's death of a broken heart nearly nine years

before the "present" of the novel. After all, if Baby Suggs, holy, models the spiritual politics of collectivity at the centre of the text, how do we account for her decision finally to "up and quit" (177) the Word because she "believed she had lied. There was no grace – imaginary or real – and no sunlit dance in a Clearing could change that" (89)? I would contend that Baby's death, rather than undermining her political vision in the novel, illuminates the necessarily dialogic and collective nature of her Call to political action as well as the demystified dailiness and accessibility of the spiritual practice of perfect love. Her death forms the brutally lucid index of the limitations of masculinist models of individualism, for she does not fail the collective in her loss of faith. Rather, her loss of faith stems from the collective's failure to be moved to act on its knowledge of and implication in Sethe's act of infanticide.

The breakdown of this dialogic call-and-response model of collectivity begins with the party Baby Suggs gives for the community during which she oversteps her own credo of "good is knowing when to stop" (87) through an excess of generosity that prevents the others from any possible reciprocation. Rather than being inspired to a holiness-model response, the community reacts by growing angry – suspicious of what it misreads as Baby's monologic power:

> Too much, they thought. Where does she get it all, Baby Suggs, holy? . . . How come she always knows exactly what to do and when? Giving advice; passing messages; healing the sick, hiding fugitives, loving, cooking, cooking, loving, preaching, singing, dancing and loving everybody like it was her job and hers alone.
>
> (137)

As if testing the necessarily *collective* imagination at the heart of Baby's Call for grace, no one in the community alerts the women of 124 when schoolteacher and his assistants ride into town to reclaim Sethe and her children by the legal word of the Fugitive Slave Act. "Maybe," Stamp Paid suggests, "they just wanted to know if Baby really was special, blessed in some way they were not" (157). The answer is clear when Baby alone cannot stop Sethe's bloody attempt to keep her children from schoolteacher's grip. Yet the community refuses to be moved – or "listened" – to speak the alternative somatic discourses of collectivity it has learned in the Clearing, such as the perfect harmony of the singing response to Baby's Call. When Sethe is taken to jail after her partially successful infanticide, the community misreads her chilly response to its own silence as haughtiness:

> Was her head a bit too high? Her back a little too straight? Probably. Otherwise the singing would have begun at once, the moment she appeared in the doorway of the house on Bluestone Road. Some cape of sound would have quickly been wrapped around her, like arms to hold and steady her on the way. As it was, they waited till the cart turned about, headed west to town. And then no words. Humming. No words at all.
>
> (152)

That Baby Suggs's "faith, her love, her imagination and her great big old heart" (89) fail her immediately after the community's betrayal allows schoolteacher to push Sethe to infanticide, illuminates the imperative toward collectivity found in Baby's political Call. The spiritual implications of this betrayal – and the community's uneasiness about them – become clear when it pointedly avoids attributing her death to the "collapse" (90) of the heart that had been the centre of Baby's Holiness doctrine, agreeing instead that "it was consumption without a sign of it in the world" (183), and refusing to acknowledge collective involvement in her spiritual death.

The end of the novel is defined by a movement from the community's bitter factions (themselves produced because Sethe had "made no gesture toward anybody, and lived as though she were alone," once out of jail, 256) to a connected, collective disposition. In this way, it traces on a larger scale the same redirection of power (from vertical divisions to horizontal connections) through gestural discourses and rememory that I have already outlined between pairs of characters. Importantly, the act of "listening" the numbed collective into a flood of nurturing and storytelling operates through Sethe's daughter, Denver, whose own ambivalence about call-and-response knowledge as a child moves her to impose upon herself two years of deafness in order to evade the terror of Sethe's act in the woodshed. However, when Denver is left as the only "mothering" force keeping Sethe alive (as Beloved slowly kills her with guilt), the rememory of Baby Suggs finally transforms isolation into a quest for help. As Denver stands paralysed on the porch of 124 rememory enables Denver somatically to experience the sensations of Baby's own body – her heartbeat and "foolish" laughter – that once marked Baby's "conversion" to somatic knowledge and eloquence: Denver's "throat itched; her heart kicked – and then Baby Suggs laughed, clear as anything." Denver's heartfelt response "listens" Baby into speech who in turn Calls Denver to act, and without the violence of the master's tools – despite the "rout" of the slavers (244). Countering Denver's caution through stories of her family's resistance to slave-holders, Baby Suggs inspirits her to reach the community beyond the porch of 124:

> But you said there was no defense.
> "There ain't."
> Then what do I do?
> "Know it, and go on out the yard. Go on."
>
> (244)

By not waiting for future grace or "vertical" political change from the "top," Denver combines spiritual and postmodern praxes by simply envisioning change and performing it into being with the motions of her body – thereby reminding others of the gestural, emotive discourses Baby once inspired. When her childhood teacher, Lady Jones, feels both the suffering and the Call bodied forth through Denver, she tellingly lapses into nurturing language, homonymically invoking Baby's spiritual power: "'Oh, baby . . . . Oh, baby'" (248). Denver's response is equally telling: "Denver looked up at her. She did not know it then, but it was the word 'baby,' said softly and with such kindness, that inaugurated her life in the world as a woman" (248).

In the name of Baby Suggs, then, the call-and-response model of "listening" others into speech and selfhood moves the community of women who have spurned Sethe for eighteen years to rememory the Clearing's gestures of "loving the flesh," and to mother the inhabitants of 124 with offerings of dialogic orality – of both food and storytelling. Reweaving the threads of monologic orality in this text – from Sethe's feeling that she had to have "milk enough for all" (100) to Beloved's vengeful addiction to sweets, stories and Sethe's flesh, to Baby's own unreciprocal generosity at the fateful party – this re-imagined collective of women re-Calls through Denver's presence the gestures and stories that bind them together. When Denver returns gratefully emptied bowls of food, for example:

> a small conversation took place. All of them knew her grandmother and some had even danced with her in the Clearing. Others remembered the days when 124 was a way station. . . . One remembered the tonic mixed there that cured a relative. One showed her the border of a pillowslip, the stamens of its pale blue flowers French-knotted in Baby Suggs' kitchen by the light of an oil lamp while arguing the Settlement Fee.
>
> (249)

Just as spirituality and politics, past and present, blur in rememories of Baby, the women are moved through Sethe's pain to understand how slavery's atrocities have blurred old categories of "right" and "wrong": "What's fair ain't necessarily right," observes Ella, a survivor herself of a brutality she can only name "'the lowest yet'" (256). Vowing to reweave the collectively inspired "cape of sound" they denied Sethe on her way to jail, "thirty neighborhood women" (261) gather at 124 and stumble upon the rememory of Baby's last party, where they must watch their own willing involvement in that generosity and feel the joy that preceded the next day's "envy." Yet it is the rememory of Baby Suggs herself, who "laughed and skipped among them, urging more" that clearly Calls the women to respond in prayer: "Denver saw lowered heads, but could not hear the lead prayer – only the earnest syllables of agreement that backed it: Yes, yes, yes, oh yes. Hear me. Hear me" (258). The prayer's diverse spiritualities, from Christian faith to folk wisdom, then shift to a wordless "holler": "They stopped praying and took a step back to the beginning. In the beginning there were no words. In the beginning was the sound, and they all knew what that sound sounded like" (259). This alternative, "wordless" discourse of private, public, spiritual and political meanings operates like "speaking in tongues," challenging schoolteacher's monologic M/master inscription of history and identity on black women's bodies and, as Henderson has argued, revisioning Scripture ("In the beginning was the Word").[37] Space, temporality, discourse and the flow of power are refigured in a moment:

APRIL LIDINSKY

> For Sethe it was as though the Clearing had come to her
> with all its heat and simmering leaves, where the voices of
> women searched for the right combination, the key, the
> code, the sound that broke the back of words.
>
> (261)

As with the other narrative gaps in *Beloved* that no one finally
"masters" with totalization, there is no consensus of interpretation among those bearing witness to Sethe's experience of
the Clearing's power at 124 – only agreement that it is a moment
of horizontal connection, with both Sethe and Denver "running
into the faces of the people out there, joining them" (262). This
collective, based on what West and hooks have described as
"compassion, recognition of difference, [and] the importance of
diversity," refigures the "sense of home" in a way that breaches
binding definitions of the nuclear heterosexual family.[38] If we
read *Beloved* as a "history of the present," as rememory surely
challenges us to do, the refiguring move from filiative to affilia-
tive collectives (to borrow Edward Said's useful terms)[39] challenges the politics of power-controlling discourses such as the
1992 presidential debate in the United States over "family
values." The racist, classist and heterosexist totalizing myth of
origins in the Republican narrative of the "nuclear family" as
the necessary home of "morality" is implicitly questioned repeatedly in Morrison's novel, as when Paul D says in surprise at
124's all-female household, "They were a family somehow and
he was not the head of it" (132), or when Halle begins to
redefine masculine roles by acting "more like a brother than a
husband. His care suggested a family relationship rather than a
man's laying claim" (25). *Beloved* also refigures "mothering,"
clearly, as a practice that tests the boundaries of biology. Not
only women like Baby Suggs, Ella and Amy Denver nurture
across biologically and racially constructed borders, but men
like Halle, Paul D and Stamp Paid also learn the gestures of
mothering, or nurturing, as a habit of being. The heart of Baby's
Call is no less than a re-invention of our selves as multipally
positioned and positionable in culture, and multipally connected
through the ways we can be moved spiritually and politically. If,
in her essay on "Postmodern Blackness," hooks cautions against
losing track of the experience of racism in postmodern theories
of "difference," she also cautions against essentialist notions of

identity that preclude postmodernism's "new possibilities for the construction of self and the assertion of agency."[40] Through Baby Suggs, holy, *Beloved* teaches us to imagine – to fiction – a "mixing it up" vision of identity-politics, as well as what we might call a "postmodern grace."

NOTES

1 The sources for the epigraphs to this chapter are as follows: P.J. Williams, *The Alchemy of Race and Rights*, Cambridge, Mass., Harvard University Press, 1991, 129, and M. Foucault, *Power/Knowledge: Selected Interviews and Other Writings 1972–1977*, ed. C. Gordon, trans. C. Gordon, L. Marshall, J. Mephan and K. Soper, Hemel Hempstead, Harvester, 1980, 193.

2 M. Foucault, *Discipline and Punish: The Birth of the Prison*, trans. A. Sheridan, New York, Vintage, 1979, 135.

3 J. Butler, *Gender Trouble: Feminism and the Subversion of Identity*, New York, Routledge, 1990. Butler argues that "Construction is not opposed to agency; it is the necessary scene of agency, the very terms in which agency is articulated and becomes culturally intelligible," 147.

4 T. Morrison, *Beloved*, New York, Alfred Knopf, 1987, 88 (all subsequent references will be given by page number only in parenthesis).

5 Foucault, *Discipline and Punish*, 1979, 31.

6 T. Morrison, "The Site of Memory," in William Zinsser, ed., *Inventing the Truth: The Art and Craft of Memoir*, Boston, Houghton Mifflin, 1987, 112, emphasis added.

7 b. hooks, *Yearning: Race, Gender, and Cultural Politics*, Boston, South End Press, 1990, 209.

8 For an overview of the debates on "revisionary" historical fiction in recent African-American women's texts including *Beloved*, M. Walker's *Jubilee*, and S.A. Williams's *Dessa Rosa*, see B. Christian, "'Somebody Forgot to Tell Somebody Something': African-American Women's Historical Novels," in J.M. Braxton and A.N. McLaughlin, eds, *Wild Women in the Whirlwind: Afra-American Culture and the Contemporary Literary Renaissance*, New Brunswick, Rutgers University Press, 1990, 326–41.

9 See L. Hutcheon's discussion of scholars like M.H. Abrams who condemn postmodernism for what they consider to be its "irresolvable indeterminacies," in *The Politics of Postmodernism*, London and New York, Routledge, 1989, 18.

10 L. Hutcheon, *A Poetics of Postmodernism*, London and New York, Routledge, 1988, 4.

11 M.G. Henderson, "Toni Morrison's *Beloved*: Re-Membering the Body as Historical Text," in H.J. Spillers, ed., *Comparative American Identities: Race, Sex, and Nationality in the Modern Text*, New York, Routledge, 1991, 62–86, at 67.

12 ibid., 72. Elsewhere in her argument, Henderson emphasizes the collective aspect of these primal scenes, as in her observation that "Beloved's implication in the lives of the collectivity of women . . . makes it necessary that all the women in the community later participate in the ritual to exorcise her," 75. This parallels A.H.A. Rushdy's argument that Beloved's primal scenes work in "inter-personal" ways: see "'Rememory': Primal Scenes and Constructions in Toni Morrison's Novels," in Contemporary Literature, 31 (1990) 300–23, at 317. However, the limitations of this model of repression become clear in Rushdy's most unrevealing conclusion that this text defers narrative origins "until only slavery stands alone as cause and curse," 318.

13 D. Fuss's discussion of the relationship between African-American texts and poststructuralist theories is especially useful here. Without ignoring the effects of the social production of race, she calls for "an approach which intervenes in the essentialist/constructionist polemic that has hitherto imprisoned 'race' in a rigidified and falsifying logic." See Essentially Speaking: Feminism, Nature and Difference, New York, Routledge, 1989, 92.

14 W.D. Samuels and C. Hudson-Weems, Toni Morrison, Boston, Twayne, 1990, 116.

15 J.M. Humez, "'My Spirit Eye': Some Functions of Spiritual and Visionary Experience in the Lives of Five Black Women Preachers, 1810–1880," in B.J. Harris and J.K. McNamara, eds, Women and the Structure of Society: Selected Research from the Fifth Berkshire Conference on the History of Women, Durham, N.C., Duke University Press, 1984, 120–43, at 130.

16 See Sisters of the Spirit: Three Black Women's Autobiographies of the Nineteenth Century, ed. W.L. Andrews, Bloomington, Indiana University Press, 1989, 5.

17 D.A. Payne's History of the African Methodist Episcopal Church, New York, Arno Press, 1969 (orig. publ. 1891) contains pertinent editorials from the early 1850s on the questionability of women preachers. See especially the editorial, "Licensing Women to Preach," 301, as well as chapter 30, "Review of Education to 1856," 393–401.

18 See D.W. Wills, "Womanhood and Domesticity in the A.M.E. Tradition: The Influence of Daniel Alexander Payne," in D.W. Wills and R. Newman, eds, Black Apostles at Home and Abroad: Afro-Americans and the Christian Mission from the Revolution to Reconstruction, Boston, G.K. Hall & Co., 1982, 133–46. Wills notes that even Jarena Lee, who was already established in the AME Church as its "first female preacher" when Payne joined in 1841, was never officially ordained, despite her recognition by the Church's first bishop, Richard Allen, who allowed her to preach on Sunday in Bethel Church, Philadelphia. (Bishop Allen is referred to briefly in Beloved as an influential, well-known member of the church [146]). Lee's autobiography, The Life and Religious Experi-ence of Jarena Lee, and that of Julia Foote, A Brand Plucked from

the Fire, are reprinted in *Sisters of the Spirit*, ed. Andrews, 25–48 and 161–234.

19 S.E. Houchins, "Introduction," *Spiritual Narratives*, New York and Oxford, Oxford University Press, 1988, xxxvii.

20 See V. Smith's *Self-Discovery and Authority in Afro-American Narrative*, Cambridge, Mass., Harvard University Press, 1987, for her persuasive argument that the slave-narrative genre, shaped by Douglass's text, "enshrine[s] cultural definitions of masculinity," 34. On the issue of Douglass's appropriation and revision of cultural discourses, see C.T. Davis and H.L. Gates, Jr., "Introduction: The Language of Slavery" in *The Slave's Narrative*, New York, Oxford University Press, 1985, xi–xxxiv, in which Davis and Gates discuss the "dialectical" relation of early African-American texts like Douglass's to the "other, racist texts against which the slave's narrative, by definition, was forced to react" (xxv).

21 Payne, *History*, 398.

22 See Houchins, *Spiritual Narratives*, xxxv, for a sketch of the scholarly arguments comparing medieval mystics and nineteenth-century black women revivalists.

23 M.G. Henderson, "Speaking in Tongues: Dialogics, Dialectics, and the Black Woman Writer's Literary Tradition," in C.A. Wall, ed., *Changing Our Own Words: Essays on Criticism, Theory, and Writing by Black Women*, New Brunswick, Rutgers University Press, 1989, 16–37, at 22, 24.

24 ibid., 22.

25 Houchins, *Spiritual Narratives*, xl, emphasis added. Houchins draws her analysis from the theologian Nelle Morton, who frames these women's spiritual autobiographies in a "feminist-style hermeneutic" that focuses on the "act" of "*hearing to speech* rather than *speaking to hearing*," xxxix.

26 See *The Life and Religious Experience of Jarena Lee*, in *Sisters of the Spirit*, ed. Andrews, 29.

27 A. Lorde, "Uses of the Erotic: The Erotic as Power," paper delivered at the Fourth Berkshire Conference on the History of Women, Mount Holyoke College, 25 August 1978.

28 C. West, *Prophesy Deliverance!: An Afro-American Revolutionary Christianity*, Philadelphia, The Westminster Press, 1982, 35.

29 D. Haraway, interviewed by C. Penley and A. Ross, "Cyborgs at Large: Interview with Donna Haraway," *Social Text; Theory/Culture/Ideology* 9:1 (1990) 8–23, at 20.

30 Butler, *Gender Trouble*, 134–5.

31 Importantly, Foucault differentiates between slavery and other disciplinary regimes emerging since the eighteenth century in Europe that "were not based on a relation of appropriation of bodies; indeed, the elegance of the discipline lay in the fact that it could dispense with this costly and violent relation by obtaining effects of utility at least as great," in *Discipline and Punish*, 137. See also, "Omnes et Singulatim," in which Foucault distinguishes between power and force as follows: "Power is only a certain type

of relation between individuals. . . . A man who is chained up and beaten is subject to force being exerted over him. Not power. But if he can be induced to speak, when his ultimate recourse could have been to hold his tongue, preferring death, then he has been caused to behave in a certain way. His freedom has been subjected to power. . . . There is no power without potential refusal or revolt," in S.M. McMurrin, ed., *The Tanner Lectures on Human Values*, 2 vols, Salt Lake City, University of Utah Press, 1981, II. 225–54, at 253.

32 Foucault, *Discipline and Punish*, 137, 143.
33 ibid., 143.
34 Butler, *Gender Trouble*, 145.
35 See, for example, L. Fultz's "Images of Motherhood in Toni Morrison's *Beloved*," in P. Bell-Scott, *Double Stitch: Black Women Write about Mothers and Daughters*, Boston, Beacon Press, 1991, 32–41. See also D. Horvitz, "Nameless Ghosts: Possession and Dispossession in *Beloved*," *Studies in American Fiction*, 17 (1989) 157–67.
36 Henderson argues that the privileging of "the other in ourselves" distinguishes black women's writing, operating through a "*dialectic of identity*" which is illuminated by what she sees as the complementary discursive models of H.-G. Gadamer and M.M. Bakhtin. See Henderson, "Speaking in Tongues," 19.
37 Henderson, "Toni Morrison's *Beloved*," 81.
38 hooks, *Yearning*, 213.
39 E. Said, *The World, the Text and the Critic*, Cambridge, Mass., Harvard University Press, 1983, 23–4, 174–5.
40 "Postmodern Blackness," in *Yearning*, 23–31, at 28, 29.

INDEX

Fogarty, Anne vii; on Aphra
    Behn xi, xv–xvi, 1–17
Follen, Mrs 96
Foote, Julia 195–6, 214–15
Foster, C.H. 114, 115, 117
Foucault, Michel xix, 191–2, 194,
    199–200, 203, 213, 215–16
"framing" of slave-narratives
    118, 123
Franchot, J. 142
Franklin, Benjamin 196
Frazier, Franklin 101, 109
freedom see emancipation and
    abolition
Fultz, L. 216
Fuss, D. 214

Gadamer, H.-G. 216
Gaines, J. 16
Gallagher, C. 16
Garrison, W.L. 139–40
Gaskell, Elizabeth: xv, xvi; and
    Mary Barton xvii, 94–117;
    and North and South 97, 112
    Gaskell's Ruth from Ruth 170
Gaskell, Reverend William 96,
    115
Gates, Henry Louis, Jr. xiv,
    xviii; on Douglass and slave-
    narratives 121–2, 139, 140;
    on language 164, 188, 215;
    on "literariness" 171–2
gazing see looking and gazing
gender see men; women
Genovese, E. 164, 188
Gérin, Winifred 96–7, 98, 114
Gibson, D. 143
Gilbert, Sandra M. and Gubar,
    Susan 114; on Brontë 64–7,
    75, 77, 87–8, 89, 93
Gill, S. 115
Gliddon, George 167
glossolalia 196
Go Down, Moses see under
    Faulkner
God: absent 37, 170; authority
    of 27–8; and self 129–30,
    134; see also transcendental
    signified

Goreau, A. 15
Goslee, Nancy Moore 48, 52, 61
Gossett, T.F. 141
Gray, B. 114
Greene, Sheila 116
Gresset, M. 189–90
Gubar, Susan see Gilbert,
    Sandra M. and Gubar, Susan
Gutman, Herbert G. 108
Gwin, M. 164

Haraway, Donna 199, 215
Hardy, Thomas 170, 171
Hauss, Jon vii; on Harriet
    Jacobs xviii, 144–65
Hawthorne, Nathaniel 114, 170
Hegel, G.W.F. xii
Henderson, Mae G. 193, 196,
    213–14, 215, 216
Henson, Reverend J. 115
"heroinism" 99, 106, 114
Hilton, N. 61, 62
history see past
hooks, bell 16, 164, 192,
    212–13, 216
Horvitz, D. 216
Houchins, Sue E. 195–6, 197,
    215
Hudson-Weems, C. 214
Hughes, Henry 166, 167, 168,
    175, 183
humanity as universal 29
Hume, David 169, 188
Humez, Jean M. 195, 214
Hurston, Z.N. 164
Hutcheon, Linda 193, 213
Hutner, Heidi 6, 16

identity and Morrison's Beloved
    xix, 193–4
imaginative reproduction of
    history see Morrison
incarnational body: "listening"
    into speech 194–9
Incidents see Jacobs
interpretation in Douglass's
    Narrative 126–34, 134–9
Irigaray, Luce 19–20, 36–7, 38,
    39

INDEX

Payne, Daniel A. 195, 196, 214, 215
Penley, C. 215
Perera, Suvendrini 83, 92, 117
performative text, Douglass's *Narrative* as 120, 122–6
Philips, W. 140
Plasa, Carl vii; on Brontë's *Jane Eyre see Jane Eyre*; on essays xiii–xix
Plato 53, 62
Platt, H.G., Jr. 15
pleasure, woman's body for *see* Blake
plurality of senses 43
poetry xiii; *see also* Blake
Poirier, Richard 182, 190
politics/political: of collectivity *see* Morrison; conflict, body as site of *see* Blake; and Douglass's *Narrative* xviii, 132; of metaphor *see Jane Eyre*; philosophy *see in particular* Wollstonecraft; struggle and allegory in Behn's *Oroonoko* xvi, 2, 15; *see also* colonialism
polygeneticism 167, 187–8
postmodernism *see* Morrison
power *see* discipline; oppression
Prince, Gerald 99, 116
Prince, Mary 64, 87
Pringle, T. 91
prison analogy in Brontë's *Jane Eyre* 65, 81
Pryse, M. 163
Puritanism 96, 129
purity: claim to 58; of readers of Jacobs's *Incidents* 155–6

Quakers 101
Quintilian 72, 85, 90

Raboteau, A. 164
race and racism xix, 166–7; of Behn 7; in Brontë's *Jane Eyre* xvii, 69, 71–2, 78–9, 83; *see also* Stowe
Rampersad, Arnold xv

Ramsaran, J.A. 15
rape *see* sexual abuse
Ray, G.N. 89
reality *see* fact
reason: and rights 22, 27–8; women without 33–7, 44–6
rebellion *see* revolts
referentiality 111–12
Reid, J.P. 38
Reidel, F. 189
reification in Brontë's *Jane Eyre* 72
"re-invention" of traditional models of self *see* Morrison
religion: traditional African synthesized with Protestantism 146, 158–9, 164; virtues of 62; visionary spirituality *see* Morrison; *see also* Christianity
rememory *see* Morrison
repetition in Douglass's *Narrative* 120, 123
representativity problem 3
resistance *see* revolts of slaves
Reuter, Edward Byron 168, 188
revisioning 193
revolts of slaves 91; in Brontë's *Jane Eyre* 71, 77–82; "heroinism" 99, 106, 114; in Jacobs's *Incidents* xviii, 144–8, 153–4, 159; possibility *see* Blake; responsibility to control *see* Stedman
rewriting the Word in Douglass's *Narrative* 126–34
rhetorical figures in Douglass's *Narrative* 119–22
Rhys, Jean 67, 88–9
Rich, Adrienne 77, 90, 93
Richardson, Samuel 115, 170, 171
Richmond, Henry 97
Ricoeur, Paul 72–3, 90
rights principle and truth xvi, 2, 5, 21, 33–4; *see also* Wollstonecraft
Ring, Betty J. viii, xvii–xviii; on

223

INDEX

suttee 83–4, 92
Swift, Jonathan 104
symbolism *see* metaphors
synecdoche in Douglass's
Narrative 120, 122
Sypher, W. 15

Thackeray, William Makepeace
69–70, 89
theology *see* Christianity
Tillotson, Kathleen 98, 101, 115
Tompkins, Jane P. 114, 162, 165
Tonna, Mrs (Charlotte
Elizabeth) 102
transcendental signified and
Wollstonecraft's *Vindications*
20, 21–6, 29; replaced and
imaginary 30–2, 36
Transcendentalists 116
transference of metaphor 72–3,
76
transgression *see* revolts
translation in *Jane Eyre* 84–6
"transsocial understanding,"
networks of *see* Jacobs
Trollope, Frances 101
Turner, Nat 159, 164
Twain, Mark 110, 117

Uncle Tom's Cabin see Stowe
Unitarianism and women writers
99, 101, 116
United States *see* America
universalism xii; of all women's
experience and *Jane Eyre*
65–6; in Douglass's *Narrative*
121–2; of slave-woman's
appeal to Northern readers
see Jacobs; universal rights
21, 24, 29–31, 33; *see also*
under enlightenment
unwed mother figure 167–71,
172–3, 175–7, 183–4

veil as symbol 77–8, 79–81
*Vindication of the Rights of
Men, A* and *Vindication of
the Rights of Woman see*
Wollstonecraft

Vine, Steven viii; on William
Blake xii, xvi, 40–63
violence: in Blake's *Visions*
42–3, 48, 49–50, 58–9; and
representation in Aphra
Behn's *Oroonoko* 1–17; *see
also* savage
virginity: at risk 103–4; control
over 36–7; and Faulkner 170,
173–4, 175
vision: specularity in Blake's
Visions 41, 50–61; *see also*
looking and gazing
visionary spirituality *see*
Morrison
*Visions of the Daughters of
Albion see* Blake

wagon symbolism in Faulkner
178, 179, 184
Walker, M. 213
Walsh: *Notices of Brazil* 91
Walvin, J. 91
Ware, Vron 5, 16
Warhol, R. 116
Warren, George 3
Washington, M.H. 165
Wasser, H.W. 61
Weld, T. 115
Welter, Barbara 145, 163
West, Cornel 198, 212, 215
West Indies: Africans and Creole
slaves *see Jane Eyre*
Whicher, George Frisbie 96, 115
Williams, Carolyn 86, 93
Williams, Patricia 30–1, 32–3,
39, 191, 194, 202, 213
Williams, R. 163
Williams, S.A. 213
Williams, W.S. 89
Williamson, J. 187
Wills, D.W. 214
Winks, R.W. 141
Wollstonecraft, Mary,
Vindications of xv, xvi,
18–39; authority 27–8;
comparison with Blake 44–9,
59, 60, 61–2; exclusion
28–33; faith 26–7; "rights of

225